Binding *up* *the* Wounds

Binding up the Wounds

An American Soldier in Occupied Germany 1945–1946

LEON C. STANDIFER

LOUISIANA STATE UNIVERSITY PRESS

Baton Rouge and London

Copyright © 1997 by Louisiana State University Press
Manufactured in the United States of America
All rights reserved
First printing
06   05   04   03   02   01   00   99   98   97   5   4   3   2   1

Designer: Laura Roubique Gleason
Typeface: Bembo
Printer and binder: Thomson-Shore, Inc.

Library of Congress Cataloging-in-Publication Data
Standifer, Leon C.
    Binding up the wounds : an American soldier in occupied Germany,
  1945–1946 / Leon C. Standifer.
        p.   cm.
    Includes bibliographical references.
    ISBN 0-8071-2094-4 (alk. paper)
    1. Standifer, Leon.   2. Soldiers—United States—Biography.
  3. Reconstruction (1939–1951)—Biography.   4. Military government—
  Germany.   I. Title.
  DD257.S66   1997
  940.55'4—dc20   96-38212
                                                                CIP

To Anna, Bridget, Gerda, Hilde, Günter, Hermann, Arbeits-
Kommando V, and especially, the men of the *Schwarze Kater;*
to all of you, my warm and sincere *vielen Dank*

With malice toward none; with charity for all; with firmness in the right, as God gives us to see the right, let us strive on to finish the work we are in: to bind up the nation's wounds; to care for him who shall have borne the battle, and for his widow and his orphan; to do all which may achieve a just and lasting peace among ourselves, and with all nations.

—Abraham Lincoln, Second Inaugural Address

CONTENTS

Preface   xiii

1. Thou Preparest a Table Before Me   1

2. Valley of the Roses   24

3. Useful Articles   38

4. Infantry, Pass in Review!   55

5. Combat Troops   74

6. Somewheres East of Suez   117

7. For Thus Shall the Lord Do   141

8. Showtime!   150

9. Never Sheathe It Without Honor   174

10. And the Lives You Lived Were Mine   190

Afterword and Thanks   199

Selected Bibliography   207

ILLUSTRATIONS

(following page 98)

American troops entering Munich

Studio portrait of the author in Solingen-Wald, 1945

The author and George Faber in Rosenthal

Postcard view of Rosenthal

General Patton reviewing troops, Strakonice, Czechoslovakia

Combat troops parading in Prague

Souvenir photo of German soldiers sightseeing in Paris

"Milky" Edwards, Joe Weiner, Leon Standifer, 1945

GIs conversing with young German women, Nuremberg

"Rubble women," Munich

German *Wochenspruch* propaganda posters

    "Germany is victorious on all fronts"

    "The woman also has her battlefield"

    "Strong hearts are those who compel victory"

    "Whatever may come, we will master it"

Ceremony at the Feldherrenhalle, 1936

The Feldherrenhalle at war's end

The Feldherrenhalle in 1992

Surrendered German troops, Bad Aibling, May 1945

Bad Aibling POW compound, December 1945

Bad Aibling base as relocation center, 1950

Former Luftwaffe cadet barracks, Bad Aibling, 1992

Café Arnold, Bad Aibling

The author and Hilda Hofer, Bad Aibling, 1992

Old Hitler Youth building, Bad Aibling

The author, Gerda Kopliks, and Hermann Böhme, 1992

PREFACE

There is an old Mississippi story about politics in the post–Civil War era.
John Mills Allen was a candidate for state representative from Lee County,
the region where the Confederate army had assembled before the battle
of Shiloh. His opponent was a proud old man who had been a general in
that army. At one of the debates the general was waxing eloquent about
his military valor. On the night before Shiloh there had been a terrible
rainstorm. While plotting strategy, the general said, he would occasionally
look outside the tent and see the lone sentry, who symbolized the brave
boys in gray—waiting, then as now, for a strong leader. Then John Allen
got up and said he could vouch for the story his opponent had told. "I
was the cold, wet sentry standing outside his tent, cursing the rain and
waiting for the orders which would get us whipped even though we out-
fought the Yankees. He is right in saying that those of you who were generals during the war should vote for a general. I only ask that the men
who fought as privates vote for Private John Allen!"

As a private first class, I outranked John Allen, but I understand what
he was saying. There are many good books written by generals and lesser
gods about the American occupation policies in Germany. This is not one
of those books. But I was there, carrying out orders, watching what the
officers were doing, and wondering if anybody really knew what was
going on. I guarded ordinary German soldiers and had long discussions
with them about the war, Hitler, and the ideals, mistakes, and brutality of
National Socialism. I met ordinary German civilians who told their own
tales of idealism, war, brutality, and racism.

"I know because I was there" is a memoir: a truth, but not the whole truth. High-school history teachers sometimes illustrate this point with a staged argument, resulting in the disruptive students' being sent out of the class. About thirty minutes later, the rest of the class are asked to write their accounts of what happened. When the papers are read, the students come to understand that people can see the same incident from different viewpoints.

History is an attempt to take individual memoirs and condense them into a broad overview. History is what the general saw, broadly accurate, but lacking the warmth, discomfort, and pain of memoirs.

Private John Allen was a wonderful speaker, but he was prone to modify facts to fit the occasion. Allen was a reconnaissance scout at Shiloh, and it is likely that he spent the night before the battle lying in the mud near or behind Federal lines. But even if his story of standing guard was somewhat embellished, its central truth was clear.

In writing these memoirs I have tried to keep embellishment at a minimum, but please remember that the incidents are from fifty years ago, and I am fifty years older. My mother saved most of the letters that I wrote home, but there are some things that a twenty-year-old boy doesn't tell Mama. Each year, when the survivors of K Company get together at the division reunion and repeat our versions of the war and of occupation times, the details vary. Even so, after all these years, we can usually agree on the main facts.

I enjoy telling tales about the old days—days that were exciting, sad, funny, and sometimes painful. I tell these stories because the old-timers are beginning to die out and because we should remember the high price they paid for the heritage we enjoy. Those men and women were dedicated, heroic, and flawed; they made mistakes during combat and while trying to learn how to serve as occupation troops. There were also heroic and flawed Germans who loved their country and paid a high price for the German heritage of today. We should remember that, too—and that is another reason I tell these tales.

Yet another reason is personal pleasure. I grew up listening to old-timers tell stories of the Civil War and of what were ironically called the Reconstruction times. Looking back, I see that the stories were embellished here and there to improve on the poverty of life, but they were basically true. They were told partly for entertainment but were also part of our southern heritage, a constant reminder that decent people can follow smart politicians up Fool's Hill—and over the cliff.

My story has bits of legitimate embellishment: the only real grandeur an ordinary soldier can rely on is that which he constructs in his mind. Our regimental victory parade, held in a dusty Czechoslovakian pasture, was not a triumphal march down Fifth Avenue, except in our minds. There, our dead and badly wounded friends were marching along with us; we saw them and felt their pride.

These are the stories as I remember them. I was there and interested in what life had been like on the German side of the war. But I was a twenty-year-old with a limited understanding of the language and a not-very-good concept of the historical setting. Also, someone with the political clout of a private first class could not engage a wide sampling of the population in meaningful discourse. As you might expect, I was only able to talk with Germans who were much like me: ordinary people, not very strong in philosophy or politics. Most of them were older than me, and many of them may have been primarily interested in getting cigarettes, coffee, and sugar. All of them had, at least for a while, supported the ideals of the Nazi Party, and most of them still admired Hitler for his devotion to the German people.

Such views, held by ethical people, are a critical part of my story. But saying anything good about Hitler, even at second hand, makes me uncomfortable. How should I go about describing a situation that was based on fraud? Over the past several years I have come to know some of the people who loved Hitler even after his death. While studying old propaganda posters or listening to Hitler's recorded speeches, they can still recall the patriotic fervor of what they called the *Hitler Zeit* (Hitler times). This aspect of the Hitler story should be told, both because it helps to explain why Germany was so fascinating to me and because we need to remember that no country is immune to the lures of a warped genius.

In most of the places where I use quotations, their purpose is to reconstruct a scene. I cannot remember conversations verbatim from fifty years ago. More than half of the names I use are fictitious, occasionally to protect someone from embarrassment but usually because I remember only a personality without a name or even a face. In telling of German people I knew, I have sometimes combined wartime and postwar experiences of several people into an account of one person. These accounts are accurate in that each part of them was told to me by someone as the truth, but attributing the various parts to the proper persons would make the story too complex.

In September 1992, my wife and I returned to Bad Aibling, the little Bavarian town where I had served as a guard in the Prisoner of War Discharge Center. We rented a small apartment and put a notice in the local paper asking people who remembered the early period of American occupation to come by for visits. The response was extremely good. Men and women, ranging in age between sixty and eighty years, came by to share memories and impressions from that era. I was surprised that they spent more time conversing among themselves than with me. For most of them, this was the first time they had felt free to talk about those days. Immediately after the war they wanted to forget the trauma. Later, their children were ashamed of the Hitler times and didn't want to hear about the excitement that Hitler had generated among German youth. In my apartment, sitting with others who had grown up in the well-crafted Hitler Youth program, these people were free to laugh, giggle, and joke about the old days.

My command of German is still rather weak, but the first person replying to my request was Gerda Kopliks, who immediately after the war had spent ten years working for the U.S. Army, first as a secretary/translator and later as a management analyst. She stayed with us for three full afternoons to serve as an interpreter in the fullest sense—not only translating words, but also explaining the real meanings of my questions and of some answers I was getting. Essentially, I was asking "then and now" questions about attitudes toward Hitler, the war, and the American soldier during the early days of occupation. Some of the answers were surprising: many of my visitors still held a deep love for Hitler (not for the Nazi Party); many said that although the war had been horrible, it had taught them to share during hard times. In some ways the experience, like our Civil War, had created a truly united Germany—perhaps the "national community" that Hitler had described for them. They had fond memories of the first year of American occupation: the war was over, the Russians hadn't come, and the sloppy, easygoing, naive American soldiers were pushovers for manipulation.

Come with me now to see postwar Germany through the eyes of a twenty-year-old boy. After six years of misery, people were no longer being killed or maimed; aircraft flying low over the devastated cities were loaded with food instead of bombs. The most powerful American army ever assembled was idle and bored, waiting for redeployment to become part of that final slaughter, the invasion of Japan. Millions of hungry, wounded, and sick German POWs were waiting for treatment and discharge. Unknown numbers of DPs (displaced persons, including concentration-camp survivors, former slave laborers, deserters from the German or Russian armies, criminals, concentration-camp guards, and other assorted debris of the war) were waiting for whatever fate held in store. Civilians in formerly occupied countries had no food reserves and were already starving. The Germans had minimal amounts of food and there seemed to be no possibility that food production could be resumed for at least a year. Only the U.S. Army had any substantial amount of food, enough to feed its troops and some POWs for several months. The army had been anticipating this situation for more than a year, but until the war had been won, postwar justice and survival were secondary concerns.

Peace brought other problems as well. The voters at home wanted their sons and husbands brought back immediately. They also wanted to see someone punished for the awful costs of war. The British and French were openly complaining that American troops did not hate the Germans deeply enough. American troops were asking: "Enough for what? We beat the hell out of them, which is more than you haters did." The voters back home didn't want to believe that their sons and husbands were having affairs with Nazi women. News correspondents did believe, and wanted to report the news—all the more so because it was controversial.

Such chaos was hardly a setting for fun and games, but we—GIs, German children, girls, women, old men, and discharged soldiers—had a ball that first year. A wartime expression in Germany was "Enjoy the war, peace is going to be hell!" But it wasn't.

Binding *up* *the* Wounds

1

THOU PREPAREST A TABLE BEFORE ME

Who knows how to drive a truck?"

First Platoon of K Company was standing in the morning formation at Solingen-Wald, near Düsseldorf, about six weeks after the war in Europe had ended. I had been back with the platoon for about a week but had soldiered with it for over a year, long enough to have learned the army's cardinal rules: Keep your mouth shut, keep your bowels open, and never volunteer for anything. But I was bored; during the entire week we had done nothing that even approached being fun. I raised my hand and nudged Frank Bucco, who looked at me as if I were stupid—but his hand went up, slowly.

"Now these are big trucks," the sergeant was saying. "You men know how to double clutch?"

My total driving experience had been in the family car, but I had once ridden in the cab of a GI truck and thought I could remember how to shift it; I had no idea what a double clutch was. Maybe someone would explain it to us.

Twenty of us crawled onto the back of a "six by" ("six" refers to the number of driving wheels, in the same sense that a four-wheel-drive vehicle is called a "four by four") and headed out into the country. That in itself was enough to make the project worthwhile. I still enjoyed seeing the neat little farming villages. The Germans kept their country a lot cleaner than did the French and Belgians. Periodically the truck would stop at a German vehicle, and two guys would climb off and listen while the mechanic started it and explained how to double clutch; it seemed that we had all lied about knowing how to drive trucks.

Then we pulled up beside a tank, scarred and rusty from shrapnel hits. "Next two!" He was pointing at Bucco and me. I looked at the boy on my other side and motioned for him to take it. Nothing doing: it was our turn and we had drawn a tank! I don't know what kind it was, just very big; Bucco called it a Tiger Royal (which it wasn't—we couldn't have possibly driven such a complex tank; it was probably the much smaller Panther). Shrapnel had jammed the driver's viewing slot; except for that, the monster was in good shape. After some sputter and stutter the engine started. The mechanic showed me how to shift and to turn by braking against one track or the other.

"The radio is monitored at the motor pool. Keep in contact and let them know if you have problems. Don't get off the road. If this thing gets stuck, it'll take all day to haul it out."

Bucco was not pleased with the mess I had gotten us into. "Leon, everybody else got a truck or a Kübelwagen." (The Kübelwagen was the German version of our jeep; it was the original Volkswagen, but their slang word meant "bucket car.") "The worst they got was a half-track. We can't drive some broken-down tank."

Looking back, I suppose they knew we would have problems, but there was only one tank and they probably didn't want to hunt an experienced driver; after all, we might be able to do it. I slipped into the driver's seat and put on the crash helmet with built-in earphones. Bucco sat in the tank commander's position, holding the microphone and looking out of the turret. My earphones would receive the motor-pool end of conversations but not what Bucco said. Periodically (about every ten minutes) we would stop, climb out, and let Bucco report to the motor pool. "This is Tiger Royal One calling Panzer Division Commander, over."

"Hello, Tiger Royal, how's it going?"

"Very well. We have advanced about one hundred yards against very light opposition. I'm giving my crew a short break."

The frequent breaks were my idea. The tank was noisy, hot, and shaking my bones; I was frightened at driving blind. We stopped at the edge of our first town, a farming village of about a dozen houses. Our road intersected with another, forming a T. "Now, Bucco, when we get to the intersection, you signal me with a kick on the shoulder and I'll make a sharp right turn." I had no confidence in my ability to turn that tank and had wanted to cut across an open field to avoid the town entirely, but the motor pool absolutely refused. Suddenly Bucco was pounding both of my shoulders as hard as he could. I stopped and looked out; the long gun barrel was pointing through a window and the tank itself had already cracked the stone wall of the house. A woman was standing in the doorway screaming at us. I quickly remembered how to get in reverse, pulled back, hit a hard right, and roared away.

"Tiger Royal One calling Panzer Division. We encountered stiff enemy resistance at Obersdorf but were ultimately victorious. Rounding third and heading home!"

It was a fun adventure. When we got to the motor pool, Bucco gave a long, detailed, and hilarious account of our trip. Nobody was much upset about the minor tank accident, except the lady who owned the house. After months of following army regulations in the hospital and the replacement depots, I was enjoying the easy atmosphere of being back in a rifle company. K Company had been my home for over a year.

I hadn't joined the army to fight as a rifleman. I had volunteered for participation in the ASTP (Army Specialized Training Program), under which I was to receive two years of college training and (maybe) be commissioned as an officer in the Corps of Engineers. When the army realized that the invasion of France might cost 35,000 casualties, and that it didn't have very many infantry replacements, we were all assigned to infantry divisions. In March of 1944 my ASTP group was sent to the 94th Infantry Division, in training at Camp McCain, Mississippi. The Division was shipped to England in August and began fighting in Brittany in early September. Three months later I was wounded during an attack and spent a month in the hospital. I rejoined the company one day after it had taken 75 percent casualties while fighting in the small German town of Nennig. I lasted three days in the bitter cold before being evacuated with frozen feet and pneumonia.

The war ended in May while I was on a boxcar, headed back into combat for the third time, hoping I could get another lucky wound.

Combat was a little like rolling dice with your life at stake. It differed in that you had minor options as to how to make each throw. By being very careful during an attack you could reduce the chances of being wounded or killed, meaning that you would remain on line: cold, dirty, hungry, and frightened. In the next attack you would throw the dice again, knowing that eventually they would come up snake-eyes. If you were going to get wounded or killed, why postpone it by being careful? Looking back over these fifty years I still don't know whether the argument was logical. Those were difficult decisions for exhausted riflemen to make.

When the war ended, the urgent need for experienced combat troops also ended. The army continued to honor—usually—its commitment to return us to our original units, but at a much slower pace. I was dumped at a replacement depot (the army was now calling it a "reinforcement depot," which was supposed to make us feel more important) in Bonn. We were staying in the plush apartments of a good residential district; I was in the apartment of Willi Hermanns, Rocküm Strasse 30. Willi had been a pilot in the Luftwaffe and was killed during the battle of Britain. The apartment was very comfortable, but there was nothing to do. I looked at photographs in his magazines; he had a lot of books, too, but they were all in German.

Technically we were confined to a compound about four blocks square. Actually we drifted over much of the town (but took care to avoid MPs). I knew exactly where my division was and could easily have hitched a ride to Düsseldorf on a GI truck. In January, when I was returning to the company after being wounded, I had simply left the replacement depot, caught a truck headed for my division, and reported for duty. That had been acceptable during wartime, but now it would have gotten me court-martialed. I had to wait for assignment orders.

Finally the day came. The division sent three trucks to take us home, about sixty riflemen who were wondering what "home" would be like. How many friends had been killed since we left? Who had been wounded? Who had gotten back from the hospital before us?

Solingen-Wald was a suburban area of Solingen, a city world famous for fine steel knives. I jumped from the back of the truck, pulled my duffel bag out, and headed for the company command post. It was in a beautiful townhouse with a large sign in the front: Headquarters, King Company. When I had left in early February, the command post had been the basement of a wrecked house; the only sign had been a GI blanket hanging over the doorway as a blackout curtain.

The first person I saw was my former squad leader, Ray Graziano.

"Hey, Standifer, where the hell have you been? I haven't seen you since Etel."

"Ray, I whipped the Krauts single-handed at Nennig after you broke and ran."

"Have you learned to drink beer yet? Let's grab a beer and I'll tell you about the platoon."

King Company had its own beer hall: Bierstube König. Liter mugs of beer cost one mark (ten cents), and yes, I had learned to drink beer. During training, my Baptist background had kept me away from the awful stuff, but I no longer felt that my body was the Temple of God. During my rehabilitation period at the hospital in England, I had learned to drink awful-tasting warm English beer and the excellent cider. I sipped a cold German beer while listening to Ray fill in long, dull details of his combat exploits and (finally) stories of what had happened to the squad.

None of my close friends had died. My best friend, George Faber, had been on a scouting patrol just before the attack on Nennig and had been knocked unconscious and taken a little shrapnel from a near miss of a German "88"—their most deadly and accurate artillery weapon. After regaining consciousness, he had crawled back to our position and gone to the aid station. His wounds turned out not to be serious, but his feet were so badly frozen that amputation was a possibility. Apparently that hadn't happened: the company had heard that George would be back soon, with both feet intact.

Ed Blake, another close friend, had been sent home and discharged with frozen feet. That was all Ray said about him, because we both knew the real story. Ed had fought magnificently at Nennig, but when it was over he had broken—mentally. None of the new boys knew about that, and they never would. Ed was a fine soldier who had given until there was nothing left.

Ray wasn't sure about another of my friends, Hubert Cagle, who had left Nennig with frozen feet; maybe they had been amputated. We just didn't know.

My platoon leader, Lieutenant Westmoreland, had been badly wounded crossing the Saar. Harry Glixon had been sure that Westmoreland could not survive but refused to let our best officer die in a shattered farmhouse. Harry loaded him into a wheelbarrow and hauled him back to a medic. The company had recently gotten a letter from Westmoreland; he was in physical therapy in the hospital and expected full recovery.

Of the original forty men in First Platoon, only Bill Henry had gone through the war without a wound serious enough to justify hospitalization. During one of the attacks, Bill had taken a large shrapnel hit on a C-ration can that was in his field jacket. The shrapnel spoiled his lunch but did little other harm.

Our company commander, Captain Simmers, had been badly wounded during the Nennig attack and was replaced by Captain Warren, from battalion headquarters. Ray didn't like Warren, who was a West Point graduate, very strict and by-the-book. Judging from Ray's descriptions, I rather liked the man. On the first day that Warren took over the company, he had seen a room full of dead German soldiers in the house directly across from our command post. He immediately began an investigation: "Nobody in King Company is going to kill prisoners!" He found that the massacre had been unavoidable. About fifteen Germans had been in the room. They would not surrender and continued firing at our troops. One of our men slipped to the edge of the door and threw in three fragmentation grenades. The result was a bloody mess. Warren had no qualms about killing the enemy, but it must be done right; he was West Point to the core.

As Ray rambled on with his complaints about Warren, I remembered that I hadn't officially reported for duty. When I stood up, I realized that the good ole German beer had a kick to it—and I had sipped a full liter mug of the stuff. Now I had to report to Warren, ready for duty.

I marched into his office, very carefully but wearing a silly grin on my face. I stood at attention, saluted, and said: "PFC Standifer, reporting for duty."

He laughed, returned the salute, shook my hand, slapped me on the back, and said: "Welcome home, Standifer. I'm sure glad I don't have to send you on patrol in that condition."

I laughed. I was home and was welcome. I had never met Captain Warren, but he already knew me because Jim Westmoreland had been a close friend of his. Bill Warren loved the men of King Company as deeply as Dick Simmers had; he was honestly glad to see me back and wanted me to know that I was still part of the family.

Warren reassigned me to my old First Platoon. Then I went to see Rosie, the mail clerk. He had a big stack of letters for me: when I had left the hospital, I had told my friends to begin writing directly to K Company.

At the supply room I dug through the stack of duffel bags and found mine. Back in England, nine months ago, I had loaded it onto a truck just before we boarded a ship to take us over the Channel. Every few weeks the company would send someone back to division headquarters with lists of things each of us wanted from the duffel bags. My bag was almost empty except for a few clothes and some junk I had collected in England. But now I was home and could get more clothes: combat boots, a combat jacket, and a Combat Badge.

The badge mattered most. When I—we—had first been assigned to a rifle company, it had felt like a slap in the face. The infantry was where eight-balls went: "You screw up one more time and you'll wind up in the goddamned infantry." The invasion of France had changed our image; wearing a Combat Badge placed you in an elite society. The Combat Badge (officially the "Combat Infantryman Badge") was awarded only to men who had fought as infantry. The combat jacket and combat boots were entirely false image: they were being issued to every soldier in Europe.

The combat jacket was a replacement for the old brass-buttoned dress blouse, which had been more expensive and required dry-cleaning. The new jacket was also called the "Eisenhower jacket" because General Eisenhower had proposed it be issued to combat units as warm clothing similar to the British "battle jacket" and the German general-purpose tunic.

The idea of its being used in combat had not gone over well because the troops, wanting to have a good dress uniform, were drawing jackets that fitted too tightly for the demands of the field.

The combat boot had a similar history. Originally proposed for combat use under wet conditions to reduce the risk of trench foot, the boots proved to be a disaster with respect to wet feet but were prized by troops as part of a dress uniform. Army regulations required that enlisted men wear a tie with the dress uniform, except when leggings were worn. (Look, I just report the facts; I can't explain army logic.) Because the combat boot had a small leather strap attached to the top, it was considered to be the equivalent of leggings. Using this gimmick, the troops could wear a dress uniform with or without a tie.

Supply Sergeant Haney issued me the Combat Badge, a combat jacket, and new combat boots. I also got a can of dubbing and some shoe polish. I gave the new boots a liberal application of dubbing, squirted on some lighter fluid, and set the mess on fire. This procedure was necessary because combat boots were made with the rough side of the leather facing out. As combat boots, there was no need for them to be polished, but I wanted dress boots. After the fire went out, I rubbed the soot off and put on a heavy layer of brown shoe polish—brown was the only color available. After two or three days I had a pair of almost black, highly polished boots.

Ray introduced me to the current First Platoon. It was nearly full strength and I knew only a handful of them. I, who had just turned twenty, was one of the old-timers.

"You came overseas with the platoon?"

"I was first scout in Ray's squad, got wounded at Etel, frozen feet at Nennig."

"You knew Proctor, guy got the DSC?"

"Yeah, he was BAR in third squad. Big, strong, tough. Played football for Nebraska." I didn't think they wanted to know that he was also a witty, sensitive man and a fine scholar.

"You were a scout at Nennig? I heard about a First Platoon scout who got captured there. He turned on the Kraut and cut his throat."

I was the scout he was talking about, and supposed he knew it, but it wasn't something I wanted to remember. "I was there for only three days and pulled one patrol. We spent most of the time trying to get warm."

I wondered why those kids were obsessed with combat. Many of them had seen virtually no fighting. The last hard fight was in early March, and the company hadn't fought at all since March 24. That was over two months ago. They seemed to regret being riflemen who had missed the war. I couldn't quite sort out my feelings; I was proud of having fought, but not at all proud of the things we had to do.

Bill Henry saw what was happening and suggested that I might want to walk around town with him. Bill was an old friend who had joined First Platoon when I did. He had been transferred to company head-quarters after the fighting at Nennig. When Captain Warren took over, he needed a messenger who knew the company well and was reliable under any conditions. Lieutenant Westmoreland recommended Bill as the best man for the job. During the next two months of hard combat, Bill was Warren's messenger, bodyguard, and companion. Warren usually worked a fourteen-to-eighteen-hour day: all night, with a few hours' sleep dur-ing the day. Bill dozed whenever possible, but while Warren slept, Bill stayed awake and alert. He received calls from battalion headquarters and from the platoon leaders. In a real emergency he would wake Warren, but much of the time Bill made the decisions himself. One day, during a lull in the fighting, the company had assembled its dead and badly wounded in an area where an ambulance could pick them up. Exhausted, Captain Warren lay down on a stretcher to take a short nap. Bill left for a call of nature. When he came back, the ambulance was loaded and ready to leave, but Warren was missing. Bill ran to them yelling, "Wait, my captain isn't dead; he's just asleep!"

Bill was a good friend to have in headquarters; he knew most of the old-timers in the battalion, and all of the gossip. Being from Wisconsin, he also knew a little spoken German.

As we walked through Solingen-Wald, I was impressed with how neat and clean the town was. There had been only one air raid on it, and only two or three houses were destroyed in our area. Then the fact struck me that, regardless of how it looked, this was the home of the enemy. This was where the filthy Boche came from. These were the people who had killed Dale, Richards, Button, Dyer—and destroyed the marvelous mind of Ed Blake. There were posters on the walls with the silhouette of a spy, and "Psst" written under it. Back home we had signs that said, "Psst, the enemy is listening," but here the enemy was us. Women were sitting at the broad, open windows watching their children play soccer in the street. Sad old men sat on benches in front of the houses, smoking their pipes and watching American soldiers strut by.

"The Yankee soldiers would strut by, smiling and hoping someone would speak to them. Ladies would go in the house when Yankees came by; old men would just sit on the porch and ignore them." Growing up in Clinton, Mississippi, I had heard countless stories of the occupation after the Civil War. On summer nights when it was too hot to sleep, the neighbors would all gather on the Pattersons' big front porch, where you could sometimes catch a breeze. We kids would be lying on quilts. I don't remember any exciting tales being told on those hot, humid nights, just the old-time, hand-me-down stories. "I remember Grandma Mills telling about when the damnyankees first came into Leake County. There wasn't any fighting because our menfolk were all gone. The captain rode his horse up to each house, looked around, and decided whether the family could stay or if troops would take over. He would allow an hour for the women to gather their clothes but wouldn't let them take anything else. The soldiers would stay about a week and leave the house almost wrecked. They stole everything that was worth anything, and some that wasn't." Then it would be quiet for a while, except for the creaking of rocking chairs, until somebody came up with a new thought.

"Damnyankees, they were pretty good fighters but pure devils during Reconstruction. *De*-struction is the word."

Sooner or later, Mrs. Patterson would have her say: "Stupid politicians had to kill off most of our young men and destroy the country just because they were too stubborn to admit that slavery was wrong."

Nobody ever argued about that: the damnyankee soldiers were barbarians, but the War for Southern Independence had been a stupid mistake.

Walking down the street in Solingen-Wald, I pondered the idea of being in the Yankee occupation army. But it really wasn't the same situation. We had come over here to free the French, Belgians, and Jews from German aggression. I knew that the Yankee soldiers hadn't really thought they were fighting to free slaves; that didn't make me feel better because they had fought to preserve the Union, the country that I loved. I became tangled in the logic but, somehow, I had to believe that this time we weren't going to act like the damnyankee soldiers and the carpetbaggers and the scalawags.

A young girl walked past us. Bill spoke to her but she made no reply. Bill clicked the bolt of his rifle and said, "Fräulein, haben einen Ausweis?" She stopped immediately, reached in her purse, and handed the identity card to him. Her name was Helga; she was sixteen. She was from another town, where she had been bombed out.

I was embarrassed. "Do we have to do that with every civilian?"

Bill laughed. "No, but we can't ever let them ignore us. It's fun to tease the girls. Just don't take them walking at night. Nothing has happened here, but they say a boy in Düsseldorf was walking with a girl and some Germans jumped him, beat him pretty badly."

I didn't know what to say. Bill was as close to me as a brother. During the long, boring days on line we had talked for hours about hometown, friends, future plans, and fear in combat. Why couldn't he see that this wasn't right? Maybe the proper question was why I thought it was wrong. That had an easy answer: I knew—from stories, anyway—what it felt like to be a defeated people. I knew that, during Reconstruction days, decent women shouldn't associate with the enemy. I knew that General Butler, the Beast of New Orleans, had ordered that any woman refusing to speak to a Yankee soldier be arrested as a prostitute.

There was a sign painted on a wall: Ein Volk, Ein Reich, Ein Führer. That had been Hitler's slogan; it meant that all Germanic people were one nation and should be under one leader. It reminded me of the Pledge of Allegiance: "one nation, indivisible, with liberty and justice for all." Our nation was indivisible because the War for Southern Independence had established that states weren't allowed to secede. Hitler had made the country indivisible, but not with liberty and justice for all. I didn't like being an occupation soldier.

The next morning at breakfast, little kids were waiting at the garbage can to beg for food we hadn't eaten. I started to give it to them, but the boy behind me said, "Hell, dump it in the garbage. If we start giving food away, the place will be jammed at noon."

I dumped it and worried all morning. These weren't the enemy; they were kids. Maybe their daddy had shot at us, but they were hungry and couldn't understand why we had no compassion. I couldn't understand, either. Maybe I had heard too much Scripture back in Clinton: "But whosoever hath this world's good, and seeth his brother hath need, and shutteth up his compassion from him, how dwelleth the love of God in him? Let us not love in word, neither in tongue; but in deed and truth" (1 John 4: 17–18).

At noon I sorted my leftovers between two kids. "Hey, don't be feeding those Krauts."

"Listen, you son of a bitch, I fought all through Brittany and at Nennig. I know the Krauts, but these are kids."

Graziano was there, laughing. "Hey, Standifer's learned to blow his stack."

At formation the next morning Captain Warren announced that orders had come down for us to have close order drill every day. He decided that the order meant for us to march with our rifles slung. The primary reason for such marching was to show the Germans that we were good soldiers. Warren knew we had been field soldiers for so long that we couldn't do the manual of arms ("right shoulder arms, present arms," etc.) well enough to impress anyone. Later we learned that the Germans already knew we were excellent field soldiers, and that they didn't care much for what they called "asphalt soldiers." We would have said "garrison soldiers," but the German term had a double meaning: most of their parade grounds were asphalt, and the original SS troops had worn black uniforms; the Waffen (combat) SS wore the gray uniform of all German combat troops.

As we stood in formation I looked down the row at my old First Squad. I was still first scout. Kevin was beside me as second scout, but he had seen no combat at all. Milky Edwards, who had joined the company a little before Kevin, was BAR man: George Faber's position. There had been twelve men in the original First Squad. That group was down to three: Herman Wendler, Ray Graziano, and me. Frank De Rosa was back as leader of Second Squad. During combat he had been platoon sergeant in Third Platoon but, like Ray, he had come back to us as a squad leader.

We began the routine army command procedure. The lieutenant said: "Platoon, left face. Column of squads."

Ray said, "First Squad, forward."

De Rosa said, "Second Squad, stand fast."

"March!"

We hadn't done this since last August in England. In my mind I could hear the regimental band playing "Stars and Stripes Forever." De Rosa started belting out the beginning of the new marching song called "Sound Off." I don't know where it originated but most of us had learned it in the replacement depots.

"The Krauts are lying in the grass. We're the ones that whipped their ass. Sound off: one, two—."

Ray said, "Let's show the Krauts what the infantry is," and he launched into "I was drinking beer in the cabaret, and was I having fun." It was the old song we had used during training. Wendler and I started singing and then the squad fell into it. "Lay that pistol down, babe, lay that pistol down. Pistol packin' mama, lay that pistol down!" I felt warm and proud. We were First Platoon of King Company, the best soldiers in the whole damned army!

That night Charlie said, "Hey, Standifer, I can line you up with a hot little girl, just cost a few cigarettes."

One of the boys warned, "Yeah, if the MPs catch you and Charlie out fraternizing, it'll cost you sixty-five bucks."

"We won't get caught. Go over before dark and spend the night. Be back for roll call in the morning."

I didn't want to go with Charlie but wasn't afraid of being caught by our division MPs. Those of us who had come over with the outfit called them "Sneaky Jesus." They were family, maybe like older brothers who were concerned with keeping us out of serious trouble. Back when we were in England they would patrol the towns, checking passes. About half of us didn't have passes, or were in the wrong town, or were beginning to get a bit drunk. Sneaky Jesus would check the pass, or whatever we handed him, and say: "There'll be a truck by here in about ten minutes. Get your butt on it. You don't want to wind up in the stockade." Or maybe: "Camp is about five miles down that road. Start walking. Maybe you'll be sober by the time you get there." Argue with Jesus and you would end up in the stockade, but he was there to keep us out of trouble. (Note: Rear-echelon MPs were as mean as snakes.)

I didn't want a Kraut girl because I—well, I just didn't want to fool around with Kraut girls. My only fraternization was with the kids who were teaching us German. I knew nothing about German grammar or sentence structure but had worked up a good vocabulary by asking, "Was ist das?" The kids adjusted to my pronunciation and grammar well enough to allow light conversation. They liked the Americans who gave them gum and candy. A few of the older kids would come by and call them "Verräter" (traitor), but we would yell "Raus!" and they would run.

The platoon was quartered in civilian homes, about six men to a house. The occupants had been given two hours to pack personal possessions and get out, leaving the rest to be "liberated." Jack Yost had a large brass bust of Hitler with der Führer's nose polished brightly and a bandage around his head. One boy had found that the women's clothes in his house seemed to be the right size for his girlfriend. He mailed her two boxfuls. Cameras and jewelry were the main items for liberation. Even during combat the boys had spent much of their time collecting trophies. Jewelry and gold were stashed in gas-mask bags (the masks themselves had been thrown out long ago). You might keep two or three cameras to trade up for a better one. Some GIs collected watches taken from prisoners, which seemed strange to me because there wasn't a good market for surplus watches. Top hats and gold-headed walking canes were hot items. One boy had a four-foot nude sculpture. Because the Nazis had glorified the strong Aryan body, there were a lot of nude paintings and sculptures, male as well as female—although the males weren't choice collection material.

Solingen was known for its fine steel and had made all of the German military swords and knives. Milky showed me a pile of sabers, short ceremonial swords inscribed with the slogan Meine Ehre Heisst Treue, and the slim bootknives that German combat troops often wore. "Look at this and decide what you want. I know where to get more of them all."

"That bootknife is good. I had one but it was stolen on the way to the hospital."

"Take it, I'll get another. What about one of these long swords?" I really didn't care for war trophies and couldn't understand why I wanted the bootknife. I had used one like it on the SS kid at Nennig and had kept it when I was evacuated, not realizing that hospital orderlies were notorious for selling trophies that they had stolen from patients. But I did take the bootknife that Milky offered me. Maybe I wanted one item to remind me of the horror.

Milky and Kevin had taken an interest in me when they found that I didn't smoke cigarettes. I smoked a pipe regularly, but that didn't count against our rations. Back during combat in Brittany, George Faber had suggested that I start smoking a pipe for relaxation when we returned from patrols. After each patrol we would sit under a tree and shake. George shook less than me because he would calm down with a cigarette. George didn't think I should smoke cigarettes because he was already smoking his ration and most of mine. Each week the squad was issued five packs of cigarettes per man, plus two packages of pipe tobacco. George got someone to buy a pipe for me in a nearby town and arranged for me to get the pipe tobacco, plus my cigarette ration. Throughout my stay in Europe I was always given my share of the cigarettes plus pipe tobacco—because no one else smoked a pipe. I can't remember any arguments over it; Leon was entitled to cigarettes even though he didn't smoke.

One day Milky and Kevin told me about a couple of girls who ran the Unterbühner photography shop. They would take studio-type photos of me for two packs of cigarettes. I got some clean clothes, put on my Combat Badge, and went over for the sitting. The girls spoke GI English and joked a lot, hoping I would relax. I kept trying to smile for the camera but they wouldn't let me: "You are a soldier, not a comedian." After the photo session, they sat and talked while smoking (my) cigarettes. The older girl (I don't remember their names) was twenty, but looked older, and was sleeping with Milky. Her sister was fourteen and sleeping with Kevin. I was embarrassed at their open attitude. They just giggled about little sister being so "mature."

Milky said, "Leon, they have a friend who wants to move in and help them. She has some great ideas about photography. You might like her. We really need another GI who doesn't smoke. These girls go through a lot of cigarettes and candy."

I tried to act sophisticated: "No, I don't think so—not just yet."

On the way back to our house, the boys told me more about the situation. The girls were running the studio because their father (Unterbüh-ner is a family name) was in the army and the mother was dead. Milky's girl was supposed to be acting as parent to the younger sister and hadn't liked the idea of Kevin dating her. She gradually relented because it wasn't really "dating," it was more like the four of them visiting and talking—with maybe a bit of lovemaking. This was allowed only if big sister was in the room to see that things didn't go too far. She absolutely refused to allow her kid sister to go into the bedroom with Kevin. There were some serious arguments over that rule; when she and Milky went into the bed-room, little sister had to go to her room and Kevin had to go home. The problem ended when Milky announced that it was a matter between Kevin and his girl. Milky said that they *would* go into the bedroom and that big sister would watch—to see that it was done right.

I walked along without comment, trying to assemble my confused thoughts. I was disgusted with Milky and Kevin but wondered if they were wrong. These girls were Krauts. A year ago that innocent, virgin girl would have killed me if she had a chance. What about the little kids who were teaching me German? Yes, I suppose so. Suppose, nothing—I was sure they would have; during the war it was common to hear of GIs being killed by Hitler Youth kids. At Nennig I would have shot any German without hands-over-the-head: soldier, civilian, girl, or kid. But that was war; that time was over.

"To every thing there is a season. . . . a time to love and a time to hate; a time of war and a time of peace" (Eccles. 3:1, 8). I thought, "Leon, what's bothering you? This is First Platoon. Four months ago we were sharing dry socks and toilet paper. Now they're offering to share women and Solingen swords. Yes, but . . ." But this was stealing and sharing the loot. Seducing a fourteen-year-old kid with candy and forcing her sister to watch was very close to rape.

I knew that these were not my kind of people; they were crude, their language as much as anything else. I had been in the army for nearly two years and knew that most soldiers were vulgar, but First Platoon had been different—a little, anyway. Lieutenant Westmoreland had discouraged foul language, and our platoon sergeant, Raymond Monti, never swore. First Squad had been run by George, Bill Henry, Ed Blake, Cagle, Herb Adams, and me; Ray Graziano had been the squad leader, but he wasn't our leader. Ray liked to cuss, yell, and swear; the squad didn't do that. Herb, a tough mountaineer and old-time Baptist, wouldn't tolerate swearing around him; I wasn't that kind of Baptist but respected Herb's beliefs.

Herb was gone; he had taken twenty-eight shrapnel wounds at Nennig and the medic had left him for dead. The squad carried him back. He survived but had a mangled leg, one lung, and a metal plate in his head. I had been lucky and was back with my old family, First Squad of First Platoon, but I was alone; my family was gone. They had been clean, dependable, strong, honest, and brave. Dale Proctor was dead; Ray Monti and Westmoreland were still in hospitals and would never be able to soldier again.

Most of all, I missed George—and knew that he would be back pretty soon. He and I had been a good team. I was tired of these idiots who hadn't fought and tried to make up for it by hating Germans. I was tired of arrogant kids acting like the damnyankees of the Reconstruction time. When I looked at things honestly, though, I knew that only a few of them were rotten. Bucco and I got along beautifully. He was a perpetual clown and could drag a dull story out for hours. We would sit in the window with a German phrasebook and practice our pronunciation on anybody who passed. When a woman passed by, we would use a phrase like "Wo ist der Bahnhof?" She might ignore us or might stop and try to explain that the railroad depot was not anywhere close to us.

Most of the boys who had girlfriends treated them decently. Captain Warren's instructions were that fraternization was permissible if it was kept discreet—and every man should keep condoms with him, just in case. He would not tolerate disturbances: fights or yelling matches with angry girlfriends would bring on the wrath of Warren. The wrath of Warren was much more to be feared than that of an MP. Most of us just played with the kids; technically, that was also fraternization, but it was friendly and fun.

The duty structure was strange, for several reasons. The first was that we had far too many noncoms. When a squad leader was wounded in combat, one of the more experienced riflemen was promoted to that position. When he was wounded, another one took his place. Now all of those squad leaders were returning with staff sergeant's stripes. We soon ran out of squads for them to lead, so the next sergeants to return were assigned as riflemen. Occasionally a tech sergeant (platoon sergeant) was serving as a rifleman under a staff sergeant, whom he outranked. A few men had their egos hurt, but in general the system worked. Most of the men had fought long enough for us to know who could soldier. A man's reputation for having soldiered well in combat carried a lot more weight than did the number of stripes on his arm. It all worked fine, for now. Things would have to change when we went back into combat, but that was several months off. We expected to be shipped home soon, get furloughs, and report back on the West Coast for the invasion of Japan.

The other problem was that there wasn't enough work to keep us busy. First Platoon was assigned to company headquarters as what we would have called the "reserve," or "patrol," platoon under combat conditions. We pulled guard duty and other minor assignments. Primarily out of boredom, I attached myself to company headquarters and helped Bill Henry on the telephone switchboard. He didn't really need any help, but the coffeepot was always full and he rode herd on the company library: a wide range of Armed Forces Edition books, generally good. For those of us who liked to read, Bill was running something of a literary coffeehouse. The liars and yarn-spinners of King Company were divided into the coffeehouse group and the beer-hall gang, but there was substantial overlap. People drifted into our coffeehouse to drink, trade for books, and swap memories of combat times. We followed a standard protocol: Everyone gets his chance to tell his version of a story. Never interrupt simply because you have heard it or were there when it happened; he might have improved the tale since you heard it last. Furthermore, his account might be better than what you remember. We were not searching for facts so much as sharing emotions, impressions of the shock, horror, excitement, and humor of combat.

No one could forget that intersection at Nennig where the 10th Armored tanks had run over dead, dying, and merely wounded troops— American and German. You couldn't blame the tankers. They were under fire, trying to protect us, and were confined to the narrow streets. We remembered the mixture of blood, snow, bits of bodies, and bits of uniforms; those were terrible times.

We all laughed about the Kraut-flavored water. The water supply in Nennig had consisted of springwater that flowed along the main street in a stone-lined trough. We would break through a crust of ice, fill the canteen, and drink. Several days later, when the snow thawed, someone found the dead German who had been lying in the spring just where it flowed out of the hillside. No one got sick, and the water tasted much better than the iodine-treated stuff that we were supposed to be drinking.

I sat there listening, remembering, needing to confess. "Man, I almost broke at Nennig. It wasn't the fighting or possibility of getting wounded; I knew the hospital could patch me up. I hated the stench, that smell of cordite and putrefying bodies. I wanted to run but was ashamed of even wanting to."

Somebody else said, "Yeah, I did too. None of us had the guts to yellow out and dump the load on men who were hurting as badly as we were." He stopped and thought. "Where could we have run? Without the platoon we would have frozen, starved, or both." I sat there wishing I hadn't said anything. Somebody broke the tension with: "Do you remember that warm-up shack, and the hot pancakes?"

"They were great, and the hot split pea soup. That room must have stunk to high heaven, all I remember is the hot food. Remember the night that rain melted the snow and exposed all the dead Krauts? Boy, did they stink!" That line of talk rambled on, sort of half catharsis, half joking. We couldn't quite say what we felt, so went on to more pleasant stories.

We laughed about the time Third Platoon was assigned to occupy Schillingen, a small town the Germans weren't defending. Ray Graziano was in charge, but he had never learned to read maps very well. As they got to the edge of town the scouts were fired on, and one was hit. The platoon fanned out, took the town, and captured about ten soldiers. Ray radioed Bill Henry to raise hell about the report of no troops being there. "Ray, you captured Nieder Kell. Second Platoon is waiting for you in Schillingen. Get your butt over there."

All of the old-timers had Lieutenant Chilton tales. Chilton was a replacement officer who joined us early in combat and never quite fit in. In retrospect, I can see that we were partly to blame for his problems. K Company was a close-knit family and he simply didn't fit our image of a good officer. On the other hand, he was short on imagination, very macho, and overly arrogant. Back in Brittany, Bob Higgins was on outpost, and bored. He called platoon headquarters to report that he saw the conning tower of a submarine coming up the stream. Somehow he made the story realistic enough to have Chilton call for an artillery barrage on the submarine, coming up a creek about three feet deep! Ed Blake had convinced Chilton that the Germans in Lorient had a launch pad from which they were firing V-2 rockets. Chilton was the butt of many jokes.

Another standard topic was how the Germans rated as soldiers. The consensus: pretty good. They weren't much for innovation, but they sure had grit. We would pound hell out of them with artillery before an attack, and the ones who survived would be ready to fight. The men of the 11th Panzer were probably the best we fought, but they were as mean as snakes: they played by their own set of rules. During the first few days of fighting against us they routinely shot medics who were tending wounded men—even when the wounded were Germans. It was something they had learned while fighting Russians, but we broke them of that habit. After about two weeks of fighting, the 11th Panzer disappeared; later the German commander said that the division had been "extracted" because it no longer existed as a combat unit.

After we crossed the Saar, the Germans threw some Austrian SS Mountain Troops at us; they were really just kids sixteen and seventeen years old. They didn't know how to soldier, but they sure had guts; the results were gruesome. They simply attacked, directly at us, running hard, firing, and yelling. They seemed to want to die, and die they did.

We were still fighting the 11th Panzer when I left, so I was just listening to the SS tales and wishing they would end. Finally there was a pause. Somebody said: "We killed a lot of brave Krauts. With no air support and not much artillery, they just kept coming. God, I'm glad that's over!"

One day Bill Henry was going over to see Third Platoon. I went along to see some old friends. Third Platoon was guarding the "potato bunker," a small storehouse with potatoes, some stale bread, and some pretty good sausage. The food was being used for the battalion's DP (displaced persons) camp. I don't know why we were running a DP camp. Bill thought that I might want to see the camp while we were there. I didn't. The awful memories of one I had seen while going through the replacement depot system were more than enough for me.

"Displaced persons" was a broad category of people who had been released from concentration camps or factories where they were being used as forced labor. Realistically, the category was even broader: deserters from the Russian and German armies, Nazi officials who had served in Poland, and criminals who had escaped during the confusion of combat. Newspaper accounts described them as honorable, hard-working people. Maybe some of them were, or once had been. The DP camp I had visited was near Bonn. Looking back, I can't remember why we had wanted to go; maybe we were just bored. I don't think we were dumb enough to be looking for women there.

I could still remember the nausea that hit me when we went into the barracks of the camp. The smell was staggering: human excrement, rancid body odors, a touch of old vomit, and a mixture of other stenches. Women in various stages of undress were lying on bunks, asleep, drunk, unconscious, or simply staring at the ceiling. These people were the dregs and debris of war. Considering what they had been through, I wondered whether there could be any human dignity left in them. Maybe they had been trash before going to Germany. Maybe all the good, decent people had already died. What kind of people could have survived the harsh life of the slave labor camps? Those who would lie, cheat, steal, and kill to get food or decent treatment? I didn't know and didn't want to go through the shock of finding out.

Those DPs had been housed in a small German military camp with

Those DPs had been housed in a small German military camp with three barracks (men, women, and "families"), a mess hall, recreation building, and toilet and shower area. The toilets had all become stopped up within a week after the DPs moved in; the shower area was converted to a toilet facility, flushed several times a day simply by turning on the shower. No one bothered to shower or even wash clothes. After liberation they had raided German homes and taken vast quantities of clothing. Now they could simply wear a dress for about a week and throw it away. The dress combinations were both funny and pitiful: formal dinner dresses too large for the starved bodies and spotted with filth. The mess hall was clean because an American mess sergeant was in charge, using German cooks and labor. He hated the damned DPs: "They're getting plenty of food, the same rations as you, but they keep stealing. Every bunk in the barracks has a box of stale bread and rotting food that they're saving in case the supply runs out. These people are like animals!"

He was right. The place smelled and looked like a zoo. Some of the women would sit on the ground all day, looking through the fence with a vacant stare. Others would stand by the fence and yell obscenities at GIs. The fence was only symbolic—the gate was always open and the guards were only there to keep order—but none of the women went out during the day. At night they would wander around town looking for anything they could drink. They weren't trying to sell their bodies for drink; no GI could put up with the stench. When DPs found booze, they stole it.

When I left that DP camp, I had sworn not to go in another one, but Bill argued that the one 3d Battalion ran was clean. I went with him only because he had to go there before we visited Third Platoon. For a DP camp, this one really was well run. It was neat and orderly; the mess hall was spotless. The inmates were still DPs. They were dirty and had the same vacant look as they lay out in the sun. Maybe they were dreaming of better times, or dreaming of nothing; maybe they could no longer remember better times. Even in a well-run camp, it was depressing to see them.

The Third Platoon boys guarding the "potato bunker" were enjoying life, on the technicality that DP women were from allied countries and were available for fraternization. Except for the observation that all DPs were dirty and German girls were clean, it was very hard to distinguish between enemy and friend; none of the DPs spoke English, but they all spoke some German. How could a poor rifleman know whether the clean, friendly German-speaking girl was friend or foe? Following the tradition of a man with a maid, Third Platoon felt they should give a little food to hungry, supposedly DP women. There was plenty of food in the bunker, and their orders were to guard against massive looting. Their defense was to use BARs with clips full of tracer rounds. Almost every night a group of the drunken DPs would charge the bunker. They seemed absolutely convinced that any building so well guarded must contain something worth drinking. The guards would fire bursts of tracers over their heads. Reports were that it made a spectacular sight, with bullets ricocheting off the stone buildings. The next day our medics would treat a few gunshot wounds, rarely serious.

Bill and I walked back to First Platoon without talking. I was ashamed of being embarrassed about the DPs. I was ashamed of King Company, of Milky and Kevin, and some others; it seemed as if my family had been invaded by outsiders. I didn't like being the victor occupying a defeated people. I didn't like the idea of being a damnyankee Reconstruction soldier. I was bothered about the slogan painted on a wall: Siegen oder Sibirien—"Victory or Siberia." If the Russians had captured Solingen-Wald, many of its people might have been sent to Siberia. Should they feel lucky that the Americans had captured the town instead? Should we be treating them as the Russian and French troops were? I was sick of the army and of war. I had only a handful of friends in the company: Bill, Bucco, and a few others. The war wasn't really over; we would soon be sent to the Pacific to invade Japan. Would I have to fight beside these no-'count troops?

How long would I last in combat against the Japanese? Would I be careful and try to last, or just blunder ahead, take my licks early, and go back to the hospital? As Roosevelt used to say, "I hate war."

2

VALLEY OF THE ROSES

I was sitting in company headquarters helping Bill Henry make up gossip about when and whether the division would be sent home for redeployment. Rapid redeployment meant a thirty-day furlough, report back to San Francisco, and head for the invasion of Japan. Some of our new boys were eager about the furlough and having a chance to be part of the next big show. Bill and I had already seen a big show; we hadn't particularly enjoyed it and didn't care for a rerun. Our hope was that the 94th would be assigned as Army of Occupation, that we would stay in Germany until the war was over.

Arrigi, the company clerk, was opening the official mail. "Hey, listen to this: 'Effective immediately, all units of the Division will begin preparations for shipment to Susice, Czechoslovakia, where the Division will relieve units of the 26th Infantry and 8th Armored Divisions. Detailed orders will follow'!"

We let out a whoop and ran over to Bierstube König to spread the news: no more fighting, misery, terror, and death. We started drinking beer and singing: "Gonna lay down that old M-1, down by the riverside, and study war no mo'. / Gonna lay me a fat Fräulein, down by the riverside, and study war no mo'!"

The celebration lasted for about ten minutes. Arrigi came over with Captain Warren's explanation of what the orders really meant. The 26th and 8th Divisions were being redeployed immediately. No decision had been made about the 94th, but we had to get out of the Düsseldorf area because it was going to be part of the British sector.

24

We left Solingen-Wald about two weeks later. I still wonder what became of the girls' photography enterprise. In preparing this manuscript I have learned that they did not own the shop and were not related to Herr Unterbühner. The shop is currently run by Unterbühner relatives; they don't know who the girls might have been. It seems likely that Milky appropriated the shop and set his girlfriend up in business.

Regardless of ownership, the girls were experienced and talented photographers. They could easily have handled the scheme hatched by a friend of theirs—the girl they wanted me to adopt. A few days after our first encounter the girls invited me over to meet her. Under other circumstances, she would have been a good match for me: not very good-looking, quiet but witty, and speaking excellent English. But I wasn't willing to date a German girl. Even so, I was impressed with her idea, which was to pose GIs with hired models. She knew some unemployed models in Düsseldorf who couldn't risk their professional reputations by actually dating the enemy but were receptive to the idea of taking part in creative photography. Her concept of "creative photography" covered a rather wide range of possibilities—but GI tastes were quite broad. I hope the girls were able to adapt the scheme for use with British soldiers.

It's possible, however, that I didn't really understand much about the girls and their enterprise. A few months later, when I told a Bavarian friend about the photographers and how shocked I had been over the way Milky and Kevin treated them, she laughed and offered an entirely different interpretation of what was happening: more about that later.

Before we left for Czechoslovakia, Captain Warren read the company a report from division headquarters about our mission. The Czechs were our liberated allies and friends. We were expected to show them that the American army wanted to help with the adjustment to freedom. We would see many Russian flags, but that was only because the language was similar to Russian. The Czechs were a friendly, freedom-loving people.

We did not learn the true meaning of this report until much later. We were being sent to the mountains of the Sudetenland, the largely German-speaking part of Czechoslovakia that Hitler had taken over as a result of the Munich Conference. Prime Minister Chamberlain had returned to London proclaiming that he had achieved "peace in our time."

But the Sudetenland had been a key point of the Czech defenses, and with it in hand Hitler was able to take the rest of the country with no organized opposition.

Hitler had claimed that the Sudetenland was "essentially German." It wasn't. It was a mixture of small villages that were either entirely German or entirely Czech. These segregated communities had existed for generations. They could not, would not, integrate because the cultures clashed. When German troops moved in, the German towns celebrated; the Czech towns resisted, and the Gestapo was probably brutal.

The 3d Infantry Division had captured, or liberated, this area against almost no opposition. Their prisoners included the "Vlasov Army" (Russian POWs who had enlisted in the German army) and the Adolf Hitler SS Division, which had originally been Hitler's personal guard division. Then the troubles began; the people from Czech towns flooded into the German towns seeking revenge on civilian women and children. The appalled GIs blocked Czech entry into the towns, which caused more trouble. I don't know the details, but some guidelines were developed and the 3d, 26th, and 8th Armored Divisions were moved out, to be replaced by us and the 90th Division.

The trip down was like a GI tour of Germany, with the plush accommodations of what we called "slide-door Pullmans." When we moved by rail during the war, they jammed forty men into each of the little "40 and 8" boxcars, but on this trip we had room to stretch out—only twenty men per car. During the war, the movement of infantry troops had priority over almost all other cargo; now we were near the bottom. Every few hours we were shunted onto a sidetrack so that a trainload of supplies or DPs could roar past us. From our perspective, these stops only meant frequent chances to get out, stretch, play ball, or just lie around. One time we were sidetracked next to a boxcar being guarded by two Canadian soldiers. The quarter-moon symbol on the side clearly indicated that the car contained rations, but the guards didn't know any more than that; they were instructed to prevent anyone from looting it. Well, one thing led to another, and the guards realized they were no match for an infantry company. We acted very much like the hordes of drunken DPs who raided the potato bunker, but we were sober and knew that no one would shoot at us. We had gotten about two cases per boxcar when our train started pulling out. We scrambled into the cars and broke the cases open to find that we had stolen Spam! (To be fair, the company that produces Spam maintains that most of the wartime "chopped luncheon meat" wasn't Spam. They are probably right, but we called it Spam.)

I enjoyed sitting in the door of our Pullman while the green countryside drifted past. Now and then we passed through towns; most of them seemed to be entirely destroyed. Of course, we usually got the worst view: railroad yards had been favorite bombing targets. Nuremberg and Munich had been popular secondary targets for American bombers when a primary target was scrubbed. The planes didn't have enough fuel to haul the load of bombs back to England, and landing with a bomb load was a bit dangerous anyway. It seemed only fitting to use the extra bombs on a center of Nazism. When we rolled through the (repaired) railyard at Nuremberg, there was nothing but rubble as far as we could see. Occasional street signs showed where a street had once existed, but the rubble was spread so evenly that the street was no different from where a house had stood. Someone had erected a hand-lettered sign that said (in German), "For all of this, we can thank our Führer." That had been a Hitler slogan in the days when he was developing public-works projects such as the Autobahns.

We were sidetracked beside the old Sportsplatz, which we had seen in newsreels with Hitler taking the salutes of cheering youth or soldiers. We climbed onto the reviewing stand, but it had been looted of everything that could possibly serve as a souvenir. A group of us stood exactly where Hitler had stood, gave the Nazi salute, and had our picture taken—from so far away that we appeared to be kids playing.

We got off the train and onto trucks for a long, dusty ride through the mountains. King Company was assigned to a little German town named Rosenthal—"Valley of the Roses." It was in a small valley, but there were no roses: the town was named for a family that had been gone for so long no one remembered them. It was a neat, clean little town nestled among some beautiful fir-covered mountains. The main street was two blocks long, but *street* isn't quite the word; it was only a cobblestone trail. The town water supply was a stream that had been diverted into a stone aqueduct alongside the street. First Platoon and the company headquarters section were quartered in town, with the other platoons on outposts (guard stations). Second Platoon had an outpost at Grosse Umlavitz ("Large Umlavitz"; I think *Umlavitz* is Czech but have no idea what it means). Because the town consisted of only four farmhouses, the platoon was quartered at Kleine Umlavitz, "Small Umlavitz," which had about twelve houses and a small school building. The citizens didn't see anything strange about the smaller town being called "Large Umlavitz" and vice versa; those had always been the names.

Over the entire area the people were friendly and glad the war was over. Most of them were old women (old by GI standards), with a few old men and children. The young men were still prisoners. There were a some teenaged girls, but not nearly enough to go around. The area had several small lakes teeming with fish, and there were miles of walking trails in the mountains. The company library was well stocked with Armed Forces Editions of good books. I was looking forward to a quiet summer vacation and wished that George or Ed or Cagle were here to enjoy it with me. Two days later George swung off the back of the ration truck. He had been chasing us all across Germany. We squealed and hugged each other like kids. George had been my anchor and mainstay throughout our time in the company. We had been assigned to First Platoon at the same time, just over a year ago. George had been the squad's BAR man while I was first scout. Those were the two most dangerous positions in the squad, but we had been proud, careful, and very lucky. I had been wounded in early December. Two days before I returned to the company, George had been evacuated with badly frozen feet. We had been separated for more than six months.

We spent hours recounting hospital adventures. He had spent the first month at a Paris hospital, where his treatment consisted of a shot of bourbon each day and having his feet massaged by a French girl, a nurses' aide. Then he had been transferred to a hospital near London. There he took exercises in the morning but had the afternoons and nights off. George had a ball in London. I hadn't been nearly that lucky, but we had both enjoyed hospitalization.

Then George started making plans for our future.

"Leon, we need to get transferred into company headquarters."

I was shocked. Why did he want to leave First Platoon? We were rifle-men. He pointed out that we *had* been riflemen and had been very lucky to survive. Before the division was shipped to Japan, we were going to be doing something in regimental or divisional headquarters. Our first step was to be reassigned to company headquarters, where we could make contacts with people in battalion and move on up the ladder.

The transfer into company headquarters was easy. I was already spend-ing most of my time there. We explained the situation to Bill Henry, who agreed that we had been riflemen for long enough. Bill suggested to Cap-tain Warren that we would make good communications men, and had us sent to a two-day school at regimental headquarters where we learned to repair German army telephone equipment (all of the company commu-nications equipment was German; it was better than ours). We soon be-came the entire communications section. The telephones themselves hardly ever needed repairs, but we had several miles of thin communica-tions wire strung (not very carefully) to the outposts, and the lines were continually being broken by horses, carts, or kids tripping over them.

Headquarters section was quartered in the Rosenthal school. We had two large rooms, where we slept on straw mats. Toilets were in the "house out back." It was something of a comedown from our luxury in Solingen-Wald, but we had been in the army for a long time and could sleep anywhere, anytime, and on anything. I rummaged through a closet and found a big stack of wartime propaganda posters called *Wochenspruch* ("weekly sayings"). Each week the Nazi Party headquarters in Munich had put out a poster, which was apparently distributed to all schools.

I learned a lot of German trying to translate the heroic slogans on the posters. One of the early ones (1940) said, "It is better to sacrifice one's life than one's loyalty." Another promoted woman's place in the home: "The woman also has her battlefield: with every child she brings into the world, she fights her battle for the nation." A poster with the flags of the Nazi Party, the navy, Luftwaffe, and army said: "Carry these flags and stan-dards and be the guarantor for the liberation of Europe from Bolshevism." The December 27, 1941, poster had a beautiful prayer: "Lord: You see that we have changed. The German people is no longer the people of dishonor and disgrace, of self-recrimination and dejection. No, Lord, the German people is again strong in spirit, strong in steadfastness, strong in its ability to endure sacrifices. Lord, we will not stray from You, only now crown our struggle for our freedom, our people, and our fatherland."

It was interesting to follow the changing themes as Germany's fortunes declined. In March 1942 a poster said: "The greatest sacrifice is the surrendering of one's own life for the whole." There was a quotation from Bismarck: "When Germans stick together, they can drive the devil from hell." In December 1943 the quote was from Goebbels: "In all that you do and do not do, in all that you say and do not say, remember always that you are German." The last poster in the collection was a quotation from Hitler, November 19, 1944: "German people: Whatever may come, we will master it. At the end stands victory."

My rough translations in 1945 were not nearly as good as those I have given here, but I understood enough from the posters to make me curious about the proud Germans who had helped to create world turmoil. I worked hard at learning what I believed were proper German phrases and customs. Actually I was learning rural mountain Austrian terms and attitudes. Translated into American, I was learning hillbilly German. The polite greeting there was "Grüss Gott," the greetings of God. It was derived from a longer greeting used in the Catholic church, but I think we were in a Lutheran area.

It is misleading to describe our situation as if it were a summer vacation. The Russian army headquarters was at Ceské Budějovice, maybe forty miles away. General Patton hated the Russians, was convinced that we would be fighting them within a month, and wanted his Third Army to drive them back into Asia. We were issued ammunition and hand grenades and told to be ready for combat on twenty-four-hour notice. Second and Third Platoons had outposts facing Russian outposts, about two miles from company headquarters. First Platoon was in combat reserve.

In spite of Patton's attitude, our commanding general saw the situation more realistically. The 90th and 94th Divisions were facing roughly two million Russian combat troops. They probably outnumbered us by something better than a hundred to one. Apparently our division commanders knew that Eisenhower was raising hell with Patton for talking so big. The American people were sick of war and were not willing to start fighting Russia when we hadn't defeated Japan. We carried our rifles at all times and had cases of ammunition available, but there were no drills, exercises, or inspections. Breakfast was 7:30 to 8:30: get up if you want to eat. I was a little worried that we would be sloppy soldiers if the Russians attacked (none of us at the company level knew how badly we were outnumbered). The company hadn't fought in three or four months and wasn't combat ready by any stretch of the imagination. But we were still a proud, experienced unit. If we had been attacked, Captain Warren's King Company would have stood, fought, and died at Rosenthal. Tactically, that was our mission: to delay the Russians until Patton could start a counterattack.

One advantage of being in headquarters section was that we got first chance at temporary duty assignments. We got a notice that regiment wanted a squad of men for two weeks of guarding SS troops. I thought that might be interesting, but George wouldn't go. Bucco thought it would be fun. He hadn't seen any SS troops. I had seen a few at Lorient and the one at Nennig. I remembered the tales told in Solingen-Wald about our slaughter of the kids in the 6th SS Mountain Division. I wasn't expecting to see any supersoldiers but was a little curious about them.

When we arrived at the camp I was surprised to find that we were to serve as a *protective* guard: the prisoners were in a Czech area where the people were very bitter toward Germans, particularly the SS. Several thousand German troops, mostly ordinary infantry soldiers but with about five hundred Waffen SS, were camped in a little valley. They hadn't really surrendered to anyone. They had just stacked their weapons and posted armed guards. Because the guards were afraid to fire, civilians had started harassing them. We had been sent to replace the German guards. The U.S. Army set up squad tents to form outposts surrounding the valley; guards had orders to let no civilians approach the prisoners.

My group was assigned to provide a very close guard on the SS troops, who had been separated from the others. They lived in small tents, had separate rations, and cooked their own food. Every day a few of them were sent up to act as our orderlies: making our beds, washing our clothes, and cleaning our rifles (they sometimes were embarrassed at having to remind us that we should remove the ammunition first). We usually gave them a few cigarettes and some C rations. We had long talks in a mixture of German, English, and sign language. Most of it had to do with what the Russians were like: the general opinion was that they were rotten soldiers and mean, cruel drunkards.

The SS boys couldn't understand why we, the strongest capitalists in the world, weren't helping them beat the Communists. Why were only the Germans trying to fight world Communism? We pointed out that Hitler's goals also included world domination and the eradication of "lesser breeds" such as Poles, Russians, Jews, Gypsies, and the mongrel Americans who represented the debris of all races. There weren't any real arguments or hard feelings because we realized that these were not bright boys. Their educational background was almost nil. Educated boys went into the Luftwaffe or submarine corps; good old country boys joined the SS. They were not stupid but simply did not have enough information to discuss world events.

One day the boy who was cleaning our tent dropped a belt buckle from his pocket. I picked it up and saw that it was just like the one I had gotten at Nennig: "Meine Ehre Heisst Treue." I tried putting it in English. "My something is named true. Was ist 'Ehre'?" He looked it up in my German-English dictionary and said that *Ehre* was honor. He was pleased that I could understand the SS motto, but "My honor is named true" meant nothing to me. He called another German over, and a couple of Americans helped us. It means more than "I am faithful to my honor." It's something like "Loyalty is the foundation of my honor." Bucco said: "It sounds a lot like the Marine Corps: Semper Fidelis." Then we tried to explain to the SS what the marines meant when they said "Semper Fi"; the SS never said "Ehre Heisst."

This discussion led to the question of why they had joined the SS instead of the regular army. There were varied answers; some had simply been drafted and assigned to the SS without any choice. One of the older men gave an interesting account: "Looking back at everything, I wish I hadn't joined. When I went in, everybody was proud of me. Now people look on us as criminals. I didn't join the SS to kill Jews. Those concentration-camp guards were an entirely different unit. They didn't have to pass the same physicals or take the rough training of the Waffen SS. I joined the Black Corps [SS] to help keep the Bolsheviks from over-running Europe. I fought the Russians for two years, and was wounded three times. I had joined the toughest outfit, and we were to be sent where the fighting was hardest. Our training was much tougher than what the *Landser* had. We ran everywhere we went, shaved and showered in cold water even in the winter. Our dress uniforms were really sharp: black with white insignia. Even our gray combat uniforms were of better quality that those of the *Landser,* and our boots would take a high polish. When I was on leave and walked into a room, everybody turned and looked. We were the pride of Germany."

To me it was a sad story. It might not be symbolic of all Waffen SS, but it seemed to characterize many of the ones we were guarding. They were simple kids who had joined for the myth and the sharp uniform (and the girls it attracted). They had fought bravely in Russia, taking awful casual-ties, and were now treated as vicious animals.

Even though we couldn't agree with them, the experience was inter-esting. We taught the SS boys how to sing the tricky lyrics of "Mairzy Doates," and they taught us all the words to their favorite song, "Lili Mar-lene." Finally trucks came to haul them back to Germany; maybe some of them were discharged quickly, but some were going to be prisoners for a long time.

When I got back, George was getting ready to leave. He was going to London so he could be with a girl he had met during his hospital stay. But there was more to it than that. Having little for troops to do, the army had developed a training program that included many professions. George noticed one that was aimed at retail marketing and entailed working at a large department store in London. During high school, George had worked on Saturdays as stockboy at a grocery store; he wrote up the "pre-vious experience" well enough to get the assignment. When he returned in six weeks, we would start working on angles to get us out of the rifle company.

I was disappointed that George hadn't told me about applying for the program. Maybe I could have gone to London with him. Maybe I couldn't have. The truth is, we were drifting apart. We were still as close as brothers and probably owed our lives to each other's support during combat, but like brothers, we were going our different ways. I had been to London a couple of times on leave, and I really didn't care for such a large city. Rosenthal was a quiet little town. It could get boring, but I had plenty of books to read and was enjoying my efforts at learning German. George hadn't tried to learn French in Brittany and had even less interest in German. The trip to London would be a good vacation, and by the time he got back we might be moving out for German occupation duty or for redeployment.

When I got bored in Rosenthal I would walk along the road and hitch a ride with the first army truck that came by. It didn't matter much where they were going. I would get off in a town and look for something interesting to buy, then hitch a ride back. One day I was headed back when a command car came by. It stopped, and I started to get in the front with the driver. "Sit back here, soldier." It was our regimental commander, Colonel Hagerty. I hadn't seen him since he had chewed out the company because Third Platoon had surrendered. That was last October.

"Where are you going?"

"Rosenthal, sir." I was a little scared. I didn't have a pass, or even permission to be away. I had just left.

"You're K Company?"

"Yes, sir, I was first scout in combat."

"Under Warren?"

"No, sir, Simmers. I left at Nennig with frozen feet and pneumonia. The company didn't get shoepacs until after the snow melted."

"That was a mess. Supplies were all screwed up. When did you join the regiment?"

"At McCain. I was ASTP."

Hagerty was beginning to loosen up: "That was a fine group of soldiers. I'm glad we got them."

I should have kept quiet but was becoming confident about his friendly attitude. "Yes, sir, we lost a lot of them in Brittany. Proctor was in my platoon."

Hagerty hesitated, trying to remember who Proctor might have been. "He's the one who got the DSC, isn't he?"

Then I hit him with the next point. "Yes, sir. He was from Nebraska. Was end on the university football team. The one that went to the Rose Bowl." (That wasn't quite true. Dale had been on the freshman team and hadn't made the trip to Pasadena.)

"Oh my God, I'm from Geneva, Nebraska."

"I know. Dale was from Bruno, near David City."

"Some fine young men died."

I wanted to say, "Yes, you stupid, egotistical son of a bitch. The Infantry School gave you some of this country's brightest and best-trained men. You wasted our abilities on stupid, poorly organized assignments and inept management. We were not your serfs; we were infantry. You let the rear-echelon troops steal shoepacs while the infantry froze their feet. I saw a nineteen-year-old boy lose both of his feet from your stupidity." I didn't say that, because I felt sure he had seen my point. I said, "Yes, sir, this war hurt us all badly."

We talked a bit about Patton and the Russians. I knew from regimental gossip that Patton had chewed out Hagerty about having so many frozen feet and pneumonia casualties. That did not mean Patton was showing consideration for the troops; he had threatened to relieve Hagerty of his command if the medics continued to send "noncombat" casualties to the hospital. Despite my bitterness, I felt sorry for Hagerty. He was responsible for mistakes his intelligence and supply officers made, but they had been competing with highly experienced German officers. (At a reunion after the war I told a man from regimental headquarters about the conversation. His reply surprised me: "Old 'Roarin' Roy' was a good soldier who was dedicated to his troops, but he had an awful temper. He was continually raising hell over the poor supply system and the matter of not getting warm clothes up to the men.")

After my encounter with Hagerty, I decided to entertain myself closer to home—I had been lucky he hadn't asked why I was hitchhiking. Besides my reading, I became more active in a loose organization called the King Company Sportsmen and Weapon Collectors Club. The several small lakes around Rosenthal hadn't been fished in a long time because no fish-hooks were manufactured during the war. There were also some small deer that came to drink at the lakes in late afternoon and early morning. We had no fishing tackle of any kind, and although several of the boys had some good sporting rifles confiscated when all the Germans at Solingen-Wald were required to turn in weapons, there was no ammunition for them. However, this was the area where large numbers of the Adolph Hitler SS Division had surrendered, plus those Russians who had been fighting for the Germans. Where Russian units had surrendered we would find the not-very-good Russian army rifles and an occasional Russian army pistol. The pistols were valuable for trading purposes, but might be hard to take home; we certainly couldn't call them captured enemy weapons. The SS surrender areas were much more promising. There were good rifles, machine guns, burp guns, and boxes of hand grenades. There were also a lot of pistols, if you looked carefully. Before surrendering, the German officers invariably dismantled their pistols and scattered the parts. If you found any part of a pistol, methodical searching would always turn up the other pieces—I found an excellent prewar Luger and several of the less-valued P-38s.

Pistols had become the prime collector's item because of a strange twist in army "war trophy" regulations. Broadly, we were allowed to send home almost anything as a war trophy—if we could pack it to fit in a mailbag and if an officer would sign a form stating that the item had greater value as a trophy than its potential value to the military. With the war over, almost anything would fit in that category; the boy who sent clothes to his girlfriend had called them war trophies. The glaring exception to this policy was that no pistols could be mailed; we would be allowed to take one with us when the division went home, but one was the limit. For this reason, each of us had several pistols, which we hoped to use in trading up to a better one. (Another reason for having extra pistols was that when we went on leave to an urban area, we could usually sell two or three at a good price.)

Rainy-day entertainment in the company headquarters section was to pull out our pistols, clean them, and brag about how fine they were. I remember a day when somebody brought in a beautiful Belgian pistol.

Eddie Morris was impressed and wanted to trade for it. Eddie was not one of our brighter boys. He had been in First Platoon back in Brittany when we slipped out near the German lines to set up a nighttime ambush. We got into firing positions and settled down to wait; Eddie went to sleep with his finger on the trigger of his rifle. The rifle fired, the ambush was blown, and the entire platoon had to run back to our lines. Well, this time Eddie admired the pistol, cocked it, aimed it at his foot, asked if it was loaded—and fired before he got an answer. It was loaded. Captain Warren put out an order: nobody will carry a pistol—anywhere—and nobody will keep a loaded pistol.

Because rifles weren't included in the order, we decided to establish a rifle range down by one of the lakes where there were deer. There was a standing company order against firing any type of weapon, but because we occasionally did bring in a deer, our officers were willing to ignore the noise, provided we fired only in that one area. One of our members got disgusted with missing so often. He loaded a machine gun with tracer ammunition and collected one badly mangled deer. We passed a rule against that, not on grounds of sportsmanship, but because rapid fire of the dreaded MG 34 aroused bad memories and caused nightmares.

Because we had no fishing tackle at all, it was necessary to improvise. We had found a large box of the small German concussion grenades, about the size of a goose egg and encased in a thin metal jacket. Once a week we would drop a couple of grenades into one of the lakes and collect the stunned fish—usually enough for a good fish fry with some left over for trading to civilians. It was a sportsman's paradise.

3

USEFUL ARTICLES

I remember most of the people in Rosenthal as being friendly, hard-working, and drab. The town barber showed a little color. He would listen carefully to our instructions as to the type of cut we wanted, and then give us the standard European-style cut. He had learned a few English phrases, which he used so randomly that he sounded like a parrot: "Sonomabitch, I cut too much!" "Morning, how you hammerhangin'?" "Gotta smoke for me?" If we spoke German, he was something of the town gossip and historian, but his tales of local history were about as useless as his gossip. The town carpenter was an excellent craftsman, but the only real business he had was in making boxes for us to send souvenirs home. There was an old man who would sit on a wooden bench in front of his house, singing old-time mountain songs while he played his accordion; we couldn't understand the words, but he sang with such gusto that we kept him furnished with cigarettes.

In Rosenthal everyone worked, regardless of age. It was a farming community without its men and with only a few horses, oxen, and cattle. Children below the age of six or seven worked as *Gänsehirten,* gooseherds. The town probably had a total of forty or fifty geese: I remember that two children could handle a flock of maybe ten or fifteen geese, and there were about four such groups. I felt sad at seeing the two little children clutching their lunch package, herding the geese out to the fields where they would graze all day. The children would sit together, trying to read from their little books; there would be no school this year. Some of the girls did simple handwork: weaving little baskets or mending clothes. Occasionally we would go out to visit, give them a bit of candy, and talk. One of the children would talk while the other kept a close eye on the geese. They had been warned never to forget their job. It wasn't a difficult task, a matter of keeping the geese together and in the middle of the field, but it hurt me to see such young children having to work all day, every day.

Old men and younger ones who had been crippled during the war mended the stone fences. They used no cement at all, just a hammer, chisel, and patience. They began by dismantling the section that had collapsed and sorting the stones according to size and shape. Then they carefully fitted them back together with only an occasional chisel blow to make a piece fit. It took days to reassemble a small section of wall, but time moved very slowly in Rosenthal.

Boys and girls over age eight worked the fields, making hay, harvesting wheat or barley, digging potatoes, or plowing the fields. Occasionally we soldiers would get embarrassed enough to go out and help, only to find that it was very hard work and we couldn't last long without frequent rest breaks. Peacetime was making us fat and flabby.

The political life of Rosenthal was simple: the people had, or showed, no particular interest in politics that did not directly affect the town. The war was over and they had lost. In this small, isolated place, the concept of war guilt did not exist. They had heard a little about concentration camps, but not very much. They supposed that some evil men in Berlin had run the camps. They knew that the Czechs hated all Sudeten Germans, and they in turn hated the Czechs, but that had nothing to do with the war; it had been that way for generations. They knew that the Russian soldiers were brutal because they were Russians. The Americans were friendly and easygoing because they came from a nice, rich country.

The Americans were also very generous, especially toward families with daughters. There were probably seven or eight girls of dating age in Rosenthal, and maybe fifteen or twenty more within ten kilometers (walking distance for a GI). The exact number varied according to the definition of "dating age": too young or too old depended on individual preferences. Most of the girls were home-grown, but some were *Flüchtlinge,* refugees who had been evacuated from bombed-out cities and were staying with families here, doing farmwork in exchange for room and board. The families considered the refugees to be surrogate daughters, subject to the same house rules as other members. The girls disagreed with that concept but were not in a strong position to argue; the alternative was to be thrown out of the house with nowhere to go.

Food, although not plentiful, was not a serious problem in a rural area that grew potatoes, grain, and some livestock. Real coffee had disappeared from the market early in the war, replaced by roasted barley. There had been no sugar for years—the younger children had never tasted candy. American soldiers, however, seemed to have limitless amounts of real coffee and sugar. The army recipe for making coffee was to bring a GI can (metal garbage can) of water to a boil, dump in a lot of coffee grounds, and wait until they settled. Strong black coffee would be dipped out to each soldier until the grounds were reached, which meant there was no more coffee (a problem that very seldom arose). My memory of GI coffee is that there was always a layer of grounds, and a little sugar, in the bottom of the cup; chewing on sweet coffee grounds was the perfect end to a GI meal. But I digress. The point is that there was also a thick layer of coffee grounds left in the bottom of the GI can. Every soldier who had a date that night would be given a canteen-cup-full of still-pretty-good coffee grounds. He could usually scrounge a little sugar and sometimes a can of the grease left over from cooking pork chops or Spam. There was never any extra meat, but the Rosenthal families used the grease to add flavor to boiled potatoes. Taking such a package of goodies to the family of your date was far more important than carrying flowers had been back home.

During the first few weeks, dating the Rosenthal girls presented problems. I don't know what the dating customs had been before the war, but they must have been very strict. The town had no Bierstube. The school had a small assembly room where people said there had been community dances every Saturday night before all the men went off to war. The Rosenthal idea of having a date involved going to the house, sitting in what might be called a living room (actually a cooking-eating-living room), and trying to carry on a conversation with Mama (Papa was off somewhere in the army). Going for a moonlight stroll was unthinkable.

Because most of the girls had come of age during the war, they had very little dating experience, but they felt that the traditional customs could stand some improvements. The GI boyfriends gave interesting accounts of American dating habits, and the *Flüchtlinge* loved entertaining the local girls with lurid tales of modern customs in German cities.

To parents adamant about upholding virtue and local tradition, daughters argued that times were changing, very rapidly. And when it came to dating GIs, they had a trump to play. They pointed out that Rosenthal was safe from abuse by the Czech police only because the Americans were there. When the GIs left, the Czechs or maybe even the Russians would take over; rape and pillage by "Ivan" was well known. The only hope, in short, was the Americans. Individual GIs were rowdy and lazy, but they were also friendly and caring, and the army as a whole not only was obviously strong, but also seemed fair-minded.

The adult population agreed with this analysis and felt sure that the Americans would not leave without providing for the protection of ethnic Germans. The most popular idea was that a small number of Americans would stay in Rosenthal to ensure fair treatment. Another theory was that the entire town would be relocated to a peaceful part of Germany.

Small towns enjoy gossip, but Rosenthal reveled in it more than most. Because the area had no German language newspapers or radio programs, the only news sources were the GIs and the army newspaper, *Stars and Stripes*, which was circulated only within the army. The practical flaw in this situation was that the GI population didn't have a clue as to future plans for Rosenthal, and most of the news in *Stars and Stripes* concerned occupation problems in Germany and the war in the Pacific. Our only information about the Rosenthal area came from the general tone of official mail to the company and from rumors we picked up at battalion or regimental headquarters. We knew that the American army was not in Czechoslovakia for the protection of a few ethnic Germans. By now we realized that, regardless of what Patton said, there was no possibility that we would fight the Russians. We were being quartered in Czechoslovakia because of a housing shortage in Germany. All of the small German towns were overcrowded with refugees from bombed-out cities. We had read that the American Military Government was working on an agreement under which the Russians would leave Czechoslovakia when we did, but nobody believed that the agreement would affect our withdrawal date. The army wanted to get us out of the mountains before winter set in. Beyond that, the plans were vague.

We also knew that the internal politics of Czechoslovakia were of no concern to the American army. When we left, the Czechs would probably move in, confiscate the entire town, and send the ethnic Germans back to Germany—which was not able to accommodate them. It was a sad situation. Rosenthal had been German for many generations, but the Czech government was determined that Germany would never again have an excuse for annexing the area.

Within the civilian population there were strong rumors that the Russian army had solved the problem in their zone by shipping all ethnic Germans to Russian labor camps. After the Germans went to Russia, the Czech farmers had simply moved in and taken over the villages. We didn't know if this was true, because the Russians allowed no one into their zone. We occasionally visited with Russian guards at the outposts, but they knew nothing about Red Army policies. Many of the Rosenthal people believed the story and were almost certain that, if the Americans left, the Czech government would sell the Russians some more cheap labor.

It was in this atmosphere of rumor and fear that the girls of Rosenthal developed their plan for revising traditional dating customs. The plan required creativity because it was impossible to pretend that we would stay indefinitely or that the Czech government would ever allow ethnic Germans to become citizens. The girls, with the help of GI boyfriends, explained to their parents that the American army was deeply concerned over the possibility of ethnic Germans being sent to Russia as slave labor and was developing a plan under which each company would be allowed to take some selected families back to Germany. Because (according to the girls' concept) our division was scheduled to serve for many years as part of the occupation army, it would need reliable German families to develop farms and businesses that would provide support services for the army base.

The idea of the American army establishing a new Rosenthal somewhere in Germany was absurd, but it was similar to the relocation theory already in circulation, and the girls were able to make it still more plausible with a little help from company headquarters. We typed up an official-looking "highly classified" memorandum suggesting that all units begin considering which families might be selected as essential employees. The quota for each company would be assigned later. Copies were then smuggled to the girls, who carefully translated the material into German. This information demonstrated the importance of not only the girls' but their entire families' staying on good terms with their American friends.

We had spent an entire day working on the document. The final draft contained enough army jargon to make it almost meaningless, especially after being translated into German. Our only ethical problem hinged on what might happen if Captain Warren were to find out what we were doing. We were not sure what the penalty might be for producing a false document and forging the regimental commander's signature. As to the matter of what Brunhilde might want to tell her parents about a secret document that her boyfriend had stolen, well, that was her business.

Beyond the fun of helping to write the order, I saw no possibility it might affect me. I knew most of the girls and would have tried dating some of them, but I really wasn't in the league with those smooth operators who had already taken the datable and marginally datable women. My involvement with a girl in the latter group was short and accidental but interesting. One afternoon before George left, he and I stopped at a small farm, probably to trade cigarettes for eggs. A girl, maybe seventeen years old, came to the door: "Yes, what do you want?" I was impressed that she could speak English. It turned out that the Rosenthal school had taught a little basic English and she had continued to study, a little. She didn't speak it very well, but she did understand the grammar and sentence structure and she wanted to practice by reading *Stars and Stripes*. I had a copy with me, which I left, promising to come back the next afternoon and explain the words she didn't understand. My idea was that she could teach me German while I helped her with English.

George laughed at me all of the way back to town. The girl was around five feet tall. I towered over her by at least a foot. And at my strapping 150 pounds, she probably outweighed me: built like a female wrestler! I kept my date the next day, met her mother and father, and sat down at the table to study. When I sat and she stood beside me, our heads were at about equal height. The procedure was for her to read a news item in English, asking about the meanings of a few words, then relay the same item in German to her mother while I listened and asked the meanings of countless words. Then her mother would ask questions about what I thought the news really meant, and the girl would translate my answers into German. I noticed that she sometimes changed the meaning of what I had said, but I didn't care what she wanted her mother to believe. I was learning a lot of German while she and her mother were learning English.

The father had no interest in English or the news. He had been badly wounded in Russia and could do hardly any work; his two sons had been killed, or maybe captured, in Russia. The girl (I think her name was Katryn, or something like that) and her mother did all of the farming. I visited them two nights each week for our lessons and got a bit of ribbing at company headquarters about my short, stout girlfriend; they called her Powerful Katrinka, after a character in the "Toonerville Trolley" comic strip.

Soon I began to realize that Katryn's mother was quite interested in seeing that I enjoyed the visits. Because food was scarce, she couldn't serve me anything except some of the coffee I brought, but when I came in, she would smile, hug me, and say a few English words she had learned (some of which were vulgar, although she didn't seem to know it). She would stay long enough to listen to the news. Then she and Papa would quietly move into the back room.

After an embarrassing silence, Katryn and I would talk for a while and I would go back to town. We differed in much more than size and stature. Katryn was a serious, quiet girl with no sense of humor and no interest in news that did not concern Rosenthal. Except for the English/German lessons we had nothing in common. As Mama grew progressively less subtle, I decided that it was time to reach an understanding with Katryn. After Mama left the room one night, I asked Katryn what was going on and got a surprising story; according to her, our "affair" had become the biggest item of town gossip. Other parents had convinced Mama that I was a prime catch, in charge of all company communications and a personal friend of the company commander; I not only knew everything that was happening but was in a position to advise Captain Warren on who should accompany us to Germany. Katryn's girlfriends, older and wiser in the ways of men, were interested in the affair for a different reason. They were afraid that if Katryn didn't perk up my sexual interests, I might tell Mama the truth about those "highly classified" papers.

Katryn had absolutely no experience with boyfriends. She was interested but wasn't very sure of how to go about perking me up; the older girls and Mama, however, had been generous with advice. The remaining obstacle was that of her virginity, which she had intended to retain for marriage. Her girlfriends looked on that as a joke; Czech police and probably Russian soldiers would be in Rosenthal as soon as we left. The only option was whether she would give her valuable possession to a GI or have it taken by a Russian. Katryn tried to smile: "Leon, I don't know what I want."

I pondered the story for a few minutes. Katryn was willing but not eager. I was a red-blooded American boy, but not that red-blooded. I didn't like being the center of town gossip. Regardless of what I decided, the entire town and most of the company would know about it the next day. After carefully weighing my options, I decided to do the honorable thing: lie. "Katryn, don't pay any attention to town gossip. Nobody knows what is going to happen, but there won't be any rape and pillage by the Czechs or Russians. The things that happened at the war's end got the Czech government into serious political trouble. Even after we leave there will still be American observers and newsmen to report on what happens. No one will be raped, and if you are moved, it will be to a safe place." Then I decided to find another tutor for my German lessons.

There was a woman at the edge of Rosenthal who washed and ironed my clothes in exchange for the bar of soap that I would have used up if I had washed them myself. By being less wasteful, Maud had enough soap not only for my things but for several washings of the family clothes. Maud was one of the *Flüchtlinge*. Before the war she had lived in Breslau with her engineer husband and two children. The only memory I can draw of her appearance is that of a worn and haggard woman; she was probably about forty, but the war had taken a heavy toll.

Maud had learned some English in school, but that was long ago, and she hadn't retained much of it. I had an army manual called *Spoken German* (EM 518; I recently found a copy in a used-book sale and bought it for ten cents). The book would have been excellent except that it didn't have a dictionary and was designed to be used with a set of records—which someone had broken. Using the manual, the German I had learned from Katryn, and Maud's smattering of English, we managed to communicate: not well, and very slowly.

I chose Maud as my alternative to Katryn because she was available, there would be no gossip about sex (I thought), and she had some interests beyond Rosenthal. Looking back, I think Maud put up with me as someone who would listen to her rage at losing a comfortable city life and having to tolerate Rosenthal. Before the war she had probably been a sharp and witty upper-middle-class housewife. Although the wit remained, she was lonely, bitter, and frequently vulgar; she took malicious pleasure in teasing me about my sheltered, small-town, church-oriented life and about my shock at the consequences of war. She had grown up in an exciting city, cared nothing about religion, and knew that the war had treated her much more harshly than it had me. Her husband, son, and daughter were in the army somewhere in Russia, or had been. They were probably dead or dying in a labor camp. Their home was a burned-out shell and Breslau was in the Russian occupation zone; she didn't want to return, and her family would not be able to find her if they did happen to survive the Russian captivity.

As a refugee Maud had been assigned to Rosenthal, where she kept house for an old man and his three grandchildren. He owned the house and paid her living costs; she hated the place. The children were not much trouble, but the old man was deaf, senile, and malicious. Maud was sick of having to live in Rosenthal; she was a city woman and thought all the locals were stupid busybodies. She complained that I was the only adult that she could talk with. Adult? I had turned twenty in April. I said, "Maud, you don't have friends because you complain so much."

"These women think only of gossip. Now they're talking about me because you come over to visit at night. That crazy old fool there told them that last week you spent the night. The gossips say that you might take me back to Germany."

I was shocked at the idea of Maud sleeping with me—surely she was too old for that sort of thing. I was less surprised that she knew all about my disaster with Katryn's mama, and that she thought it was funny. She had been telling the town gossips that the GIs were lying about being able to take their girlfriends back to Germany. The women kept saying, "No, I myself have seen the secret document." I confessed that I had helped write the document. Maud promised not to quote me but said that most of the women knew it was a fraud; the story persisted partly because it offered a glimmer of hope but also because the mothers wanted their daughters to have a brief fling before things got really bad.

Maud thought the women were enjoying a bit of vicarious pleasure: she had heard Katryn's mama tell about our "affair," especially the tricks that Mama had suggested—clever moves that she felt sure would have worked if only Katryn hadn't been so shy. Maud described the plotting in vivid detail while I squirmed and protested that I had only wanted to learn German. "Oh, but you learned much more, didn't you?" Sometimes in the middle of a discussion Maud would start laughing and tease me about having "played with little Katryn's boobies."

Maud was an interesting woman who seemed to have opinions about everything. Over a period of about six weeks, I dropped in to see her once or twice a week. Every time I came I brought a can of coffee grounds; Maud put them (some of them) in her pot and made coffee. I also brought some sugar, condensed milk, a little candy for the kids, and a little pipe tobacco for the crazy old fool. Then we would sit and talk. Maud discussed whatever was on her mind. Frequently it had to do with the Hitler times. (Maud was the first German I met who would talk honestly about her views of Hitler. The others would just shake their heads and say, "Aw, he was crazy!")

Sometimes what Maud said would contradict what she had told the week before. I don't know why. (When I pointed out such a discrepancy, she would smile and change the subject.) The account I am giving here is an amalgam of her more logical stories. I cannot say that I remember them exactly or that they were true when she told them, but they are consistent with her personality and with some of the written accounts of that period.

Maud had never cared much about politics and only heard of Hitler in 1933 when he ran for president against Hindenburg. She heard him speak in Breslau and thought he was wonderful. She remembered that when he started speaking, his voice was low and calm. As he began explaining what he wanted to do for Germany, his delivery became more exciting. At the end, he would be hoarse from emotional exhaustion. Having grown up in a Baptist community, I understood what she meant. I remembered preachers who would start off quietly and end the sermon with a voice that sounded like a gravel truck. This emoting was taken as a sign of true dedication. Maud had certainly believed that Hitler was dedicated, and she liked the things he said. He said that Germans had been forced to try democracy for fifteen years and the system was too weak to protect them from vengeful countries like France. When he was elected, he would be the absolute leader and do what was best for the country despite criticism from fringe lunatics.

Maud's husband had laughed at her for supporting Hitler. "You don't understand what he is saying. He's going to force all women out of their jobs, send them back into the home, and have them raising children for him." Maud didn't think that was so bad. She enjoyed being a housewife and raising children for the country; I pointed out that she had only two children and Hitler had urged women to have at least eight. Because of Germany's tremendous losses in World War I, the nation needed a lot more children and didn't have nearly enough young men for the women who wanted to marry. Furthermore, a lot of the men didn't want to marry; they were enjoying single life with the large number of available women. Hitler promised that, when he was elected, there would be more incentives for men to marry.

Hitler lost the election badly but was able to take over anyhow. Maud wasn't sure how he did that. She was glad to see him become a strong leader but rather disgusted that he had let the rowdy Storm Troopers arrest all Communists and Social Democrats. Except for that, he seemed to have done a good job and kept most of his promises. Breslau became a pleasant, law-and-order city. The streets were safe for women to walk anywhere, anytime, day or night. Hitler pushed through laws to help young couples buy and furnish homes. Abortion had been illegal before he took over, but the laws weren't strictly enforced. Hitler changed that quickly. He was strongly opposed to the killing of unborn Germans. Children were an investment in the future. Although Hitler praised German family values, he said that it was not a disgrace for unmarried women to get pregnant; people should recognize that there weren't enough men for the large number of young women. Maud hadn't agreed with him on that point; she thought that single women should not get pregnant. But she was proud of the Fountain of Life program, under which unmarried women got excellent prenatal and postnatal care until the babies could be adopted by married couples. (Unmarried girls were not allowed to keep their babies because children needed a man in the house.)

Maud had been strongly opposed to the things Hitler said about Jews. There were a lot of good patriotic Jews in Breslau who were embarrassed by some of his accusations. The Nazi Party pressured some Jewish teachers and civil servants to leave the country, but successful professionals were not bothered. Occasionally some drunk Storm Troopers would curse or even beat on a respectable Jew, but most citizens of Breslau understood that Jews were an important segment of the city. Some of the best department stores, for example, were owned, and run efficiently, by Jews.

Hitler had campaigned with a promise to abolish the "filthy literature" that was supposedly damaging the German culture. After proper warnings, his men raided the pornography shops, hauled the stuff out, and burned it in the streets. I argued with Maud about that because, back home, we had heard that Hitler burned the books of great Jewish philosophers and artists. Maud wasn't particularly interested in that sort of literature and couldn't remember any stores that sold such books. She had been in the crowd near her neighborhood bookstore and saw them burning books with naked women and dirty stories about homosexuals. She also knew of a store where decadent modern art had been burned. Maud felt that the act was justified because, as an artist himself, Hitler knew what would be bad for the German people.

In Hitler's first years of rule, large families became popular again. The population was growing and life was improving throughout Germany. Other countries were in a depression and enduring massive unemployment, but Germany had jobs for everyone. The government was building wonderful highways and bringing electricity to the small towns. Besides the construction jobs that were available, there were good opportunities for young men to get vocational training in the army. On weekends the soldiers would drive trucks out to communities and have town picnics. They would play with the children and hand out good, nutritious bread to everyone. As the army grew larger and stronger, other nations began respecting Germany. Hitler took back all of the land that had been stolen after the war and didn't have to fight for it. Maud's husband quit arguing with her about Hitler and even joined the Nazi Party. She knew that he still didn't like the Nazis and had joined only because they were responsible for giving out government engineering contracts. Becoming a Nazi made good business sense.

In 1938 the SS and Gestapo began arresting Jews and taking their property. This new tack had worried Maud, but her friends pointed out that the Gestapo was focusing on Jews who might cause trouble if Germany had to go to war. Patriotic Jews would always be safe.

Hitler had many wonderful slogans. One that appealed to Maud was "Gemeinnutz geht vor Eigennutz"—"Common good goes before personal advancement." Hitler was developing a classless society. Individual worth would be determined by what a man or woman did for the country, rather than how much money he or she had. I tried to needle Maud a bit over this; she had lived in the "better" part of town, her husband had made a lot of money from Nazi contracts, and Maud had produced only two children. She laughed and teased me about Katryn's "boobies"—*that,* she said, was for my personal gain rather than common good. "Maud, I didn't play with her boobies, but if I had, it would have been for the common good: Katryn deserved a little entertainment."

Because Maud was the wife of a Nazi Party member, she had to join the women's auxiliary, the NSF (Nationalsozialist Fräuenschaft). It was a boring group of simple-minded women who gossiped about what fine positions their husbands had. The only consolation was that it didn't meet

very often and sometimes they invited good speakers. Her son had enjoyed the HJ (Hitler Youth—the German term was *Hitler Jugend)* for a few
years before tiring of it. From her description the HJ seemed a lot like
the Boy Scouts. They had weekly meetings, wore uniforms, and marched
a lot. At camp they had lectures about the meanings of the Nazi symbols
and the history of the party, along with lurid tales of how bad the Jews
were. Her son kept his membership but didn't go to the meetings very
often. He had no serious complaints about the program except that it
took up so much time. I remembered Boy Scouts who dropped out for
the same reasons; they had nothing against scouting except that they
wanted time to themselves.

The girls' branch of the HJ was the BDM (the full name translates
simply as Organization of German Girls). Maud's daughter hated the program from the time it was installed at school. She at first refused to join,
but the teachers pressured her into at least trying it. She tried, still hated it,
and found that it was not possible to resign. BDM met once a week, but
she was only required to attend once a month. The girls were taught to
be obedient wives and to raise children for the country. That sort of talk
was embarrassing for teenaged girls, and the boys made it worse by coin-
ing bawdy names that had the initials BDM. One translated as "Baldur,
take me" (Baldur von Schirach was a national HJ leader). Another was
Bedarfsartikel für deutsche Männer—"useful articles for German men."

With a few exceptions, such as the BDM and Hitler's tirades against
Jews, Maud had liked the prewar Nazi Party. She had felt that Hitler was
great because he restored honor to the country. He had proved that other
countries will respect power. He claimed that there was no risk of war if
you were always strong. His approach worked for a while, but England
and France declared war when Hitler invaded Poland. Bitter memories of
the First World War frightened Maud, but Poland fell after minor resistance and the French only blustered. At dinner parties, everyone said that
the French were afraid of the German army and would probably ask for
a peace settlement. When Hitler invaded Holland and Belgium, Maud's
husband said, "Now you will see why I was worried about Hitler's bluffing. The French and English are going to destroy us." But he was wrong.
Maud realized how brilliant Hitler had been in developing such a

powerful army. Even if other countries tried to resist, the war would end quickly.

Hitler's decision to invade Russia still baffled Maud. He had promised that the army would be entirely for defense; the very name *Wehrmacht* meant "defense or protection force." The newspapers explained that Russia was invaded in order to obtain room for German expansion; the German people needed more "living space." But this was entirely different from the goal of defending Germany, and everyone saw obvious parallels to Napoleon's experience in Russia. The newspapers tried to reassure people by saying that the German blitzkrieg would bring victory within a few months. The blitzkrieg had worked beautifully at first—until the fall rains came, bogging vehicles, animals, and soldiers in seas of mud. Even so, the army penetrated nearly to Moscow. Then winter hit—the hardest Russian winter in fifty years. Grease and diesel fuel froze; trucks and tanks could not operate. Because the fighting was supposed to have been over by now, the troops had not been issued winter clothing. Rumors trickled back that large numbers of the men were dying from hunger, cold, and disease. Long hospital trains filled with winter-weather casualties rolled through Breslau. The papers kept saying that the war would end quickly with the next summer campaign, but it didn't. The Russians had millions of soldiers and endless supplies from the United States. They held out at Stalingrad, then counterattacked. In the winter of 1942–1943, with whole armies being captured on the Eastern front and American bombers staging the first daylight raids on the homeland, people gradually came to realize that Germany was in serious trouble.

Food became scarce. Household items like pots and pans disappeared from the stores. Army quotas for more men seemed insatiable. Soon all of the men were gone, including Maud's son and her husband. Her daughter enlisted as a radio operator for the Luftwaffe and was sent to Russia; she still despised the Nazi Party, but her country was in a war that it couldn't afford to lose. People in Breslau began to say that Germany couldn't defeat Russia. They speculated that Hitler would offer peace in exchange for the land already taken. They never said such things publicly because it was dangerous to discuss the possibility of losing the war: even at small parties there might be someone who would report to the Gestapo, and people expressing "defeatist opinions" were being sent to camps for "political reorientation."

Early in 1943 Goebbels announced that Germany was mobilizing for "total war." This was a bitter joke because there wasn't much left to mobilize except the women, who Hitler had said should stay at home with their children. Until the total-war announcement, Germany had depended on the use of foreign volunteer labor to replace men who had been drafted. These people were called *Hiwi* (pronounced "hee-vee"), from the initials of the German word meaning "volunteer." Unfortunately, the Hiwi were not very strongly committed to quality control: it wasn't their countrymen who depended on having the ammunition and weapons work properly. Maud, with no children to care for, was assigned to work in a factory; it was dull, useless labor that ended when the factory was destroyed in a bombing raid. She and many other less-essential workers were moved into rural areas because they had nothing to do and no other place to live. Some of her friends were sent to Dresden, which was much nicer than Rosenthal (neither she nor I knew that Dresden had been fire-bombed to almost total destruction in the last stages of the war). Those who remained in Breslau had lived through horrors during the siege and fall of the city. A weak force of Volkssturm—old men and boys—had held out against Russian attacks week after week, surrendering only because the war had ended. When the Russians realized that they had been bested by a rag-tag army, they were humiliated and angry. Their pillage and rape of Breslau were even worse than in other cities. Squads of ten or twelve Russian soldiers would round up the women in an entire block. Ages ranged from mere kids to old women. They would then select one woman and rape her repeatedly while the others were forced to watch. The woman who wrote to Maud about it said that nobody even tried to understand a Russian soldier's logic, except that he was determined to humiliate German women to avenge the atrocities committed by German soldiers in Russia.

I remember being so shocked that I couldn't say anything. Maud was furious—not at me, but at fate. "Now you ask what I thought of Hitler;

he was awful. I think he was lying to us all along, but I'm not sure. The SS and Storm Troopers were awful thugs. But people say that if they hadn't been so cruel and tough, the Communists would have taken over, and things would probably have been just as bad that way. England and France would have destroyed us. I'm ashamed of the things the Nazis did. I'm mad that we lost after working so hard. I'm bitter about having to live in Rosenthal. When you Americans leave, the Czechs are going to ship us all to Germany. Will they make me go back to Breslau? The Russians are there and my home is rubble, but if I don't go back, my husband won't be able to find me—but he is probably dead."

It had been a horrible war for everyone.

4

INFANTRY, PASS IN REVIEW!

Carl Nance and I were in Pilsen on the day that Japan surrendered. I can't remember why we were there, except to take a break from the excitement of Rosenthal. There was an army hospital in Pilsen where the doctors were bored and would cooperate with any sort of excuse offered by GIs who wanted to get a taste of city life. Once, I had a bullet fragment removed from my arm. It wasn't hurting me at all and probably never would, but the doctor said, "Yep, that thing should come out." I went to the hospital dentist several times: one filling per visit.

Carl was an old friend from ASTP days and had been first scout in Third Platoon during most of the war. Carl had a keen mind, a wonderful dry wit, and was what we would now call a quick study. After only a few days in combat he seemed to develop an instinctive feel for survival—an ability to sense danger and never be a conspicuous target. During the bitter cold, Carl was one of the few who did not get frozen feet. Although he took a lot of small shrapnel, he was never seriously wounded, and he never shirked his duty. He was an absolutely reliable soldier and friend; I had no doubt that he would risk his life to help me out of a tight situation.

Because Carl was an excellent leader, he was often acting platoon sergeant or acting platoon leader, but his actual rank fluctuated between private and private first class. Carl was much like Bill Mauldin's Willie and Joe: he was a good combat soldier but prone to speaking his mind, especially when it involved the safety of his comrades. He would tell officers specifically why an order was stupid. He would also explain the facts of life to soldiers who hadn't quite realized we were all interdependent. Once he was in charge of Third Platoon and told one of the replacements to lead out as scout on a patrol. The boy said, "Man, I'm not crazy. That's the way to get killed." Carl slipped a round into the chamber of his M-1 and replied very calmly: "No, if you follow orders there's only a chance of getting killed. The sure way to get killed is to stand where you are." At the age of twenty, Carl was an old soldier. He made frequent trips to the Pilsen hospital for removal of shrapnel fragments: one at a time.

Undoubtedly another reason we had gone to Pilsen was because it was obvious that the war would end soon and we wanted to be in the city for the celebration. Absolutely nothing happened. The local GIs must have had a party somewhere, but we couldn't find it. There was no parade. At the Red Cross Club everybody was sitting around the radio listening for more news. I don't think there were any discussions about whether dropping the atomic bomb saved lives; we didn't know very much except that the army had dropped a helluva big bomb on Japan and the emperor had surrendered. *Stars and Stripes* published a good, simple explanation of how an atomic explosion was caused. The article said that even after the blast, the remaining fragments emitted energy that could probably be converted into electricity. The rest of the article discussed possible future applications. Atomic generators could be made small enough to replace gasoline engines in cars and to provide electricity for individual homes. In the future all houses would be heated and cooled by atomic devices that would be installed in the basement much like the soon-to-be-outmoded furnaces. We enjoyed reading about the future of atomic energy, but the matter of whether the bomb should have been dropped had no meaning to us. We didn't know that the army had projected invasion losses for Japan that made the cost of the Normandy invasion—about five thousand American lives—seem minuscule. All we knew for sure was that no more bombs would be dropped and nobody would die while storming the Japanese beaches. The war was over and we were still alive.

Carl and I left the Red Cross Club and wandered the streets. We met a Czech army officer who congratulated us—not that we had done anything to help beat the Japanese, but he was glad to see the end of all war. We talked a bit about how great we had felt when the Germans surrendered. He had been with a Czech armored brigade attached to the American army. He invited us to his house, where he opened a bottle of wine and we told some more tales. Then we went back to our hotel, depressed. Through most of the war, the Armed Forces Radio had played a song they called "The Victory Polka": "We'll go marching down Fifth Avenue, the United Nations in review." I had dreamed that, somehow, I would survive the war and, somewhere, I would march in a victory parade.

Actually, the U.S. Army did stage a victory parade in Pilsen about two weeks later. It was for the entire XXII Corps and included one battalion from each of the regiments in the 94th, but not my battalion. During our stay in Czechoslovakia, I was in only two parades. They weren't victory celebrations, but they were a lot of fun. In mid-July, General Patton came to review the troops of each regiment. We suspected that his real purpose was to drum up our support after his political blunders.

Patton, as commander·of the Third Army, was in charge of occupation duty for eastern Bavaria. In his typical pragmatic fashion, he had landed in political hot water about his attitude toward Germans, especially minor Nazi Party members. As the most popular American general in Germany, Patton felt he had earned the right to speak his mind. His wartime aggressiveness was legendary: Old Blood and Guts ("our blood and his guts," ran the GI version). When the 94th Division joined the Third Army, Patton went to each battalion and gave pep talks to the line officers. The gist of these talks was that we were there to kill Krauts: never hesitate when you see one—just shoot him. We were going to keep killing the sons of bitches until Hitler either surrendered or ran out of Krauts: he expected the latter to be more likely. Throughout the war he kept a detailed count of the German soldiers the Third Army had killed versus the number of Americans lost: the ratio was seven to one.

Patton praised his troops as the finest soldiers who ever wore shoe leather, and drove us to absolute exhaustion—both physical and emotional. To give the devil his due, the man was an excellent general; the German commanders were often cowed simply by the fact that they were facing the famed Third Army. But when Germany surrendered, Patton believed that was that: the war was over—period. He respected the German soldiers and commanders as worthy foes. He did not think they were the equal of his Third Army, but he considered them far better than the soldiers of England, France, or Russia. He also respected the German people and was shocked at our letting the Russians—he called them "Mongolian barbarians"—rule even a part of Germany.

Although Patton was also shocked at conditions in the concentration camps and the way American POWs had been treated, he attributed those things to the small group of Nazi Party leaders who had looted Europe. He did not accept the idea that all Germans were Nazis or that all Nazi Party members were criminals. To his wife he wrote: "I had never heard that we fought to de-nazify Germany. What we are doing is to utterly destroy the only semi-modern state in Europe so that Russia can swallow the whole. . . . Actually the Germans are the only decent people in Europe." Patton considered that, as commander of the Third Army, he was responsible for developing a civil government that could restore order, including the repair of utilities such as electricity and water, and the regeneration of manufacturing and food production. He felt cramped by Eisenhower's orders that no former Nazi Party member would be allowed to hold any position of authority; virtually everyone with experience in civil government had been at least a nominal member of the Party. Pragmatic Patton decided to obey the Eisenhower order, to some degree, and ignore it when he saw a better method; that was the way he had operated during the war.

Even in wartime, however, the press had enjoyed baiting Patton into making brash statements, and now they were having a field day. So, during July, Patton decided to visit his combat divisions, essentially to thank them and to say good-bye. He had not yet been relieved of his command, but he was not going to change his attitudes, and he knew that Eisenhower was not going to tolerate much more Patton controversy.

Official orders said that Patton wanted to review the 301st Infantry Regiment on July 17 and to review them as combat troops; it was not to be a spit-and-polish parade—an excellent pragmatic decision. We had not marched as a regiment in over a year, and most of the men from that time were gone; some were dead and many were at home with severe disabilities. On the morning of July 17, the rifle companies began assembling in a nearby field. We were to march in after the other units: regimental artillery, service company, headquarters, and such. The division band had been practicing for a week. During the war they had done filler duty such as carrying supplies or helping with the wounded. Finally they were back at the job of playing spirited Sousa marches and any other music they liked; everything was loose and easygoing for this parade.

As part of the Third Battalion, K Company was near the end of the column: "King Company, 'tention. Sling arms. First Platoon, forward, march!" We strutted into the field where Patton had a reviewing stand. The band was playing "When the Saints Go Marching In." I was proud beyond any description. This dusty pasture was not Fifth Avenue, but we were the finest soldiers who ever wore shoe leather. We were hardly saints, but we were the Queen of Battle and Patton was proud of us. The actual parade began with Patton "trooping the line": he stood in the back of a jeep, saluting, as it drove by each company. Emblazoned on the front of the jeep were the words "War Eagle!" Patton returned to the reviewing stand and made a short speech (my letter home said that it was full of profanity) in which he recounted our accomplishments while fighting under his command, thanked us, and praised the men who had died in order that this victory might come about.

Then came the honored command that I had learned to love at The Infantry School in Fort Benning: "Infantry: Pass in review!" "King Company, forward, march!" The remnants of Captain Simmers' King Company stepped out smartly. He was still in the hospital with severe head injuries. Westmoreland had just gotten out of the hospital and had been discharged. In my memory, in my heart, Simmers was strutting in front of us, carrying his swagger stick. Dale Proctor, Jack Button, and Richard Thomas were marching with us. They were not dead because I would not allow them to die. This was the last parade in which the guidon of King Company would lead combat troops: men who were grit to the core. It seemed fitting that our final parade should honor Patton, who had become the symbol of courage and daring.

My other big parade was in Prague, the capital of Czechoslovakia, located in the Russian zone of occupation; we were to be the first American soldiers the people of Prague had seen. One Monday morning an order came down: "The following men will report to L Company head-quarters, prepared to remain for approximately one week. . . ." There were about fifteen names, including mine.

Packing our gear for a one-week stay was no problem at all; we had learned to travel light. In late 1944 the army had begun issuing the "bag, sleeping, wool, w/case," known affectionately as a "fart sack." The inner lining was composed of ordinary blanket material, sewed in the shape of a sleeping bag, with a zipper running down the front. The zipper was de-signed for quick release in an emergency: simply pull the zipping device to the top and it would slip off and disengage. The outer shell was a light-weight water-repellent cotton fabric, which snapped into place. Accep-tance of the fart sack by combat troops varied according to weather con-ditions. We liked it in Brittany, where the weather was cool but not cold. We were careful to clean our muddy boots off before slipping them into the bag. Once a week we would dump the mud, debris, and DDT pow-der out of the bottom. We would replace that with a new can of DDT, about half a cup of the powder, and be ready for another week. We knew very little about DDT except that it would saturate our clothes and keep away fleas, lice, and most of the flies. During January and February the weather was much too cold for simple fart sacks—we tried to keep our foxholes lined with blankets that we got from dead German soldiers.

The fart sack really came into its own after the war ended. It was ideal for short trips: toss in a change of underwear and socks plus some toilet articles, roll it up, and you were ready to go for at least a week. The bundle was about eighteen inches long and eight inches in diameter; it weighed about three pounds. It was the standard GI travel outfit. You could eat at a transient mess and sleep on the floor if there were no beds available. Most of the transient billets would even arrange to have your shirt and pants washed and ironed overnight. Only very meticulous sol-diers used this service on a daily basis; most of us felt that shirts and pants needed washing only once a week.

To start the Prague trip, we crawled on a truck and bounced over dusty roads to L Company's Camp Gass. The camp was a small German military post, complete with barracks, mess hall, beer hall, and parade ground. L Company had named it to honor Lieutenant Glenn Gass, who had won the Distinguished Service Cross when he was killed during our final big push in February. We were assigned to an empty barracks with a long line of double bunks that had straw mattresses and no pillows. All German wartime camps had identical buildings: prefabricated wooden units painted light green. The modular panels (about three meters square, I think) were bolted together; they could be dismantled, shipped anywhere, and reassembled. They were versatile enough to be formed into mess halls, lecture rooms, beer halls, or barracks in concentration camps.

After dropping our gear we went to the mess hall for lunch. As I walked through the door a GI yelled: "Hey, 'Sippi, you rotten son of a bitch. Where the hell have you been?" Macho protocol required that I honor him with an equal insult: never admit that you are glad to see an old friend. I was ready to comply but couldn't recognize the face or bring up a name. I hadn't been called Mis'Sippi since basic training, so he must have been in ASTP with me. As I stood there grasping for a memory, he said, "Hey, Pinky, look who's here." I remembered Pinky; I also remembered hating his guts. But at least the connection brought me back to the first boy. His name was Steve. He was gay—most of us knew that he had a boyfriend in the navy—but that hadn't really mattered back then, and I suppose it hadn't during combat. Steve had helped me to fit into the squad when I was transferred to ASTP's Fifth Company during the middle of basic training. Because cliques had already been formed, I was an outsider; Pinky had been the leader of those who harassed me.

I went over to Steve's table. "You useless eight-ball, how come you didn't get shot?"

"Didn't get shot? Man look at this, and this, and this."

Pinky stepped up. " 'Sippi! Long time, no see."

It was a friendly greeting, but I was still mad—cold, mean mad. I looked at him for a minute and said: "I wonder why the good men got killed and rotten bastards lived."

At Benning, a fight would have landed us in the stockade; now I was ready to break his neck. We stood toe to toe like two dogs sizing each other up. I was a bit taller than Pinky but he had a big weight advantage over me: about thirty pounds. I knew I could take him. At Benning I had faced him in the hand-to-hand combat exercises; he was slow and pudgy.

Besides, I had no intention of fighting fairly. Ray Graziano had taught me about Brooklyn street fighting. I would wait until Pinky shifted his weight to swing, duck into it, knee his family jewels, and give a karate slash to his neck.

It dawned on me that I wasn't planning a fight: instinct was telling me to kill him; I had reverted to a combat animal. I didn't want to fight like that and didn't know how to back down. The entire mess hall was quiet, watching these two fools acting like high-school kids. I had made the challenge and should be the one to apologize, but I didn't want to. Then Pinky smiled and said, "Aw, 'Sippi, the war's over." He stuck out his hand. I was relieved but not enough to shake; I still hated his guts.

I went over to the K Company group. Somebody said, "Good God, Leon, what was that about?" One of the boys who had been in Fifth Company explained, but the general opinion was that I was wrong in holding the grudge for eighteen months. They were right, I had made a fool of myself. Looking back, I can't remember a single postwar fight in K Company. I don't know why there weren't any. I can't believe we made a conscious decision to avoid fighting because our combat instincts were to kill—that notion had come through to me only because I realized that everyone in the mess hall was watching. It seems more likely that we didn't fight because of emotional exhaustion, or maybe simply because we were afraid of what Captain Warren might do.

After lunch we assembled for orientation. We had three days to learn to march properly. We were to form a composite company representing the regiment in a Czech Independence Day ceremony on Friday, September 27. It was to be something of a victory parade in that it included units from the British, French, and Russian armies. Symbolically, the occasion was to transfer command of the First Czech Armored Brigade from the American army to the Czech government. We were told that it actually meant transferring command of the government from the American and Russian occupation forces to the Czech army; there was no civil government in place at the time. There were to be companies from each of the three infantry regiments plus one from division artillery to make a composite battalion of roughly five hundred men. This group, plus the 94th Division band, was to represent the entire American army. The review-

ing stand was to have Generals Eisenhower, Patton, and Harmon (XXII
Corps commander) plus generals from the British, French, Czech, and
Russian armies.

It was to be a highly ceremonial parade, but Patton had specified that
the American army be represented by combat troops. The 94th had been
selected because it was the only infantry division remaining in Czechoslovakia. The problem with using combat troops for such a parade was
that they couldn't march. General Harmon knew that the British were to
be represented by a Scottish bagpipe band and the French were sending
their finest drill team; he assumed that the Russians would also send some
sort of ceremonial battalion. He sent down orders that we *would* look
good. We were going to practice marching every day, all day, and would
be weeded out until we were a company of very sharp soldiers. There
would be a movie every night and the beer hall would be open from
seven to ten—drink all you want, but reveille would be at six. Punishment
for missing formation: the regimental stockade.

After formation the ASTP boys got together to spin yarns. Eighteen
months earlier, the 94th had lost about 2,000 men to the 8th Division,
which was ready for overseas shipment but understrength. The army, in
its wisdom, had replaced those men with 1,500 ASTP boys—eighteen to
twenty years old, all with IQ scores above 120. Most of us had come directly from basic training at The Infantry School. The Infantry School
had been established to give advanced infantry training to West Point
graduates; it also ran the infantry Officer Candidate School and the paratroopers Jump School. Before the ASTP came, it had never conducted
basic training, and I don't quite know why they attempted it. Maybe they
decided that because we would receive commissions after our college
training, this would be our only experience at learning to be officers.
Whatever the reason, they planned to give us the entire wagonload: basic
training, OCS training, the physical conditioning of the Jump School.

We never quite lived up to those high expectations, but we were well
trained, in good physical condition, and had a broad understanding of infantry tactics. We were as tough as leather and hard as nails, but we were
also cocky, arrogant teenagers. Because the division had assigned nearly
all of us to rifle companies, we represented about 25 percent of the rifle-

men, working beside men almost old enough to be our fathers. Many of them were barely literate; they resented us crazy college kids and were sure that we couldn't soldier. The two groups fought like cats and dogs. Because of tight discipline, the battles were usually verbal, but there were a few "let's go to the woods" fights. Gradually, we compromised and became good combat teams. ASTP brought stamina and self-confidence but we soon learned patience and caution. We raised the average IQ level of the rifle platoons by several points. I don't think academic intelligence, of itself, made much difference in our combat ability, but I do believe there is a strong correlation between intelligence and self-confidence.

Eighteen months later, it was difficult to remember who had been ASTP. Six months of combat and 400 percent rifle-company casualties had aged us all. We had all gone overseas with the rank of PFC but now ranged from private (lost the single stripe for drunkenness) to technical sergeant. A sergeant's stripes did not reflect leadership ability so much as random chance. Because combat resulted in a continual shortage of noncoms, anyone with a little common sense was promoted sooner or later to squad leader. If you survived until that fight was over, and the company clerk had spare time, the promotion was made official. I had been a staff sergeant for three days but went to the hospital before I was promoted. I have no idea whether I would have been a good squad leader. I was very good at taking care of myself, but playing surrogate father to eleven green replacements was an entirely different matter.

Because the war was over and most of the older men had been sent home for discharge, ASTP boys had become the old-timers: experienced men who had come over with the division. We would never be kids again but for that afternoon we could relive the days when we really had been kids. "What happened to old Eight-Ball Riley?" "He got it in our first firefight near Loc Maria. Raised up to shoot and a Kraut shot his finger off. They sent him back to the States on limited duty—lucky bastard." One boy from I Company had been on a scouting patrol and got caught by two Germans who happened to have four bottles of wine but no food and no cigarettes. He traded them two packs of cigarettes and some K rations for the wine, and they let him go. Somebody told the tale of when old 'Sippi had put down his rifle to chase a rooster but ran into a German. The German still had *his* rifle, but he was as surprised as I was. We sprinted in opposite directions.

We talked about how many ASTP boys had been made scouts or BAR men, the most dangerous and critical positions in a squad. We decided that the high number was probably due partly to our intensive tactical training at Benning and partly to the fact that we were kids—fool enough to take chances. The topic of luck led naturally to those for whom it had run out: the good men who had died, or had lost a foot to the Schü mines (wood-encased and hard to detect). One of our bright, sharp kids had been offered admission to West Point. He planned to make the army his career but wanted combat experience before going to the academy. He fought well but cracked up during an assault on the SS position at Munzingen Ridge.

The tales were getting emotional, we had talked too long and told too much. Somebody suggested that we meet in the beer hall that night for a reunion, no more war talk, just fun and games. Everybody agreed that it sounded good.

The beer hall was identical to the mess hall except that the prefab modules were put together in a six-meter width instead of three meters. There was a bar and several long tables and two or three German barmaids. That night we had the place to ourselves, possibly because the replacements knew that we old-timers were having a party, but probably because there was a good movie being shown.

We began with a series of toasts: quotations from our cadre at Benning. "You have been selected into the ASTP because you are the cream of the crop, the pride of our nation." That was from the battalion commander's standard welcome speech. "You are a bunch of worthless, yellow-bellied Jew bastards who couldn't fight your way out of a paper bag." I don't know where that was from; Sergeant Cohen and his assistant, Corporal Finkelstein, expressed similar sentiments to us but never in those terms. "You think I am chickenshit; well, you are chickenshit too" (from First Sergeant Smith, Fifth Company). "Sergeant, instead of digging a four-by-four-by-four-foot foxhole tonight, could I dig four one-by-one-by-ones?" (Sergeant Swords fell for that once, but never again.) "Goddamn ASTP kids, you don't deserve such good training—you'll never see combat" (every paratrooper in Jump School). Finally, someone said: "Gentlemen, I toast the infantry: the Queen of Battle!" "Hear, hear, the Queen!"

As the beer began to take effect, we sang, and sang, and sang. "Cheer, cheer for Old Notre Dame, call down the echoes praising her name. . . ." "On Wisconsin, on Wisconsin. . . ." Some of the boys had been taking classes at Ole Miss when the program collapsed: "From Peabody's lobbies to Whitie's Saloon, we're doing the town tonight." We ran out of college material and started on army songs: "Roll me over, in the clover, roll me over, lay me down and do it again!" "Drunk last night, drunk the night before, gonna' get drunk tonight like I never got drunk before." "There's the SS Deutsche, and the Wehrmacht Deutsche, the Nazi Deutsche, and the other damn Deutsche. Sing glorious, victorious, one keg of beer for the four of us, sing glory be to God that there are no more of us, for one of us could drink it all alone."

Eventually, there were no more of us; one keg of German beer was more than we could handle. The last I remembered was the K Company group heading for our barracks, holding each other for mutual support and singing garbled verses of "I've Got Sixpence": "Oh happy is the day when the Yankee gets his pay and we all roll 'im roll 'im home!"

At five-thirty, the CQ opened the door, blew his whistle, and gave the time-honored reveille call: "Cocks and socks. Drop 'em and grab 'em!" I crawled out of my fart sack, slipped on pants and shirt, started to the door, remembered my boots, and went back. My head ached, I could hardly see, the cottony mess in my mouth tasted awful. It was my first hangover. I regretted all those jokes I had made back during training about hungover boys falling out on Monday morning. Or maybe I didn't; I certainly didn't regret the glorious drunk we had thrown last night. We had vindicated ASTP, we had called down the echoes praising her name: maybe not praises, just vindication. We, the pampered yellow-bellies, had paid our dues. The parachuters had laughed when we sang "Gory, gory, what a helluva way to die," but we did fight: tooth and nail—rifle, knife, rifle butt, and fists. We had taken more combat casualties than most of those famed parachute-infantry rifle companies; we had spent more time on line and killed a lot more Krauts than they did. We had never pretended to be assault troops, we were the straight-leg infantry. The Krauts were afraid of us because when American infantry closed with the enemy, we stayed until the job was done. We would not, could not, be stopped.

The K Company group formed into a reasonably straight line. The lieutenant yelled, "Report!" Our ranking sergeant responded: "All present or accounted for, sir!" *Or accounted for* was a stock phrase, but on that morning it also meant that some of the group hadn't quite gotten out of bed. We hadn't stood reveille since . . . I couldn't remember when, maybe back in England something over a year ago. We went back to the barracks, finished dressing, got our mess kits, and went to eat. I decided that I wasn't going to like this new army.

At eight o'clock we formed into twelve-man squads and began learning to march. We drilled all morning. At every break a lieutenant from regiment went around and tried to shape us up. He was expecting us to become a "crack drill team" in three days. The program reminded me of daily drills during basic training, except that this was amusing; we were not worried about being "washed out." Most of us wanted to parade in Prague before General Eisenhower, but not badly enough to take a lot of yelling and harassment. We weren't particularly pleased about standing reveille and retreat, and the idea of rifle inspections was a bad joke: after combat, our rifles were pitted, rusty, and shrapnel-scarred—uncleanable.

Over the three days, we got to be pretty good at keeping in step, and our lines became reasonably straight. Learning to do the manual of arms all over again was a hassle. Even during basic training, I hadn't been able to master the trick of getting the rifle off my shoulder with a simple wrist movement; my simple wrist wasn't strong enough without a little boost from my shoulder. Joe Weiner had even more trouble, but that was because a piece of shrapnel had ripped through the muscles of his forearm just after we had reached the Rhine River. About half of the boys limped a bit, from bullet wounds or the effects of frozen feet. Once, during a break, Joe said: "You know, we look a lot like the painting *The Spirit of '76.*" We weren't quite that bad, but we weren't any "crack drill team" either. Very simply, we were combat troops who had paid the price. Most of us would never again be able or want to march properly.

At the end of each day the officer in charge would read out names of men who should return to their companies. Each day we would try to figure what his basis for culling was. Joe and I were still there; we could keep in step but were barely able to do the manual of arms. Early in the training the lieutenant had wanted us to do the "marching manual." That meant going from right shoulder arms to port arms, to left shoulder, and back again—while marching. He gave up on that dream because we kept hitting each other on the head with our rifles. His final goal was to have men who were close to the same height and were physically able to hold up for four miles of marching at attention.

Even though we couldn't march very well, we looked great; quartermaster had cleaned and pressed our combat jackets and issued us new Combat Badges, plus all of our ribbons. They took our helmet liners, stenciled a "9/4" on each one, and gave them a heavy coat of varnish. We loaded onto trucks at eleven Thursday night and went to sleep. They woke us up when we got to the Russian border post at four in the morning. Everyone had to unload and be searched. We were carrying rifles and had cartridge belts, so they wanted to be sure that we had no ammunition. There was a bit of tension. We cursed the Russians in German and they returned the insults, in German, our only common language. About twenty armed Russians were trying to control an entire battalion of unarmed (or at least unammunitioned) American combat troops, but it wasn't a dangerous situation; they were under orders to search us and we were ordered to cooperate. We took turns peeing on the wall of their guard shack. They tried to scare us off with rifles, but we knew they were afraid to create an incident.

We reached Prague just at dawn (my letter says 6:30) and the Red Cross Clubmobile girls were waiting for us. When we had pulled back from the line during combat times, dirty and exhausted, a Clubmobile was usually there. The clean, neat, smiling girls would laugh and hug their filthy, stinking heroes. The Clubmobile girls were our cheerleaders; we loved them and they loved us (figuratively speaking; in the army ranking system, they were considered to be officers). This wasn't the same group that had carried us through combat, but the spirit was there: coffee, doughnuts, smiles, hugs, and encouragement.

After typical army delays, we were standing in formation along the edge of the road at about 8:00 A.M. when the Czech army battalion marched by, followed by the Scottish bagpipe band. The Scots put on a show: the sergeant major strutted by in his colorful uniform twirling his big baton, then the bagpipes began skirling out their music. The parade hadn't really begun, but the Scots wanted to intimidate the Yanks—and were quite successful. They were followed by the French drill team, which was good, far better than us, although a black American quartermaster company would have put them to shame. Then the 94th Infantry Division band stepped out, blaring a Sousa march loud enough to drown out the bagpipes.

"Infantry, forward. First Platoon, forward." We were the first platoon, marching under the L Company guidon but representing the entire 301st Infantry Regiment. Down the line there were the commands to "Stand fast" or "March!" We led off briskly, practically all of us in step. We marched for almost four miles through one of the most beautiful cities in the world: "the city of a thousand spires." The streets were lined with cheering crowds, people were leaning out of windows throwing flowers at us. We were the first American troops they had seen. We were the army that could have, would have, and should have rescued Prague from the brutal German army during the last days of the war. At noon on May 5, Patton had been in Pilsen with an armored division, riding hell-for-leather toward Prague. He sent a motorized patrol to the outskirts of the capital, where terrified troops of the Adolph Hitler SS Division offered no resistance (in fact, they were desperate to surrender before the Russians came). Patton had orders to halt at Pilsen, but he reported to Bradley that he could occupy Prague by dark. The answer was absolutely no. The Russian army wanted the honor of liberating this Slavic capital.

The Czech underground began an uprising when they saw Patton's vehicles on the outskirts of Prague, but the patrol returned to Pilsen and the German army began slaughtering civilians; the Russian army arrived on May 9, four days too late. Everyone in Prague knew this story, and there were many opinions as to why the Russians were so slow. The theory most widely accepted was that they waited until the Germans had destroyed the leadership of the underground movement, leaving a vacuum in which the Russians planned to set up a puppet Communist government. Prague had no love for the Red Army, but we were General Patton's combat troops, and it didn't matter whether we could march. All of Prague was yelling "Nazdar!" or bits of British English they had learned in school: "Cheerio, Yanks!" "Good show, Yanks!" "Hooray for General Patton!" They were also yelling "Vojáčku Zlàtý." The phrase doesn't translate well: "My golden little soldier" means something like "precious, beloved warriors." It meant God Bless America!

On the Charles Bridge, which crosses the Moldau River, we halted to allow the color guard, followed by the band, to parade across the square and get into position. The bridge was the most impressive I have seen. About every forty feet there was a niche with a beautifully carved statue. Then came the command "Infantry, forward, march!" and the representative battalion of General Patton's Third Army strutted across the Old Town Square, the centerpiece of beautiful Prague. The band blared out "Stars and Stripes Forever." At Fort Benning, Smitty had taught us the words to it:

> Sing out for liberty and light,
> Sing out for freedom and the right,
> Sing out for union and its might,
> Oh patriotic sons!

I was glowing with pride. No bagpipers could compete with Sousa's finest. We took up our position and waited while the nondescript Russian battalion marched in.

The Russian uniform was a tattletale-gray cotton blouse held in place by a black belt. The soldiers' heads were shaved, and there was no Russian band. The troops carried long infantry rifles with gleaming bayonets attached—not chrome-plated, just cold steel hand-buffed to a mirror sheen. As the Russians came off the bridge they began doing the marching manual of arms—with fixed bayonets! The procedure ended with a movement that we couldn't possibly have done, the rifle pointed forward with the sharp bayonet over the front man's shoulder and about one inch from his ear. Then they began to sing, the sound reverberating across the square; this was not only a crack drill team, it was also a trained chorus. We cringed.

We stood at attention for about an hour, listening to speeches in various languages. The only ones in English were by the British general and our General Harmon. Patton and Eisenhower, it turned out, weren't there. (On September 22, Patton had made a statement that the press misquoted slightly as: "This Nazi thing is just like a Democrat-Republican fight." Eisenhower was preparing to relieve Patton of his command and could not afford to be seen in public with him.) We marched out behind the division band, which was playing beautiful music, but somehow it wasn't quite as great as before: the Russians had skunked us.

We were served an excellent meal prepared by various chefs of the Prague hotels. They used GI rations, but no GI cook could come close to making such food. After eating we went to the soccer field, where the 94th Division played a demonstration football game against the XXII Corps team. The announcer explained all of the plays in Czech, and the people cheered at the right places. The Russian battalion sat in stony silence from start to finish. The 94th won, but it wasn't much of a game. Maybe I should hedge by saying that I thought it was slow and dull, but I had grown up watching fast, flashy teams. Our division had some men who had played at leading universities, and a few had professional experience. They, too, had been through a war and were in poor physical condition. I remember one play in which a 94th player caught a long pass and began running for the goal line with a defender chasing him. They both decelerated to a slow trot before the ball carrier collapsed on the five-yard line. After the game we loaded onto trucks and got back to camp at 11:30; we had spent just over twenty-four hours with only catnaps while bouncing along in a truck.

The next week we received orders to pull out of Rosenthal and go to an area near Strakonice where the regiment was assembling for movement to Germany. It wasn't a big move because there were only about fifty of us left in K Company. In early September the army had accelerated its demobilization plan. The plan was based on a system of points for time in service, battle stars, combat wounds, and medals. But it also awarded points for married men, for the number of children, and for age. The older men of K Company left immediately. Captain Warren was replaced by a captain from an armored division who knew absolutely nothing about running an infantry company and didn't care. It didn't matter much because Bill Henry, still a PFC, had already been handling routine matters for Warren. It was very much like the TV show *M*★*A*★*S*★*H,* in which Radar ran things and told the commanding officer what papers to sign. Radar ran things because he was the company clerk; Bill was the company runner, but we had lost our clerk. Fred Thomas and I, both PFCs, were the entire communications section (I can't remember what George was doing). We operated the switchboard and tried to keep the line to battalion repaired. We were supposed to have lines to the outpost platoons, but repairing them was a nuisance and the men on outpost were glad to be isolated. We spent a lot of time drinking coffee, reading, and swapping jokes.

When we moved to Strakonice, the company really ceased to exist; those of us in headquarters section helped in packing records and equipment to be shipped back to the States. For about two weeks we got detailed reports on the fate of Rosenthal. Czech police and civilians had moved in the day after we left. But my lie to Katryn had been surprisingly accurate. There had been no rape and very little pillage. The police had searched every house for "contraband," which meant anything they thought was of value. They didn't find much because the GIs had bought most of it with food and cigarettes and mailed it home. (It had seemed like fair exchange at the time, but looking back I wonder if it wasn't just a slower and more congenial version of looting.) The police took the carpenter's tools; he protested, and they beat him up a bit. Because no food was taken, the people had enough to get them through the winter rather comfortably. They weren't moved out until the next summer. I understand that they were all sent to badly crowded relocation centers in Bavaria, but eventually did settle on small farms and establish new businesses. To some degree our highly secret document had been true, except that the resettlement was under the sponsorship of the United Nations rather than the American army, and that GI boyfriends had no influence at all. Rosenthal still exists. It is about fifty miles south of Pilsen. The population is entirely Czech, and its name has been changed to Rozmital.

The 94th Division was designated as a 55-to-60-point division, meaning that anyone with 55 or more points would go home with it. I had 52 points, but George had one more battle star and a cluster to his Purple

Heart. He was headed home and I would stay in Europe for another six months. I was mad, disgusted, with the army. I had gone overseas with the division. I had carried the load when things were rough. I had fought. We had won, but my division was leaving me behind.

There was a parody of "Lili Marlene":

> Dear Mr. Truman, when do we go home?
> We have beaten the Master Race,
> And now you say, "No shipping space."

I was sick of the army.

5

COMBAT TROOPS

I was transferred to the 243d Field Artillery Battalion at Bad Aibling, a small town about thirty miles east of Munich. The battalion was quartered in what had been a large Luftwaffe training base for fighter pilots. The official name had been Flughorst Kaserne. *Flug* referred to fliers and *horst* meant "eagle's nest." Most of the Germans in Bad Aibling called the installation the Kaserne, which simply meant "the barracks." We called it "the base," and the official army name was POW Discharge Center No. 26.

I was housed in what had been the cadets' quarters. Never before, in or out of the army, had I lived in such luxurious housing. The barracks was much like a dormitory in a very elite college. Two large entrance doorways opened to a terrace where, on warm days, you could sit and enjoy the view of snow-capped Alps to the south. The lobby had lounge chairs, a fireplace, a reception desk with mailboxes for each room, and impressive murals painted on the walls. Several murals showed glorious air victories, and one had a slogan saying essentially that all opposition would flee when "in the field, a Bavarian stands." That must have been a traditional slogan about the Bavarian soldiers; it didn't quite make sense in reference to the Luftwaffe.

The entire building was steam heated; coal was scarce, but we used wood cut by the POWs. The living quarters were spacious—they had been designed to accommodate four cadets, but we had only two or three men to a room. I requested, and got, a private room because I liked to read and to go to bed early. I remember the beautifully tiled shower and toilet area; it was hard for me to believe that this had been a barracks. The toilets had hardwood seats constructed into the ceramic bowl—at least, they had originally been built that way, before someone knocked one wooden side from each toilet. You could still use them, by sitting with your weight on the good side. We made some bad jokes about the half-assed Germans. The toilets flushed into a septic tank. During the war it had been pumped out every week and the sewerage spread over adjacent pastures; Germany couldn't afford to waste fertilizer.

On the day of my arrival I started practicing what George Faber had taught me: there are always good assignments for someone who knows what he wants. The key is knowing what to ask for. I began by walking the area and asking questions. All buildings on the base were constructed of the same cement-covered limestone blocks. There was a large barracks that had housed enlisted troops (the training cadre; noncoms and officers had lived off base), an administrative building, lecture halls, and a spacious multipurpose theater that we used for movies, USO shows, and Sunday church services. My letters home tell Mother that I was going to church pretty often, but the services were dull. I don't remember much about the chaplain; his assistant led a Sunday-night Bible-study group, which I attended once. Its focus was the Bible as the infallible word of God. I tried to stay diplomatically quiet—but didn't succeed. I had grown up in a strongly religious town, but we were taught on a basis of integrity: when passages of Scriptures conflicted, one of them was in error. When I quoted one of the obvious conflicts, the group got disgusted and called me an atheist. They didn't realize that I was playing dirty pool. The sound argument against my stance is that because the original form of the Bible doesn't exist, we don't know which parts might be transcription errors: maybe the "real" Bible *was* infallible.

The base had a magnificent dining hall, which opened onto a terrace much like that of the cadets' quarters except that it overlooked what had been the parade ground. The terrazzo floor in the lobby had a large black swastika in the center. The lobby provided entrance to four individual dining areas with highly polished wooden tables. The plate settings were decorated with Waffen SS insignia; the word *Dachau* was stamped on the bottom. I don't know how SS chinaware came to be at a Luftwaffe base, but the concentration camp at Dachau had contained several small business enterprises, including some making decorative ceramics, chinaware, and pottery.

There was continuous music while we ate. The speakers were completely recessed into the wall so that only the grille showed. I suppose there were sound boxes behind the speakers because the tonal quality was excellent, much better than that of our GI public-address loudspeakers. The music was usually via radio from the army station in Munich; at noon they featured classical and semiclassical works on a program called "Lunchin' in München." The radio program at suppertime featured country-and-western music, also on records but hosted by the ETO Ridgerunners. The Ridgerunners had their own theme song, "It's Rough in the ETO": "Like the talking dog says, ruff, ruff, ruff, it's rough in the ETO." We got some relief in that the supper program was occasionally local requests—records played by our own disc jockey. These were Army Special Services records: a lot of Glenn Miller, Judy Garland's "Trolley Song," and such. I remember "One Meat Ball" as the funniest and worst song of that time. Most recordings of the song have mercifully been lost, but it told the story of a poor man who went into an expensive restaurant with only fifteen cents. He studied the menu and found he could afford an order of one meat ball. The waiter took his order and called out for the entire restaurant to hear: "This here check wants one meat ball." When the order came, there was no bread, and the customer complained. The waiter then called out the refrain of the song: "You get no bread with one meat ball!"

The airfield was less impressive than the buildings. It had about ten short bays that had been used to service and refuel planes. The bays were paved with brick. The landing area was entirely grass. At the far end of the field fifty or sixty German planes sat stacked together—nose on the ground, tail in the air. When American troops captured airfields toward the end of the war, they had used Bad Aibling as a collecting point for operable enemy aircraft. They supplied each plane with just enough fuel, put a Luftwaffe pilot at the stick, and told him to fly to Bad Aibling. The plan didn't work very well because the pilots didn't want the Americans to have usable planes, and especially not the fantastic new jet fighters. So as each pilot came in he would retract the gear and skid in for a belly landing, destroying the plane's engines and much of its underside with relatively little danger to himself. On warm days, several of us would go over to the junk pile and play fighter pilot. The cockpits and instrument panels were in good condition. It was fun to sit in the planes and pretend we were zooming down to strafe the enemy. But the enemy for those planes had been us, and we had heard tales of jet planes that suddenly appeared, flying so fast that you didn't hear anything until they had passed. We didn't want to guess what might have happened if the Germans had perfected the jets just a little sooner.

The prisoner compound stood on the near side of the airfield. It was divided by wire fences into fifteen "cages"; I didn't like the implication that we were keeping men caged like animals, but that was the term everyone used. Each "cage" contained ten barracks, which could hold 110 men each. The total capacity was more than 16,000 prisoners, but the camp was only about 75 percent full. Immediately after the war, though, the airfield had been packed with hungry prisoners. On April 31, a cavalry recon unit had captured the base without opposition. Within days, word spread that Americans had arrived in Bad Aibling. Thousands of German soldiers, fleeing westward to escape the Russians, descended on the air base.

The handful of Americans, with enough rations to feed themselves for a few days, were suddenly responsible for about 35,000 German soldiers. The GIs simply stood at the entrance to the airfield and watched them stream in. It was impossible to keep records as to how many prisoners there were or what units they represented; thousands of Germans were simply herded into the airfield, with no food, water, or shelter. The weather was cold, with occasional snow or freezing rain. The GIs who weren't on guard huddled in one of the hangars and looked out at the miserable prisoners. When the people of Bad Aibling heard about the situation, they came out and threw loaves of bread over the fence. It was a humane gesture, but it caused so many fights between hungry men that the guards had to quit allowing civilians near the fence. A week later some rations arrived, enough for one K-ration box per day for every three men—in other words, one-ninth of the normal combat ration. The prisoners were issued German army pup tents, which were simply ponchos that could be buttoned together into four-man shelters.

After that awful first week, the place gradually became a camp. The very young and very old men were released and told to go home. There are no records on them because they weren't really "soldiers." Also, some of the prisoners were postmen, firemen, even schoolteachers; during the early chaos, everyone wearing a uniform had been sent to the camp. Sick and badly wounded soldiers were shipped to a hospital at Dachau. Able-bodied prisoners were taken to an abandoned German army camp, where they dismantled the barracks; they then reassembled the buildings on the airfield. By the time I arrived, the accommodations were good. The men slept in double-deck bunks on straw mattresses. There were two stoves in each barracks, and wiring for electricity was almost complete. Each cage had a heated dayroom with books, magazines, and the weekly POW paper called the *Rat und Tat,* "Information and Action." The camp library had a wide selection of books.

There were three large hangars, originally used for aircraft repair and maintenance, that had been converted into various support facilities. There was a good machine shop, facilities for shoe and clothing repair, and an extremely large store of new uniforms, boots, blankets, and so forth. The clothing stocks, for reasons that I would understand later, were under the supervision of an American officer, but everything else was run by the Germans. The prisoners also ran a well-equipped dispensary with a little thirty-bed hospital. Men who would be hospitalized for longer than five days were sent to Dachau.

Cage Number Seven was heavily guarded because it contained the SS officers: 772 of them. I never did go in it, but the guards said that the SS men were mean and arrogant. Many of them were nearly invalids, part of a prisoner shipment we had received from the Russians; the Soviets only returned Germans who were no longer capable of manual labor. The German doctor was trying to get the invalid SS men transferred to a physical-therapy unit at Dachau. It seemed strange to me that a notorious concentration camp could provide such outstanding medical care; it even had an artificial-limb factory.

The prisoners' only serious complaint was about the food: they didn't like it and there wasn't enough. They had my sympathy; I didn't like the food either and didn't get enough of it (although I got more than they did). They didn't think much of the scrambled eggs made from dehydrated egg powder or the dehydrated potatoes that tasted like paste. The coffee was good, and they often had canned fruit for dessert. The Germans, who were used to heavy "farmer's bread," thought the stuff made from white GI flour tasted like paper. We occasionally got pork chops or beef stew, but the prisoners didn't.

The GIs who had been there for a while said that I would probably be assigned as a guard. There were three kinds of guard duty: cage guard, gate guard, and work-crew guard. Cage guard, sitting in a machine-gun tower for eight hours, was the dullest, and guarding the gate was only slightly better. Having learned this, I became acquainted with the company (the proper artillery term is "battery") clerks to find how the assignments were made. They didn't make the assignments but told me which officer chose guards for work crews. Again applying the Faber system, I learned that the officer had been an artillery forward observer with an infantry division. We talked about the old days and how much we riflemen had appreciated artillery support. At some point I mentioned that I would prefer guarding work crews because I spoke some German and, from combat experience, knew how to manage prisoners. The officer said that he would try to help but hadn't been in the battalion long and didn't expect to be there much longer; he had enough points to go home. He also made a vague statement to the effect that the battalion commander was not the kind of man he cared to serve under.

The next morning all of the newly assigned men were sent to the theater for a welcoming address by the commander: Major Muller. I must hedge here by saying that I don't know much about him personally or about the orders he was under. I remember him only by that introductory speech, but it was enough for me to rate him as a first-class, number-one, all-time, all-American son of a bitch and bastard. He was known in the battalion as "Major Miracle": a living, breathing man who was both brainless and gutless. Gossip said that when he arrived in September he had tried to run the place like a concentration camp. The situation got so bad that the prisoners appealed for a Red Cross inspection team. That must have frightened him because by the time the team arrived in late November, the camp was being run pretty well. The Red Cross team did note that because Major Muller was not present, they could not voice their complaints to him directly.

There were about thirty new men assembled in the theater. Seven or eight of us were from the 94th Division; most of the others had just arrived from the States. Major Muller was late but finally came strutting in: " 'Tention!" "At ease, rest, be seated, smoke 'em if you got 'em." He started out pleasantly enough by welcoming us to the battalion. He had studied our service records and was pleased to see some good combat records. He was particularly interested in using guards who had seen infantry combat, been wounded, and understood what German soldiers were really like. His first remarks were directed at the combat veterans: "Unfortunately, you will find that the rules have changed since the war ended. You are not allowed to give Krauts the sort of treatment they handed out at concentration camps. Lieutenant Kelly will explain the regulations later, and I want them followed to the letter. However, I expect you to treat all prisoners with the contempt that they deserve."

He then gave the newly arrived men a long lecture, saying that they would not be assigned to work with prisoners until they had completed orientation, which consisted of a training film and a lecture on the rise of Nazism and racism in Germany. He went into a tirade about prisoners who tried to say that they had only been soldiers following orders and that the blame for concentration camps lay with Hitler and the Nazi leaders. "Absolute garbage! They all believed that they were the super race and that the rest of us were subhuman. Talk with these veterans from the 94th Division. They saw Panzer troops shooting every American medic who came out to care for wounded. Many of these friendly German girls that you will see around here used to live in Munich and Stuttgart. American airmen who parachuted from disabled planes were beaten to death with clubs by those sweet, smiling fräuleins." He said that no German, man, woman, or child, deserved any sympathy whatsoever.

My southern traditions had not taught me that Abraham Lincoln was a glorious leader, but as I sat there fuming, the words of his Second Inaugural Address came back (not the whole thing; my high school English teacher had only required us to learn the last paragraph): "With malice toward none; with charity for all; with firmness in the right, as God gives us to see the right, let us strive on to finish the work we are in; to bind up the nation's wounds; to care for him who shall have borne the battle, and for his widow, and his orphan—to do all which may achieve and cherish a just and lasting peace among ourselves, and with all nations."

Major Muller was not a disciple of Lincoln. Maybe his hero was General Butler, the Beast of New Orleans. The man rambled on in the same vein for nearly an hour, repeatedly saying that the German people did not deserve acceptance into the civilized community. When the tirade ended he sent the new men over to see a film, and we combat veterans went to a hangar for guard-duty instructions. During the walk we took turns venting our rage about Muller. Those of us from the 94th explained to the others that during the first few days, men of the 11th Panzer really had fired on medics, but they had learned about combat on the Russian front. Generally, the Germans we fought against were good soldiers. During the occupation period most of us had come to like the German people—men, women, and children. They were cleaner, friendlier, and more trustworthy than the French we had known during the war. Back in September, General Patton had said that he was proud of his Third Army for having killed 144,500 German soldiers, but that the war was over: the Germans had been good soldiers and would make good civilians.

At the hangar, I realized that Lieutenant Kelly was the man I had already met, the one who had said he didn't like Muller. Kelly made an excellent talk: "Gentlemen, you have already had the Muller treatment. I will explain how the camp is run and what I expect of you. I will not tolerate men who think they are here to punish soldiers for having surrendered. Most of you have seen some degree of combat duty; remember that when these men surrendered they still had weapons and plenty of ammunition. If they had followed Hitler's orders to fight to the last man, a lot more Americans would have died—including some of you. I am very glad that they decided to stop the killing. Once when Stonewall Jackson was criticized for taking good care of Union prisoners, he said, 'I would rather feed them than fight them.' Any time you decide to get rough with prisoners, stop and remember what fighting them was like."

Kelly also pointed out that we were not to carry loaded rifles. "The old 'lock and load' days are over. You will be issued one clip of ammunition, but it will stay in your cartridge belt and is to be used only in extreme emergencies." He said that the possibility of such emergencies was almost nil. If any prisoners decided to escape, we should bluff a bit but let them leave. They were probably just homesick; they would go home, find that everyone needed a food ration card, and come back. Their only punishment would be placement at the bottom of the list for discharge.

Kelly was a good man, and I was embarrassed about having tried to con him into giving me a soft job. But he did remember me, and I usually got work-crew assignments. It was easy work. I gradually realized that not being able to go home with the division was a lucky break. I was living comfortably and had free time to see Bavaria as a GI tourist. Someone has written that when Germany was divided into occupation zones, the Russians got the productive farmland, the British got the industrial area, and we got the scenic tourist area; ours was the best deal.

I was disgusted with having to serve under a man like Muller, but it didn't matter much because I never really had to deal with him. My main personal disappointment for the moment was at losing my 761. Job descriptions in the army were based on MOS (Military Occupational Specialty) numbers. For the past eighteen months I had been classified as Infantry Scout (761) and was proud of it: in Rosenthal, I had turned down a promotion to communications sergeant (T-4) because I wanted to be discharged as a 761. Officially, I had now become a Guard Patrolman (522), but I still felt like an Infantry Scout and wore my Combat Badge every day.

The boys who lived next door to me in the barracks had arrived from the States about three months earlier. They listened in awe as I told them what combat was really like. Mike and Stud (that is all I remember of his name) were older than me, maybe twenty-three or twenty-four, and Mike was married, but I was the old veteran. They did some sort of work in the ration depot and envied me for being a guard "because of my combat experience"—but that was only the tale Muller was telling. The truth was much more pragmatic: I was a guard because it doesn't require special training to stand out in the cold and watch prisoners who don't want to escape. Guard duty went to men who had almost enough points to go home; training would be wasted on us because we wouldn't be there very long.

Although I spent a lot of time talking with Mike and Stud, it was just trivia. I don't remember having any close friends during the entire three-month stay, probably because we had such mixed backgrounds and many of us were just waiting for shipment home. The battalion must have been understrength. All of the enlisted men were quartered in the cadets' barracks, and it was not nearly full. My letters home tell about the excellent library of Armed Forces Edition books and frequent sightseeing passes. I spent the week of Christmas at Grindelwald in the Swiss Alps. The sudden change of going from a devastated nation to the clean, neat, German-speaking Swiss mountain communities was fantastic.

Broadly, in spite of Miracle Muller, the battalion's attitudes toward Germans were positive. During the entire month of December there was a candy collection box in the office dispensing PX supplies. Everyone was urged to donate his candy ration as a Christmas gift for German school-children. The week before Christmas, a large box of American candy was sent over to the public school. (When I returned to Bad Aibling in 1992, several adults remembered that their first postwar Christmas was celebrated with gifts and candy from the Americans.)

One night while sitting in my room smoking my pipe, I began to realize just how lucky I was. The old army expression was "You've found a home in the army." The army was not my home, but my living style was much better than any I had known as a civilian. As a child of the depression I seldom had new clothes, mainly just patched hand-me-downs from relatives whose sons had outgrown them. My family had enough food, but just enough. The idea of having meat at every meal was a dream, and I usually left the table hungry. Of course, I was still leaving the table hungry, but no more so than I had back then. I was also wearing new, freshly washed and pressed clothes. True, the clothes were an army uniform, but each of us was allowed some individuality. I was supposed to be wearing a Third Army shoulder patch but was using my divisional patch instead, and had outlined it with the stainless steel beads that were issued as dog-tag chains. I had bought a small replica of wooden shoes, which I usually wore dangling from the pocket of my combat jacket. Directly above that pocket I wore the Combat Badge, which said that I had earned the right to dress as I liked; I had already paid the price. As my preacher back home would say, I was wealthy beyond my wildest dreams, both in spiritual and material goods.

In fact, most of the occupation GIs were living better than they had ever expected would be possible—but none would admit it. All of us, including me, wanted everyone else to believe that "back home" we had lived even better than this. It was particularly important that the German girls believe all Americans were rich.

Guarding work details was easy and interesting. We spent a lot more time sitting around and talking than we did working. A work crew was a prized assignment for the prisoners because they got to eat at the extra-rations table. Food was scarce throughout Germany. According to army records, we were on 75 percent of standard rations, but I remember it as closer to 50 percent. The Geneva Convention required that prisoners of war be given the same rations as their guards, but the army had decided that these men were not POWs but DEFs—"disarmed enemy forces." According to the November Red Cross report, the Bad Aibling prisoners were getting 2,100 calories per day, and the extra-rations tables about 3,000 calories. In a sense, the army had decided that these men were civilians who should be getting the same low rations as everyone else. The prisoners grumbled about this system frequently, but it was probably sound. The war was over, and there was no reason for them to eat better than their families did. That argument didn't satisfy the prisoners: "But why do the Ami get to eat so well?" I thought the reasons were obvious: it was our food, and we had won the war.

I was usually the guard for Work Crew Number 5 (the German designation was Arbeits-Kommando V; they used the term *commando* much more loosely than we did). Number 5 was a motley crew of ten men from all branches of the service. The assortment varied as some men were discharged and others replaced them from the central pool. There were usually a few Luftwaffe, with the rest being what we called Wehrmacht. (Actually, *Wehrmacht* referred to the military forces in general, including the navy, Luftwaffe, and army; the proper term for the army per se was

Heer.) Most of the Wehrmacht were infantry, with a few panzermen and occasionally someone who had been a clerk. They ranged from fifteen-year-old boys to one man who was fifty-five, older than my father. We operated on an informal, first-name basis, except that they called me "Sheriff Leon." The nickname was part of the game that they admired Americans. In Germany, Bavarians had the reputation of being wild, crude, tough, and uncouth, much like Wild West cowboys. They were Bavarian cowboys and I was their sheriff.

I was in charge of my cowboys only in the sense that I carried the rifle and would be responsible if we got into trouble. The crew chief was a prisoner with experience in general repairs. He received the work assignments from a central agency, which was also run by prisoners. So far as I could tell, the general operation of the camp was entirely in the hands of German officers. It was a pragmatic solution to the management problem: German soldiers could be handled more efficiently by using German military procedures. Our main goal was to get these men back into the civilian sector as quickly as possible, within the guidelines assigned by Washington. Politically, the Americans were in charge. They screened prisoners for war crimes and Nazi connections, issued discharges, assigned men to guard duty, and supervised the warehouses (rations, clothing, and general supplies). The American army must have also set regulations and general policies; I wasn't in a position to know the full protocol. Certainly it appeared that German officers had routine control.

The guards tried to make a show of being in charge, but it was difficult. I would go to the gate and ask for my group, and a German noncom would shout, "Kommando V, Appell." Technically, *Appell* refers to inspection, but it is also the term for roll call. The work leader would simply look down the line and tell me that everyone was present; it meant nothing to me because I didn't know how many there were supposed to be. Then he would tell me what our work assignment was. I would call them to attention, in English, and march them off calling cadence. I enjoyed calling "Hut, tup, thrup, fourp" again. The "Sound Off" songs were everywhere now, and there was something of a competition among the guards to show what we could teach our groups to sing. The basic Sound Off song described Jodie, the 4-F who was at home with our women. For the

POWs we changed his name to Hermann. "Every time you stand Appell, Hermann rings yo' Fräulein's bell. Ain't no use of sounding off: Hermann's got yo' gal and gone." We recycled old cowboy songs into the Sound Off pattern. "I got a gal, she lives on a hill. She won't do it but her sister will. Sound off . . ." I liked to have my group sing "Pistol Packin' Mama." They agreed that it was funny but preferred cowboy songs: "Deep in the Heart of Texas" was a favorite. They loved to strut along clapping their hands and slurring the words. We sang in English, but I tried to translate so they could enjoy what they were singing. Some of the words were very difficult to put into German. "The coyotes wail, along the trail" became "Die Koyoten heulen auf der Fährte."

One day I collected my crew and we were sent off on a truck to get some lumber. The crew chief said, "One of the men lives only a short way from where we are going. Could he stop off to see his family?" Sure, how long would it take? Well, that depended on what I thought we could get away with. I decided that if we had a flat tire in front of his house, it would take at least an hour to repair. That worked beautifully; the driver pretended to repair the tire while we all went in to visit. It was the prisoner's mother's house, and someone went to get his wife, who lived down the street. He hadn't seen them in three years. After Mama laughed and cried, she went into the kitchen for a "little cooking." The wife and neighbors came in. Everybody was jabbering so fast I couldn't understand anything. They sang a German song in which I couldn't understand even one word. Then, "We sing the Ami song 'Pistol Packer Mama.'" I laughed until I was crying. They would sing a phrase and translate it into German for the women, then start again. Mama came in with the "cooking." She was able to celebrate her son's homecoming with half of a small boiled potato for each person. Then it was time to leave. I reached for my rifle, and it was gone! *Gewehr, Gewehr,* where's the *Gewehr?* We were all scared. If we had to go back with my rifle missing, there would be hell to pay. I felt like a fool: the guard losing his rifle. Mama came in from the kitchen with the M-1. With so many kids around, she had been afraid and had taken it to a safer place.

My group had a lot of fun and we joked a lot, but there were some bad aspects, such as the "quota draft." Under the Allied surrender agreement there was a provision that each month, the American army would provide a group of prisoners to be sent to France for war reparations labor. Around the first of each month a French officer would arrive to select new workers. The officer boasted, both in English and to the Germans, that these men were to receive the same kind of treatment that the Nazi government had meted out to captured French soldiers. His concept of reparations was simply vengeance—a fact that was emphasized by what we called the "salvage detachments." The term *salvage* came from training camps back in the States, where we had been able to turn in worn-out or damaged gear to the company supply room and receive new equipment in exchange. At irregular intervals, both the French and Russian armies would send us groups of German soldiers for "discharge." In fact, these men were too sick or badly injured to be discharged; they had been driven until they were of no further value as laborers. We would send them to hospitals, where some died and some recovered enough for discharge. As far as I know, there was no real relationship between the number of disabled soldiers that the French shipped us and the monthly labor quotas; we called them "salvage detachments" as a joke. Apparently we had no agreement for sending prisoner quotas to the Russians. I know of only one such shipment that left from the Bad Aibling camp. These were ex-Russian POWs who had volunteered for the German army. Forcing them onto boxcars was a painful experience because we had no doubts about their fate.

The French quota officer seemed to have complete authority to select anyone in the camp. He would spend some time looking at soldiers' records and then call for certain men; to fill the rest of the quota, he would simply go down the formation of prisoners and select groups at random. The November draft came up a few days before I arrived at the camp. The officer selected an entire ten-man work crew that was going out on an assignment. Because they would not leave until the next day, the crew was allowed to continue on its project. A little after noon the guard returned with the sad news that the entire group had suddenly escaped; he had fired his clip of ammunition and missed with every shot.

The guard received an official reprimand but was not punished. I would have done the same thing if my crew had been selected for almost certain death in France.

I remember several men in my crew by personality, but names and other details elude me. We spent a lot of time talking shop: war. We compared weapons, equipment, and tactics. The Germans agreed with me that our M-1 was the finest combat rifle used by any army. They laughed over my admiration of the Schmeisser machine pistol—what we called the "burp gun." It had used 9-mm pistol ammunition, large, heavy, and underpowered; a target twenty yards away was nearly out of range. Its rate of fire, 500 rounds per minute, meant that a 32-round clip lasted four seconds; with the standard six clips, the total firing time came to twenty-four seconds. During assaults, the Germans had used the Russian version whenever possible. It fired 7.65-mm (.32 caliber) ammunition with greater range and many more rounds per clip.

The Germans claimed that our .45-caliber "grease gun" was even more useless than their burp gun. They said that our praise of their officers' pistol, the Luger, was misplaced. It was machined with such precision that a little dirt would cause it to jam. The cheap-looking Walther P-38 was a much better pistol for combat. They liked our .45 pistol. It kicked like a mule but was very effective in stopping a man at close range. (I said, "Yeah, we learned that from the cowboy shootouts in Western bars.") Our artillery was about the equal of theirs, but we used it much more lavishly. The Russians had attacked behind rolling artillery barrages, but theirs were nothing compared with our saturation shelling. The Russian tanks were by far the best used by any army. German tanks were next, with ours a distant third: fast and maneuverable but with ineffective weapons and skimpy armor. Luckily, the Russian commanders didn't seem to know how tanks should be used. A man with the nerve and daring of Patton would have been a terror if he had had tanks like the Russian T-34. (Patton seemed to be the only American commander the Germans knew of.)

The German infantry had been terrified by our P-47 fighter plane. They called it the *Jabo,* a shortened combination of the German words for "hunter" and "bomber." Our pilots had called the P-47s "jugs" for their bulky shape. The planes were slow and heavy but very accurate in dropping bombs. During combat we could call them up to knock out a tank or any fortified position. They would roar in, blast the target, circle back, and fly low over our troops wagging their wings. The jug pilots were part of our team.

The Germans admired our vehicles for a reason that had never occurred to me. Individually, their Daimler-Benz, Porsche, and BMW vehicles were extremely reliable. The problem lay with poor planning. Rather than using uniform specifications, the government had simply contracted with each company to furnish vehicles of a certain general type. Even among trucks furnished by a company, very few of the parts were interchangeable. In contrast, the United States had contracted with companies to furnish vehicles with detailed specifications. All parts on a Chevrolet truck were exactly the same as those on a Ford or Dodge. If one of our trucks broke down in the field, parts could be cannibalized from another. Sometimes the Germans had seven or eight disabled trucks and were unable to repair any of them.

We had long talks about the relative fighting qualities of various troops. Their accounts of combat against Russians were frightening. Individually, the Russian soldier was not very good; he could be easily fooled and was poorly trained. The Russians fought as a mass, usually outnumbering the Germans three or four to one. Even at those odds, the Germans could win through discipline; if they held their positions, the Russians would eventually panic and retreat. But cold weather and lack of food seemed to have no effect on Russian soldiers. They were tough and could live on grass seeds or roots. Their winter uniforms were better than those of the German army and far better than ours. The Russian occasionally carried a blanket but never had a tent, and it didn't seem to matter. Medical care for wounded Russians was terrible; it was nil for captured Germans.

In the face of a Russian attack, the only alternatives were to stand and fight or to retreat in an orderly fashion. Surrender was out of the question. Prisoners were used as pack animals to carry ammunition and supplies, usually until they collapsed and died. The greatest hazard was of being captured after you were wounded. Russian soldiers seemed to take great pleasure from torturing wounded men. Most of my crew knew horror tales of what Russians would do to dying men. At night they could hear German prisoners screaming from behind the Russian lines. In some cases a captive was stripped naked and tied spread-eagled on the frozen ground. When he became cold enough to start feeling numb, the Russians would douse him with warm water. I was shocked, and remembered part of a Kipling poem about advice to British soldiers who were wounded and left on the field in Afghanistan: "Jest roll to your rifle and blow out your brains./An' go to your Gawd like a soldier."

When I quoted that, one of the men smiled: "I don't know Kipling, but he knows war."

When I asked about German treatment of Russian prisoners, my crew admitted that the road ran both ways: they had worked prisoners to death and knew of Germans who had tortured wounded captives. Their war in Russia had been as brutal as ours in the Pacific. The Japanese soldier set the tone for our brutality there. I think he was a much better soldier than the Russian but was fully as vicious.

I was almost afraid to ask what kind of soldiers we had been. They laughed and said that they would much rather fight the Ami than Ivan. The primary reason was that we treated our prisoners well. They weren't afraid to surrender to American troops, with one exception: paratroopers had a terrible reputation for abusing prisoners. They also said that our paratroopers took heavy casualties because they fought too aggressively. (I had heard that same criticism even back at Fort Benning. Some of The Infantry School instructors had used the cocky paratrooper as an illustration of what overconfidence could do. In an attack you should stay as calm as possible, move slowly, and wait for the right opportunity. Don't let hatred blind your decisions, don't hurry or push your luck, keep pressure on the enemy until he makes a mistake.)

I pointed out that American troops had felt the same way about the SS. My remark stirred up a serious controversy. Some of the older veterans argued that we had never fought against the real Waffen SS because most of them had been killed on the Russian front. Those half-trained kids that we had fought were just trying to get themselves killed. Others argued that even the old Waffen SS had been too cocky and aggressive. They had looked good against the Russians because the Russians were poor excuses for soldiers. It became an endless argument. Everyone agreed that in Russia it had been good to have SS on the line because they would never surrender or retreat.

What I really wanted to know was how the American straight-leg infantry compared with its counterpart, the German *Landser.* "You were more like German troops than any we had seen before. We hadn't fought against well-trained, confident troops until we met the Americans. We had rolled over the British and French. The Russians were animals." The Germans had heard reports from Africa and Italy that the Americans were well equipped but poorly disciplined; they had also been indoctrinated with the idea that we were a 'plutocrat army' that would break under stress. Maybe we would have, but they had never been able to put enough pressure on us.

Part of the problem was our tactics. Those American panzers! They weren't any good, but the Ami sure knew how to handle them: "You drove like Chicago gangsters." Then there was the artillery. A long, heavy barrage always preceded an infantry attack. "The ground would shake for hours. We would be dazed, deaf. Then the infantry came up, but there was nothing to shoot at. One man would get up, run a few steps, fall to the ground, and roll. Another would get up somewhere else, but there was no system to it." And the Ami wouldn't break under fire pressure or artillery. When they decided to take a position, they kept coming until they won. There were no yells or screams, but the cold efficiency was frightening. One man summed it up: "The Ami knew they were going to win."

There was also an odd psychological element that I hadn't considered. Men who had served as occupation troops in France said that it seemed strange to call the Americans "Ami" because it was so close to the French word for "friend." But that was a minor point. The fact was that, at first, they had felt awkward just to be fighting against Americans. They had always seen the Russians as their real enemy, and they hated the French because of memories from the World War I occupation times. But German boys had grown up watching Hollywood movies. Now they were fighting boyhood heroes: Tom Mix, Ken Maynard, and the Chicago gangsters.

I am summarizing many different conversations and opinions, but there seemed to be general agreement that, even in their prime, the German army could not have run over us as it had others. There was no consensus as to why, but I remember a story told by a man who had been with an engineering unit in France repairing bomb craters in the roads. Using wheelbarrows and shovels, it took twenty men about eight hours to completely repair a crater. On the day of his capture he marched down the same road and saw one black GI, operating a bulldozer, fill a bomb crater in thirty minutes. "That was when I realized we had no chance of winning the war."

For my work crew, the superiority of American equipment and supplies was a given. Whether the individual American soldier was the equal of a German regardless of that advantage was another matter. I conceded that the American soldier was far less disciplined than the German but pointed out that an army is composed of men, equipment, and supplies. A group of men without weapons is not an army. Although the American rifleman went into battle on foot, he was supported by machines. The German army relied heavily on horse-drawn artillery and ammunition hauled up on wagons. We attacked behind massive artillery barrages because that was the way our army was organized. In the process of establishing air supremacy before the invasion, we had suffered heavy losses of aircraft and airmen, far more than the defending Luftwaffe had. We ruled the air because we had been willing to pay the price, building more planes and training more men. I think we were the first truly technological army. Germany had some excellent weapons, but they were hand-crafted, not the uniform, mass-produced equipment that all modern armies now use. We were, as Patton said, the finest army that had ever worn shoe leather, partly because of our highly developed mechanization; but we should never forget the men who operated the machines, many of whom died doing so.

Most of my crew eventually agreed that the Ami soldier could not be judged separately from his equipment, but I knew some German soldiers who were never convinced that we were anything but pampered plutocrats. They thought we had too much equipment, too much food, and far too much ammunition. The British and French held the same view; they also called us naive because we didn't hate the Germans enough. But blind hatred is a dangerous emotion in combat, and I don't think any of them,

German, French, or English, could call us cowards. American troops would moan and complain even when they were living better than anyone else, but they fought to win and continued to fight until they did win.

My opinion (from a limited viewpoint) of the German soldier is that he wasn't nearly as well-trained as we had expected. But then, we were not fighting the German army that had conquered Europe and much of Russia. We faced an experienced but badly weakened enemy. They had very good reasons to be demoralized and to surrender after halfhearted attempts at fighting—but they weren't and didn't. The German soldier had grit. Which raised another question: why had they continued to fight, against such odds, for a government they knew was corrupt, and while their country was being destroyed? It wasn't a fair question because there were many reasons. "We fought the Russians to keep them out until the Americans came." Or: "We fought against the American army as a delaying action to help civilians escape from the Russians." Or: "I fought because of the *Sippenhaft* [kin arrest] rule. My family would be sent to prison if I surrendered."

One man summed it up nicely: "I fought for my country, probably more for Bavaria than for all of Germany. I was proud of the country when we defeated France, I was ashamed of some things we did in Russia, but we all fought, and fought—even after we realized that victory was impossible. I kept fighting because my country needed me."

I could understand that. There is a Civil War story of a Tennessee soldier who said: "I fought because I loved my state and country. I've been fighting for three years. If this war ever ends, I'm damned if I'll ever love a country again."

I enjoyed these discussions and I think my crew did. These men, like me, were the ordinary soldiers; they were glad the war had finally ended and that they were again free to express opinions. With the exception of a few well-indoctrinated Hitler Youth, most of them had known for the past two years that a German victory was impossible and that absolute defeat was likely. They hadn't been able to discuss this knowledge with anyone but very close friends because of a regulation against "defeatist attitudes." You could be sent to prison or, in extreme cases, shot. Many of them seemed to understand that Hitler had led them into the disaster and that the only solution had been for the Allies to invade. In a sense, we Americans had liberated Germany. This attitude did not extend to regarding the Russians as liberators. The Germans hoped, and expected, that we would fight the Russians before they grew too strong. "In one month Patton could be in Moscow. The Russians aren't good soldiers. There were just so many of them, and we didn't have the kind of air and artillery support that you have. Think of it: a combined German-American army could whip anybody in the world." (This belief was common among the prisoners I spoke with, but most historians say that an American attempt to fight the massive Russian army would have been catastrophic for both sides.)

The work crew had two boys, only slightly older than me, who had grown up in the Hitler Youth. All I knew about the HJ was what Maud had told me. It sounded a lot like the Boy Scouts and not like much fun. But these boys had absolutely loved being in the HJ. To them, it represented the true values of National Socialism; they would have explained those values except that the rest of the crew continually made fun of them. One of the men would pretend to blow on a trumpet and another would beat on an imaginary drum, and they would sing one of the many HJ songs. Together, we would translate them into English—often in a not-very-glorious manner.

I laughed with them but was impressed at the beauty of the thoughts, wishing that the Boy Scouts had used songs like that; I only remembered singing "Trail the Eagle," to the tune of "On Wisconsin." One of the HJ songs described Germany as a new cathedral:

> Now the cathedral is standing, standing squarely in the light.
> The suffering is gone, that tore our Volk apart.
> Our song makes us strong and sure.

Another song had been written about the coming battle for new lands in Russia:

> Raise the banners in the east wind,
> for they wave so strongly there.
> They signal our departure
> and our blood hears the call.

The final verse went:

> Our morning stands in the East,
> this is Germany's future.
> Cares of our Volk lie there,
> victory and danger await there.
> Comrades, raise the banners,
> let the drums thunder forth!
> What the others only dream of
> will blaze in our hearts.

A song called "The Oath of the Cadet Sergeant" proclaimed:

> Thousands die, thousands tower up
> a mountain of bodies on the battlefield.
> Though I am felled a thousand times,
> I will get up on my knees and attack!

Jokes about the HJ were both good-natured and serious. The older men strongly resented the way the ex-HJ boys had kept insisting that the army fight to the last bullet. The boys were disappointed to hear Germans saying that Hitler's national community had been a cruel myth that no one believed. *They* had believed; they still believed that Hitler hadn't known about the evil things that were being done in his name. It was as if I were to be told that the Boy Scouts had been rotten at the core.

My cowboys were a lot of fun. We worked well together and never got caught goofing off or completing a project too quickly. Occasionally we would get a new man who didn't fit; if I couldn't manage him, the prisoners would do it themselves. I don't know how the system worked, but apparently they could go to the German officer in charge of work crews and explain that we needed a replacement. In theory, I could report a prisoner as "unmanageable," but the informal method was easier. It became routine that when I had guard duty, I would get the cowboys. Then came a black day.

We had received group of former Afrika Korps men, fresh from two years in the States (we called them "stateside" Germans). They had lived well in America and loved to tell about it. The joke "over there" had been that POW stood for "Pensionierung of Wehrmacht," a mix of German and English meaning "German army retirees." They seemed to know the Geneva Convention rules of POW treatment by heart. Their first complaint was that POWs were entitled to the same rations as GIs. We told them that they were now DEFs, not POWs. They then complained that everyone who wanted to be on a work party should be allowed to—in order to eat at the extra-rations table. Somehow, this argument worked. They were given work instructions, and I was assigned to guard a group of them.

I protested that I was the guard for Crew Number 5 and didn't want a new group; Lieutenant Kelly, the assignment officer, laughed. As we marched off I called cadence for a few rounds and asked, in German, what they wanted to sing. They replied, in very good English, that they didn't want to sing or listen to me calling cadence. We stopped and I explained to them, in English, that they damn well would sing and I would call cadence. They began a German song, using a strange accent, but I recognized the tune and some of the words. It was "The Oath of the Cadet Sergeant": "Though I am felled a thousand times, / I will get up on my knees and attack!"

We stopped again and I said, "All right, you will not sing that song, or anything else. Now move out!" I realized that they had won a round and might test me again, but at the time it didn't seem important. We got to the area where the fence was to be repaired, and they wanted to build a fire first. It wasn't very cold, but we didn't have much work to do, so I agreed. Then they started complaining about the short rations and how we were violating the Geneva Convention. I just listened; I was getting disgusted and really didn't care what they thought was fair. I knew that they had studied both the Geneva Convention and U.S. Army regulations on handling of POWs; but why did they think I could, or wanted to, do anything?

Finally I had heard enough of their complaints and told them to get to work. Two of them started toward the fence but came back when someone spoke to them in fast German. The ranking sergeant walked up to me and said, "You don't seem understand who is in charge of this work group. They start working when I give the order."

I began to realize what I was up against. Through pure carelessness I had let them think they could manipulate me. Somehow, I was going to have to regain at least the semblance of control.

I backed up, keeping eye contact, pulled out my bayonet, and fixed it on the rifle. In basic training we had learned that a bayonet was the best way to intimidate prisoners. Maybe it would work here.

It had no effect at all. The sergeant stared me down and said, "Quit bluffing. You can't use that rifle against prisoners."

I took the clip of ammunition from my belt, slipped it in the rifle, put a round into the chamber, and took the safety off. My hands were sweating and I could hear my voice of command wavering. "Just try me. If I put a round in your gut, they will court-martial me, take away my PFC stripe, and send me home for discharge. Do you think I care? *Feldwebel,* line your men up, we're going back to the cage!"

He stared at me. I stared back, neither of us knowing whether I would pull the trigger. Then he turned around, got the men in a line, and started them off, singing that Hitler Youth song again.

I couldn't let the bastard win and didn't know what else to do. "Halt. You can sing if you like, but get those hands on top of your heads!"

He stopped, turned his head around, and said: nothing. I was pointing the bare bayonet directly at his face. "Have your men get their hands up or this thing will be sticking up your ass!"

This time both of us knew that I would carry out the threat. In fact, I wanted to: the dull bayonet wouldn't do much damage, but it would bring about instant discipline. The crew marched off with their hands resting on their heads. This was the way The Infantry School had taught us to handle newly captured prisoners, which is exactly what these men were.

Lieutenant Kelly was laughing when I brought them up to the gate. "Run 'em in the chute, cowboy!" I followed him into the office to raise hell about what he had done, but he was laughing so much that I couldn't stay mad. He explained that he wasn't to blame. The German officer in charge of work crews had asked for me to be assigned as the guard.

The next day I got my cowboy crew back. They laughed all day. The stateside prisoners had been bragging that nobody could make them work because they knew more about American army regulations than any of the guards. The cowboys had told the work crew officer about it and suggested that I could teach them the facts of life. But why me? They wouldn't say, but I suspect it was all a joke. The stateside group would see this shy, skinny kid as a pushover for manipulation, not knowing that I had an ego about being a tough soldier. Also, it was pretty obvious that I wasn't so stupid as to try shooting anyone. At least it had seemed obvious to them; no one realized how close I had come to being that stupid.

Troops riding on tanks of the 20th Armored Division advancing into the heart of Munich, April 30, 1945.

National Archives, 111-SC-206195

Glamorously lighted portrait of the author taken in June, 1945, by the two young women operating—apparently illicitly— the Unterbühner photography studio in Solingen-Wald.

Courtesy the author

The author (right) and former BAR man George Faber in front of the church in Rosenthal, Czecho-slovakia.

Courtesy the author

Postcard view of Rosenthal, probably taken in the early 1930s.

Courtesy the author

General George S. Patton trooping the line at a review parade, Strakonice, Czechoslovakia, July 17, 1945. The K Company guidon appears above the jeep window to Patton's left. Rather than referring to Patton, the words "War Eagle!" probably indicated that the driver had gone to Auburn University.

National Archives, 111-SC-227620

Composite company representing the 301st Infantry Regiment passing in review in the Old Town Square, Prague, October 19, 1945.

National Archives, 111-SC-214898

German soldiers sightseeing in Paris, August 9, 1941. The man in civilian clothes is apparently a French guide. The author found this photograph in the house of Willi Hermanns, Bonn, 1945. Hermanns had been killed as a Luftwaffe pilot. His connection to anyone in the photo is unknown.

"Milky" Edwards flashes a con man's smile, probably in Solingen-Wald, June 1945. Behind him to his left are Joe Weiner (laughing) and (partial profile) the author. To Milky's right (in glasses) is the boy called "Kevin" in this book.

Courtesy Harry Glixon

Two American soldiers in Nuremberg chatting with German girls despite the rule against fraternization, April 25, 1945.

National Archives, 111-SC-234642

"Rubble women" cleaning bricks for reconstruction work, Munich, May 18, 1946.

In Rosenthal, the author found a cache of *Wochenspruch* propaganda posters, which were distributed weekly by the Nazi Party. This one, for the week of August 17–23, 1941, proclaims that "Germany is victorious on all fronts."

Courtesy the author

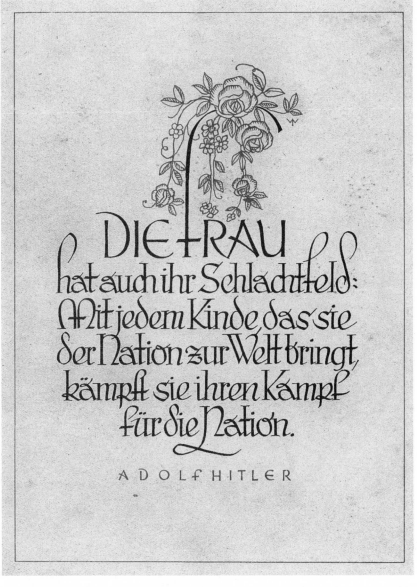

A *Wochenspruch* poster for May 18–24, 1941, quoting Hitler: "The woman also has her battlefield: with every child she brings into the world, she fights her battle for the nation."

Courtesy the author

The tone of the *Wochenspruch* changed subtly as the war turned against Germany. On the poster for November 7–13, 1943, a wounded but unbowed man carries a banner: "Strong hearts are those who compel victory."

Courtesy the author

Wochenspruch, week of November 13–19, 1944: "German people: Whatever may come, we will master it. At the end stands victory. Adolf Hitler."

Courtesy the author

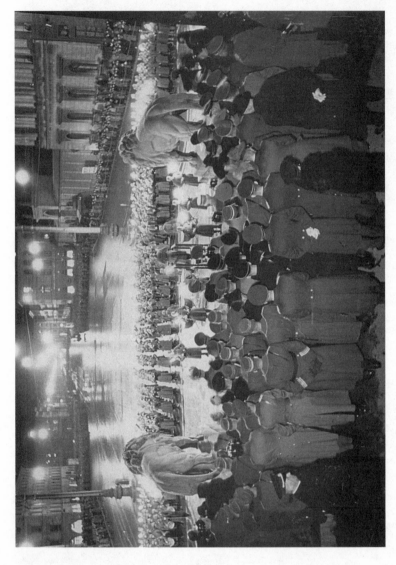

Ceremony at the Feldherrenhalle, Munich, March 16, 1936, at the height of Nazi prewar glory.

Nazi Party memorial plaque being removed from the side of the Feldherrenhalle, June 1945. The plaque commemorates the men who were killed on the Odeonsplatz during the failed Nazi putsch of November 1923. The graffiti on the right says, "Goethe, Diesel, Haydn, Rob. Koch. I am proud to be German." That on the left, not shown completely, says, "No shame! Only the swastika."

Courtesy Otis B. Wheeler

The Feldherrenhalle in 1992. As this view shows, the "hall" is actually a facade.

Courtesy the author

Surrendering German troops stream into Bad Aibling Air Base, May 5, 1945, four days after the U.S. Army arrived. Apparently POWS are being unloaded in the foreground to be sent to join the much larger group beyond the aircraft. Records suggest that the Americans belonged to the 2d Chemical Mortar Battalion, attached to the 3d Infantry at the time. The thousands of prisoners represented a serious problem for a small unit with barely enough food for its own men. Note also the lack of shelter for the POWs.

National Archives, 111-SC-206061

Bad Aibling Discharge Center, December 1945. The former air base had become a work camp for German DEFs awaiting discharge. Prisoners in the cage on the right are assembled for work assignments.

National Archives, 111-SC-227620

Bad Aibling base, May 19, 1950. At this time the base was being used as a relocation center for Germans from nearby countries. The German residents of Rosenthal were sent to a center such as this (although probably not, in 1945, such a good one). The former air-cadet barracks that the author occupied stands at the extreme lower right of the housing compound. The field that housed prisoners is beyond the photograph on the left.

National Archives, Mun-50-116 EUCOM-6071

The old air-cadet barracks at Bad Aibling in 1992. It is now used by the U.S. Army for offices.

Courtesy the author

The Café Arnold in Bad Aibling, 1992. This is the beer hall where, in 1945, the author and Anna had long visits.

Courtesy the author

The author with Hilda Hofer at the Café Arnold, 1992. Hilda was working at the café, which belonged to her father, in 1945. She later took it over and ran it until her death in 1995.

Courtesy the author

The building that once served as the home of the Hitler Youth in Bad Aibling.

Courtesy the author

The author conversing with Hermann Böhme, a former Luftwaffe officer, in Bad Aibling in 1992, Gerda Kopliks translating.

Courtesy the author

6

SOMEWHERES EAST OF SUEZ

My work crew told fascinating tales about the old days before Miracle Muller had come. None of them had been in the camp that long, but stories of pre-Muller times had become legendary. Except for that chaotic first week when nobody had food or shelter, the GI guards had been, well, GIs. The war was over and they saw no point in following regulations that didn't make sense. One of the prisoners, who was from Bad Aibling and hadn't been home since Christmas of 1942, wanted permission for his family to visit him. Because regulations prohibited civilians from entering the compound, one of the GIs requested the man for help as an expert in some sort of problem. He picked the man up right after breakfast, drove him home, and left him with the family until just before suppertime.

It was common for American units in the area to request detachments of prisoners to help with chores. One Signal Corps company in a nearby town had five Waffen SS officers (who spoke English) assigned to live in a house next to company headquarters and perform "general maintenance": serve food, wash dishes, do a little cooking and cleaning, and help GIs learn some German. I suppose the SS officers felt degraded at having to serve enlisted men, but they came to enjoy the relaxed atmosphere of the American army. Although their textbook English was very British, they picked up enough army slang to sound almost like GIs. They were efficient workers and wanted to visit the local town during their off hours but couldn't do it while wearing German uniforms. The solution was typically Ami: they were given GI clothes and told to stay within a few miles—there could be trouble for everyone if an MP caught them with no pass and no identification. With their new freedom, the SS men would swagger into the local Bierstube and order beer in GI-accented German. They had expected to pick up girls and have a bit of fun. That didn't work at all. Girls on the sidewalk would cross the street to avoid meeting them. Women sitting in their yards would go inside and close their doors. Wearing GI uniforms, the German men had become the enemy, and no girl who cared for her reputation would speak to them. Identifying themselves was too risky. It couldn't be "our little secret" because the girls would have to explain to the local gossips. If the truth became public knowledge, no more GI uniforms and visits to town.

When the signal company was transferred, the prisoners were returned to Bad Aibling, where they met Muller. He made a show of asking them what they thought the American army should do with them. The answer was obvious: discharge them so they could go home and start rebuilding Germany. Muller smiled and assigned them to the notorious Cage 7, where they were kept under close guard and tight restrictions.

I enjoyed the stories, knowing that they must have improved with time. But later I met a daughter of the man who was taken to visit his family and one of the SS officers who had been with the Signal Corps company: the stories apparently were true—and probably fairly typical of early GI management of prisoners.

In telling me about the SS men, however, my work crew was making a different point: Times were changing. The local women no longer crossed the street at the sight of an American uniform, and even if prisoners couldn't go into Bad Aibling, I could and should. "Hey, a great soldier like you can go out and capture a fine German girl anytime you want to." There was some bitterness in the remark—the prisoners didn't like the idea of their women dating the Ami, although they knew there was nothing they could do about it. There was also a touch of sarcasm: to some extent, they were teasing me about being too shy to find a girl. On that point they were absolutely right. In the rigidly controlled moral climate of Clinton, my high school "dates" had consisted largely of walking a girl home from Sunday-night church services or Saturday-night church socials. I had dated a girl while I was in the hospital in England, but we had both been shy and uncertain about the proper way to act on such occasions; our most exciting sexual experience had been the goodnight kiss.

My first effort locally was a rather halfhearted attempt at dating some of the girls working on the base. We had far more female employees than were needed. They were all good-looking and all loud-mouthed idiots. My crew said, "Hell, Mr. Sheriff, you don't need those *karbolische Keks.* Go into Aibling and find you a nice widow-woman. The town is full of them, and they are hungry for a good man." (*Carbolic cookie* was German army slang for "prostitute." I don't know the derivation; maybe it had to do with the use of dilute carbolic acid as a disinfectant.)

Mike and Stud, the boys who roomed next to me, had also been saying that I should find a girl in town, but not a widow-woman. They were having a lot of fun with a fifteen-year-old and her fourteen-year-old sister: "Get 'em young and teach 'em proper respect for a man." The girls had been bombed out of Stuttgart and were living with an old-maid aunt who had tried unsuccessfully to keep her charges in line. Now the boys were keeping the aunt in line, partly because the girls were crazy about them, but also because the aunt appreciated the food they were smuggling out of the ration depot.

Given a choice between taking advice from my work crew or from Mike and Stud, I decided to look for a widow-woman. My first effort was another failure. Bad Aibling was a clean, neat, rural Bavarian town; clustered along the old Munich-to-Rosenheim road, it was about four blocks wide and maybe eight blocks long. I found that the local people called it simply Aibling; *Bad* (bath) referred to the famous local hot mud baths, reputedly an effective treatment for various orthopedic ailments—some resort spas on the edge of town were being used as rehabilitation hospitals for German soldiers. The town had some fine old homes and a picturesque, undamaged downtown district. Because it had escaped bombing, it harbored a lot of refugees from the cities. There were plenty of girls—and widow-women—to choose from; it was the first time I had been in a town where the GIs didn't outnumber the available women.

I had expected to stop a prospective date on the street, strike up a conversation, and proceed from there. I didn't even consider the possibility that anyone might still think of me as an enemy soldier. We hadn't been the enemy since our stay in Solingen-Wald. In Rosenthal we had been the American army that was protecting German nationals from Russians and Czechs. To my work crew I was just another soldier, bored with the army and anxious to get out. But in Bad Aibling, I soon realized, people resented me as much as my grandparents had hated the damnyankees. They were courteous and obedient, but aloof. If I asked for directions or information, they answered civilly. If I tried to make conversation, they didn't seem to understand a word of my German.

The next morning I reported to the cowboys on my failure: "I got nowhere. Those people hate my guts!"

My crew just laughed: "Man, they don't hate you; it's the way you are acting. You want to find a date, not pick up a whore, use a little common sense. Look around in the shops until you find a woman who looks good. Buy something and make some small talk. Do the same thing at several stores and decide which ones you like. Then come back the next day and talk some more. Do it this way and you can choose what you want."

I followed their instructions, and voila! Anna worked in a bakery that made wonderful bread: moist, with whole grains of wheat in it and covered with fine wood chips. (The GI explanation said that the wood was filler, to produce more bread from the flour ration, but I vaguely remember that the chips kept the loaves from sticking together.) Technically, I couldn't buy anything at the bakery—bread was strictly rationed. But American cigarettes were the standard currency for everything. I made a little small talk with Anna and asked if people ever had extra ration tickets that might be traded for cigarettes. She smiled and said that, yes, she knew of a little old lady who couldn't eat bread but loved cigarettes.

Anna was not especially attractive, a short stocky blonde. She could have looked much better with a little makeup and some sexy clothes, but she felt that if neat and clean weren't good enough for men, they should look somewhere else. She wasn't the kind of girl they would have hired at the base; her English was good and she made intelligent jokes about translation problems. I decided that this was the girl I wanted to date, even if she was a little older than me. For nearly a week I went in to joke with her and occasionally buy something. Finally I mustered the courage to ask for a date. She smiled and said that German girls shouldn't date American soldiers, but it was a weak refusal. I tried again a few days later and she agreed, with a stipulation: instead of going to her house, I was to meet her at the Café Arnold, a little beer hall on a side street close to the bakery. The café had been a popular Luftwaffe cadet hangout, and the Americans would later adopt it in the same way. When I was there it had a small orchestra, not-very-good beer, and no other GIs.

On every date Anna and I talked a lot, working on her English and my German. She had taken English in school and had a good grasp of the fundamentals. My understanding of German grammar was almost nil, but I had developed a fair vocabulary. We usually spoke English, with me trying to translate words or expressions she didn't know. Because I was also trying to teach her American slang, our conversations didn't go very smoothly. When one of us had trouble with a word, we struggled through several ideas before looking in her dictionary. Occasionally we would meet at the beer hall and go to the movie theater: American movies with German subtitles. (Most German movies were now banned as Nazi-related.) I was amused at the subtitles for *Abe Lincoln in Illinois.* For example, Lincoln comments on the Todd family, his future in-laws: "They must be important. They spell their name with two d's and God only uses one." The German version simply said, "They must be important. They spell their name with two d's." The Germans spell *Gott* with two *t*'s.

At first Anna had said that she was twenty-one. That didn't hold up well when she started telling stories of her past. After a while she changed her age to twenty-six, which was still a few years shy of the truth. She was originally from Stuttgart, where she and her husband had run a small bakery. After he was drafted, she ran the bakery until it was bombed. Then her house was hit, killing her young son. She moved to Bad Aibling when she heard that the local baker, Mrs. Bachmann, needed help.

This information worried me a bit. Anna was much older than me, and she didn't seem to be a widow-woman; she was married, and her husband might come home at any time. I was sure he wouldn't be as tolerant of my dating her as the soldiers in my work crew seemed to be. I tried to think of what people would say if this happened back home in Clinton. Maybe trashy people ran around with older, married women, but my kind of people didn't. I didn't feel trashy, but in the last year I had done a lot of things that my kind of people didn't do: strip clothes, boots, and wallets from dead soldiers, or cut an innocent man's throat because he had thought I was a friend—which I wasn't.

I wasn't ashamed of being with Anna. She was a nice Christian girl. Well, she wasn't really a Christian. She had once been Catholic but was now what she called a "God Believer." I remembered Abe Goldstein as having said that Jews, Christians, and Muslims had reached their under-standing of God by different paths, but it was the same God. All right, Anna wasn't Christian and wasn't a widow. I could rationalize all of this because I enjoyed being with her and listening to stories of Germany be-fore the war—except that we weren't just talking. I was holding her hand and kissing her occasionally, and it was obvious that she was willing to do more; it was also obvious to her that I was afraid we were already doing too much, and obvious to both of us that she was in control of what we did. I was more than a little apprehensive, but I kept coming back be-cause . . . because I wanted to.

I kept asking Anna about her husband, but she very clearly did not want to talk about him. For weeks her answer was, "He is probably dead." Then one night, without my suggesting it, she decided to tell me. She started by explaining that he was a Waffen SS officer, but only by accident. "Accident" meant that Hans had been drafted in 1941 and put in the SS. That had embarrassed both him and Anna because one of the Waffen SS divisions—the infamous Death's Head Division—had trained near Stuttgart just before the invasion of France and had earned a terrible repu-tation for drunkenness and rowdiness. The joke was that the intelligence test for admission to the SS required that a man be able to count to ten using both hands.

Although the SS was an embarrassment, Anna and Hans were strong supporters of National Socialism: the concepts of community spirit, hard work, a classless society, and dedication to the improvement of Germany appealed to them. They were both surprised when it turned out that Hans enjoyed SS training; the work was tough and demanding, but it built unit pride. He got long lectures on the ethics and responsibilities required of an elite unit. Besides loyalty to the corps, he was taught the virtues of absolute honesty and reliability. The word of an SS man was his bond, and he could be relied upon to carry out orders precisely.

Hans knew that some of his assignments would be difficult. An SS man must realize that he could not take soft, civilian ideas of ethics into the corps. He must be hard, even harsh, with himself and in carrying out orders. "Are you able to walk over dead bodies without feeling any emotion at all? You must learn to value the needs of your country, you must serve with honor and courage wherever you are sent." There was an expression that Waffen SS men must be as hard as Krupp steel and as tough as boot leather. They were taught a careful distinction between the Waffen (combat) SS and the General SS, which used its men for guard duty in concentration camps. (Although the Death's Head Division that trained at Stuttgart was technically a Waffen unit, it had been organized and was run by the man who was also in charge of the concentration camps.)

Anna had enjoyed seeing Hans in his sharp uniform. It was the same color and design as that of the regular army but made of better material; the SS had the best of everything. At first, though, she was bothered by the "Blood and Soil" ideas he was bringing home. Roughly, the slogan referred to the German race defending its land, violently if necessary. Gradually she came to see that a race must be proud both of its genetic heritage and of the land that had produced such a strong people. She still found some of the SS ideas extreme, but others made a lot of sense.

Hans was selected for the SS *Junkerschule*. As Anna explained it to me, the program resembled our Officer Candidate School in that graduates became officers. The graduation ceremony took place in Munich at midnight in front of the Feldherrenhalle ("Hall of War Heroes"), one of the great Nazi shrines. The candidates marched into the vast Odeonsplatz in front of the monument, and someone read the roll call of dead heroes. After each name, there was a distant answer: "Here!" Then Himmler, head of the entire SS, made a not-very-good speech. Each candidate was called to the front steps of the Feldherrenhalle and given a sword inscribed with Meine Ehre Heisst Treue and a certificate that admonished him never to draw the sword without cause or sheathe it without honor. Anna glowed with pride. That night she and Hans had a remarriage using the new SS wedding ceremony. Rather than calling on the Jewish God to bless them, it was based on the old Teutonic blessings. Now I understood why Anna had described her religion as "God Believer"; her name for God was Wotan.

Hans was assigned to train troops for an SS division that was already fighting in Russia. The combat-experienced officers who were helping him train recruits told plentiful stories of how brave and tough the SS was in battle. Under direct orders from Hitler and Himmler the division was continually being moved to places where the fighting was thickest. Hans was impatient to take part. He knew that the Slavic animals would have to be destroyed or all of Europe could become their slaves. Anna was frightened and beginning to wonder whether she still agreed with his ideas. In her mind, National Socialism had been a plan for improving Germany. Hans seemed to be talking of conquest, of capturing rich farmland, of expelling the owners and establishing German villages.

Finally, in the spring of 1942, Hans got his chance to fight. His letters from Russia sounded encouraging but lacked the enthusiasm he had expressed earlier. He was wounded and sent home after about six months of combat. Then Anna began to understand what he had seen. Hans was thin, sick, and broken. He said that the Russians really did fight like vicious animals, and anyone who surrendered to either side was tortured and killed. The SS were better soldiers than most of the Russians, but that wasn't enough. Russia seemed to have unlimited manpower and equipment (like every German I talked with on the subject, Anna emphasized a belief that the Russians' supplies and vehicles came largely from America).

Hans soon realized that victory was impossible. It wasn't the sort of thing an SS officer should be saying, but he added more. He told Anna that Himmler had made a serious mistake in treating Ukrainian civilians so harshly. During the invasion, they had welcomed German soldiers because it meant liberation from the Communists, but Himmler's General SS looked on all Ukrainians as subhumans who were of value only as laborers. Action squads would raid a village and send all adults back to Germany to work in factories; the children were killed. The Ukrainians formed guerrilla teams that attacked German supply dumps to obtain food and weapons. Then they began surprise attacks on German troops. The only practical means of fighting back was reprisal: the Waffen SS would round up some citizens of a nearby town and threaten to hang them if the attacks continued. The attacks continued and the people were hanged—and there were more attacks and more hangings. Then the SS began burning entire villages for reprisal, but that was futile because it only increased the hatred.

Hans broke down and cried as he told Anna these things. He was sent back to Russia in the spring of 1943. Anna received occasional letters that said nothing about the war. Then the letters stopped, and she was notified that he was missing. She knew nothing about when or where. When the war ended, his division had surrendered to the Americans in Austria but had been turned over to the Russians.

Anna's manner in telling all this was more matter-of-fact and resigned than it was sorrowful. She had held out hope for victory a little longer than Hans, but by early 1943 she had known that Germany was losing the war and could not win it (in February of that year, the entire German Sixth Army was captured at Stalingrad; in May, Rommel's Afrika Korps surrendered). She was still proud of the original National Socialism concept but knew that it had been corrupted by Nazis like Himmler. For a while she had hoped Hitler would ask for a truce with Russia and then work out some agreement with Britain and the United States. When his speeches made it clear that he wanted to fight until Germany was victorious, she began hoping someone would kill him. Failing that, she only hoped the Americans would conquer Germany before the Russians did. I wondered then, as I do now, what she had been like when Germany was winning. Maybe she no longer remembered; maybe she didn't want me to know.

Anna was very firm in saying that the Nazi Party had become brutal and corrupt, that it had betrayed both Hitler and the German people. She enjoyed telling about the old days, before the war, when National Socialism offered a dream for the future. Hitler had wanted Germany to return to its old ethics of integrity and hard work. He said that city life and the strong influence of French occupation troops had corrupted the national sense of honor and cooperation. The true strength of Germany lay with the farmers and small rural communities. The youth in the cities were soft and corrupt, with no sense of obligation to the family or the country.

Anna was proud of the entire Hitler Youth program and told me about its good points in more detail than I would have gotten from my work crew. Boys aged ten through thirteen belonged to the Jungvolk; the girls' organization was the Jungmädel. At fourteen, the boys went into the Hitler Jugend (HJ) and girls into the BDM. The terminology was a little confusing to me; the umbrella name for the youth program was Hitler Jugend, which was also the name for the older boys' section. It seemed to be clear to Anna; she had been in the BDM section of the HJ. (Or so she said. Later, I realized that this version made her seem younger than she was. In fact, she would have been about seventeen in 1933—too old for membership. Probably she was one of the youth leaders who worked with the younger girls. With this background she would have had a good understanding of how they saw the program, which may have been her attitude as well.)

Almost every city neighborhood had an HJ home with meeting rooms for each group and a full-time youth leader (in small towns the leaders were often part-time volunteers). The HJ home in Aibling was a large two-story building constructed for that specific purpose, but Anna's HJ home in Stuttgart had been a former residence; I didn't ask who had lived there. After school, girls could go to the home and talk, play games, or get help with their homework. Wednesday night was known as "home evening." At seven o'clock the girls met at the home for a background talk by the leader on the topic of the week. At 8:15 they gathered around the radio for the "Young Germany Hour." The program might be a play, a discussion among youths, or a lecture from a national authority, but it was always related to the weekly topic. Afterward, the girls held group discussions of what had been said. The topics were extremely varied, covering German heritage, current events, or international problems.

The young people were also given booklets on subjects that would be covered on weekend outings or at summer camp. The American Boy Scout and Girl Scout programs had monthly dues to be paid from our own earnings, and parents were not supposed to pay for our uniforms—

we did without until we had earned the money. In HJ and BDM, everything was paid for by the government, including all expenses at summer camp. On weekends and at summer camp the girls learned about German history, old customs, folk dances, and how to make things for the home. There was plenty of recreation and athletics; they learned to swim and to ride horseback, and could learn marksmanship if they wanted. There were lectures and discussions about becoming German women. The BDM taught that proper German girls never used makeup because it attracted the wrong kind of men. There were lessons on nutrition and the proper care of children.

BDM girls had several volunteer programs to help in the war effort. One involved the repair of socks sent back from the Russian front. The girls unraveled wool from the socks that were beyond repair and used it to reknit the worn-out heels or toes of others. They were allowed to attach a note to the repaired socks, giving their name and address together with a message of encouragement. Occasionally there was a thank-you letter from a soldier who had received the socks.

Anna was shocked when I told her what Maud had said about the HJ boys teasing BDM girls as being "useful articles for German men." That sort of thing hadn't happened where Anna lived. The boys were taught to respect girls and faced discipline if they were rude in any way. Hitler, who was their role model, respected women as the foundation of German culture. He also did not smoke or drink and was a vegetarian. The HJ did not expect its members to live up to such high standards, but smoking was usually forbidden and beer drinking was allowed only in moderation. The summer-camp instruction for boys was essentially the same as that of the BDM except for a heavier emphasis on athletics and the concepts of *Volk* and *Volksgemeinschaft*.

Anna made several attempts at explaining these terms, but I never quite understood. *Volk* seemed to be such a simple word: the dictionary said that it meant "people" or "the folk." Anna tried to explain that it meant all of the German people, as a single unit. The English word *community* didn't quite match it, and the German *Reich* ("government") wasn't even close. Anna had learned about *Volk* and *Volksgemeinschaft* in the BDM, but the ideas weren't from National Socialism; they were part of German tradition from long ago. *Volk* meant, approximately, the total of all Germanic heritage and traditions. She thought that *Teutonic* might be a better word because the Vikings and Viking ships were part of the Volkish heritage. Teutonic knights, who defeated the Romans, had used the swastika as their symbol: it was an ancient Aryan sign for the eternal circle of life. To be Volkish meant that you were a patriotic German. I remembered the prayer that I had seen on a poster in Rosenthal; using a dictionary, I had translated *Volk* as "the German people." My translation had been accurate as far as it went, but that wasn't very far. Similarly, it was obvious that *Volksgemeinschaft* meant a lot more than the translation "national community."

Anna told me more about the German youth programs. At the age of seventeen, everyone owed the country six months in what was called the Labor Service. For the boys it was much like our Civilian Conservation Corps, except that it was obligatory. They worked draining marshes, preparing land for the new Autobahns, planting forests, and performing other useful tasks. Girls had the same obligation, but it was not strongly enforced; deferment was allowed if a girl was already doing work of value to the community. Girls who did go into the Labor Service were usually assigned to work with poor families. After a short training period, they would go into slum areas to help mothers raise healthy children. They would give demonstrations on nutrition, sanitation, and preschool education. Some girls participated in what was called "Mothers' Day in the Country." Mothers took their children to a child-care center run by the Labor Service girls, then rode by train to a country area—often an estate the government had confiscated—where they could rest, talk, hike, and play games. The holiday was given at no cost to the families.

When I returned to my work crew with these stories of how wonderful the youth programs had been, I encountered mixed reactions. The ex-HJ boys were enthusiastic over Anna's account. They had been inspired by the organization; it had helped them in their schoolwork, been their sports club, and taught them strict ethical rules for life (the Hitler ethic: respect women, work hard, be honest, never smoke or drink). Some of the older men agreed, but only up to a point. Although the HJ had claimed to be nonmilitary, it promoted the discipline, marching, and drama of an army. It taught boys that they must eventually fight for the honor and survival of the Volkish people. It glorified the concept of dying for Germany. After the war began, the HJ became extremely militaristic. The boys were taught assault tactics and marksmanship. A good record in the HJ meant special consideration for becoming a Waffen SS officer. Discipline in the HJ had been aimed at conformity; the boys were encouraged to haze anyone who was weak or came from a wealthy family; plutocrats could not be real Germans. They were particularly vicious toward Jews or half-Jews who tried to be part of the group. Anyone who was only one-quarter Jew was also three-quarters Volkish, so was generally acceptable—but not good enough for SS service; boys who expected to join the SS could have no trace of Jewish blood.

Men whose daughters had been in the BDM told a similar story. It was useful, highly disciplined, and extremely intolerant. Generally, Anna's account of the girls' Labor Service was considered accurate. The girls had done a lot to help poor families, and the Mothers' Day in the Country program had been very popular.

I decided not to let Anna know that I was checking her stories with other sources. She was obviously telling me the truth as she believed it. She saw her former way of life as a good one because she had been taught that it was good. She and I disagreed strongly, though, when she started trying to explain the German attitude toward Jews.

There hadn't been any Jews in Clinton, but I had liked most of those I met in the army. Anna argued that I couldn't really know Jews until I saw how they operated as a group. Non-Jewish people were called *goyim* and were excluded from Jewish business and social opportunities. Although that sort of situation was beyond my understanding, I could remember the problems of Yankees and of non-Baptists trying to break into the social system of Clinton. I had known a few Jewish boys in the army who always seemed to have a grudge against the *goyim*, particularly (I thought) against the redneck types. Every group, including Jews, has intolerant people. My point was that no one should label an entire group on the basis of a few of its members.

Anna said that I just didn't understand. She claimed that although the Jews had made up only a tiny part of the German population (a little less than 1 percent), they were concentrated in the large cities and dominated business. Before Hitler took over, Jews controlled the entertainment industries, most of the banks, and the large department stores. Many universities were dominated by Jews and gave Jewish students preferential treatment. In Bavaria, Jewish intellectuals took over the government and made it Communist. They wanted to establish an international Communism, run from Moscow, instead of helping to build a strong German republic.

I didn't know anything about that. It didn't seem logical, but my argument was on a more fundamental point. The Nazis had put all Jews, even German citizens, in concentration camps and killed most of them. Regardless of what some Jews might be alleged to have done, mass murder was not a reasonable solution.

"Leon, that isn't what Hitler meant when he said we must get rid of them. He planned to take all the Jews who didn't want to be patriotic Germans and send them back to Jerusalem. Most of the Communist Jews liked the idea, and we sent several shiploads over there. The British made us stop because the Arabs were getting mad. We tried to send a shipload to America, but you didn't want them either."

I sat thinking that surely it wasn't true, but even if it were, "Anna, it's wrong to deport people from their native country just because the majority doesn't like them."

"You tried to do it with the Negroes. You wanted to send them all back to Africa."

"That's just political talk." (In fact, Theodore Bilbo, a vilely racist senator from my own home state, was making himself notorious at that very time for his ship-'em-back-to-Africa statements.)

"No, you established a colony called Liberia."

I saw that the BDM had taught Anna very well. She could still recite the lessons to justify, or at least explain, the things that had gone wrong in Germany. The one group she blamed most, though, was the Nazi Party. Her disillusionment with them was complete. She couldn't say just when she had turned against the Party. It had happened gradually as the Gestapo and General SS became stronger and harsher. Anna's BDM group kept believing that when Hitler realized what was going on, he would step in and correct the evils. The girls even tried to devise a way to write Hitler and tell him what the Party was doing in Stuttgart. They couldn't simply send him a letter because they were sure the local Gestapo would open it—and it was said that the Gestapo had a file of the handwriting and fingerprints of every student in the schools. The letter never got written because the parents found out about the plan. It was generally laughed off as girlish naïveté—most of the parents no longer thought that Hitler was unaware of his party's doings, even though they still supported him because Germany needed a strong leader. But the laughter must have been a little nervous. Anna knew of people, family friends, who had been arrested for criticizing the Party and sent to a reeducation camp. It was a rare event, she said, and the people usually returned in a few months with a much more supportive attitude.

Throughout the war Anna had been proud of Germany's victories and had felt that no other country could have done so well. She wouldn't say it openly, but I got the strong feeling that she still thought Hitler's leadership had been sound and that an authoritarian government was more efficient and effective than a democracy. The whole thing made me uneasy. I couldn't see why this soft, gentle woman still loved Hitler. I couldn't understand how anybody could have stood by and watched while the country was being destroyed through bigotry. Ten years later in Mississippi, I wanted to apologize to Anna: I didn't know how or when to protest when my community was being destroyed through bigotry.

I had dated Anna for a couple of weeks before she let me come to her house. It was in a quiet neighborhood near the edge of town. There were no street signs. The signs had been removed when the Americans came: the area was where the Luftwaffe cadre had lived, and the streets had been named after German pilot heroes of World War I. Anna lived on what had been Freiherr von Richthofen Strasse, named for the famed "Red Baron." (The main street of Bad Aibling, once Adolph Hitler Strasse, had regained its original name, Rosenheimer Strasse: the street leading to Rosenheim.)

As we walked to her house, Anna explained that she had wanted to know what I was like and what I believed before introducing me to the girls who were living with her. Inge and Hilda were the fourteen- and fifteen-year-old daughters of friends of Anna's in Stuttgart. Their social life had been rather restricted during the war, both because of the bombing raids and because the HJ training had kept young boys busy. When Stuttgart surrendered to French troops, rape and pillage were common. The girls had hidden in their basements for nearly a week. Americans moved in as the war was ending; the girls thought the Ami were cute and wanted to start dating them. Their parents disagreed. The compromise was that they could move to Bad Aibling and stay with Anna. Everyone at home would assume that—well, it didn't much matter what they assumed. I asked if it weren't illegal to move from Stuttgart to Bad Aibling. Anna hedged a bit and said, "There are ways to accomplish almost anything."

Listening to her story, I realized that the girls were the two Mike and Stud had been telling me about; the "old-maid aunt" was Anna. I kept my mouth shut about all that. I didn't believe half of what Mike and Stud said and didn't like the rest of it. They used the words *Nazi* and *German* interchangeably, something we had never done even during combat. In their minds all Germans were ex-Nazis who should be repaid for the awful things they had done. Their current idea of revenge was to dominate these girls and their maiden aunt.

I had felt sure that Mike and Stud were just spinning yarns about their conquests, but their descriptions of Inge and Hilda were right on the money; the girls were good-looking and rattlebrained, typical adolescents. After dating the boys for almost two months, they still knew no English except for a few dirty phrases. Inge had a good voice and was trying to learn some of the songs she heard on the Armed Forces Radio network. She wasn't making much progress. Hilda knew most of the words to a dirty song that Stud had taught her.

Being a rattlebrained adolescent isn't the same thing as being stupid. The kids were so smart that I was sure they could learn English quickly if they wanted to. Apparently they didn't: the Armed Forces Radio had a German-oriented program called "Let's Learn English," but they wouldn't listen to it. They showed interest only in the words to American songs. During the early Hitler years, American "swing" music and Hollywood movies had been popular. As the American government began to oppose Hitler, such decadent entertainments were banned. German young people were supposed to prefer folk songs and folk dancing—but they didn't, and they were delighted when the Americans brought swing music back. "The Trolley Song" was a favorite of the time, but Inge and Hilda couldn't catch the fast lyrics. I tried going very slowly, teaching them to pronounce each word; it didn't work. Another song they liked was "The Yellow Rose of Texas." I saw some hope there because the music was much slower. After I went over each word, they would sing part of a verse correctly, get mixed up, and start giggling. I finally gave up; they didn't really want to learn the words, just wanted to sing.

For a while I enjoyed listening to a story from Mike and Stud, then hearing a different version from the girls. I suppose that lasted for about two weeks; Anna and I didn't date often, and I left before Mike and Stud came. But one night while I was helping Inge with a song, the boys barged in (they never bothered to knock on the door of a Kraut house).

"Stan! What the hell are you doing here?"

"I'm the GI who's been dating the old maid."

They laughed and then started getting mad: "Why the hell didn't you tell us you were dating her?"

"You didn't ask, and there wasn't much to tell. Anna and I don't do anything very exciting."

That I was dating Anna didn't bother them nearly as much as the possibility that I had been telling the girls about them. Mike and Stud calmed down when they realized that the girls knew nothing about my friends at the base; I wasn't a gossipmonger. They decided that I might be just what Anna needed to get her straightened out. She came in about then, and they were impressed with how much her English had improved since I began teaching her. Anna had spoken very good English when we first met; if she had used broken English while talking with them, there must have been a reason. Even then, I didn't suspect that the girls might also be pretending about their poor command of English.

"Say, Stan, what do you say we all go on a triple date sometime soon?"

"Yeah, maybe we can do that, sometime." But to myself, I said we would do that when hell froze over.

I was wrong; the next week Anna insisted that we join them for a night at the Kurhaus to celebrate Hilda's fifteenth birthday. I argued that I didn't like the Kurhaus and didn't like being around Mike and Stud because of the way they treated the girls. Anna didn't argue back; she said that we were going.

Literally, *Kurhaus* means a spa or bath hotel. In Aibling the Kurhaus was a large recreation center where the bath hotel patients had been entertained. Before the war it had been the place where aspiring local musicians, dancers, and actors could hone their skills. During the war it had been used for tea dances and light entertainment for the air cadets and for wounded soldiers who were being treated at the hotels. Now it was a noisy GI beer hall with a little German oompah band trying to play American songs. The beer was excellent, much better than the stuff they served at the Café Arnold. The army had furnished the Lion Brewery (Löwenbräu) with hops and malt and had bought its entire output. I loved the cold beer, served in big mugs with the Bavarian lion on them. The only problem was that it had a real kick. We were told that it contained 10 percent alcohol; the actual strength was probably more like 6 percent, but it was still pretty potent compared with the 3.2-percent stuff that had been served to GIs back in the States. I had learned to nurse it along, but a lot of the new boys got very drunk before they realized that this was he-man beer.

The six of us sat at a table, drinking beer and singing old songs: "Roll Me Over," "I've Got Sixpence," and such. Anna and I tried to translate the words into German, having a lot of fun but not much success. Hilda and Inge saw some girls they knew and went over to talk. Mike was beginning to get drunk, and I decided we had been there long enough. When Anna and I got up to leave, Mike saw a GI he knew from some trip they had made. He introduced me as an old combat man who had been here "when the Krauts shot back." He didn't bother to introduce Anna but began bragging about Hilda.

"Man, you ought to see the girl I found, she's only fourteen and built like a—wait, I'll call her over here."

He yelled across the room for Hilda to get her ass over here. She bounced over, giggling and happy. As Mike introduced them he was unbuttoning her blouse almost to the waist. He pulled it back and said, "Look at those tits, sticking straight out. Ever seen anything like that on a fourteen-year-old kid?"

That did it. I was already disgusted with Mike, and this was too much. I pulled back to hit him. Fortunately, I couldn't swing because Anna grabbed and hung onto my arm. She said, very firmly, "Leon it's time for us to go home and leave the partying to these young people."

Anna began talking fast as soon as we got out of the hall. It turned out that she had told me several half-truths and some lies. Hilda was nineteen. Inge was twenty and had been engaged to Anna's brother, Kurt, who was reported missing and presumed dead on the Russian front over a year ago. Both of them spoke much better English than did Anna. They *were* daughters of some family friends but were also friends of Anna's. They had left Stuttgart to get away from brutal and wild French occupation troops. So they actually *had* come to Bad Aibling in order to date Americans and do other things that would not be allowed for nice girls in Stuttgart.

Anna explained that the game of being innocent virgins was often played on Luftwaffe cadets during the war. When the girls started dating Mike and Stud, Anna had played the game with them, but only for a while. Because two virgins were enough, they had decided that Anna should become the conscience of proper German society: a frustrated maiden aunt who wanted to protect the poor girls. It had worked at first, and she enjoyed it, but Mike and Stud were a bit too dense—and rough. Continuing in her maiden-aunt role, Anna had agreed to let the girls have more freedom, on the condition that the boys begin acting somewhat civilized. It wasn't really a compromise, only a cover story that allowed Anna to take a less active role in the game. The girls were in no danger and were manipulating the boys as if they were puppets. Mike and Stud still believed that by using large words, they could speak English in front of them without being understood. That gave Inge and Hilda a big advantage; they always knew what was going on and could speak German between themselves when they wanted a private conversation. And if there had been any serious physical threat, they would have called the MPs; the Bad Aibling MPs played rough.

I was embarrassed at my gullibility. How could I have believed that the girls were so young? They had acted like junior-high kids—but they certainly didn't look that way. I was a bit angry that they had lied to me and that I had worked so hard at teaching them English. Anna pointed out that I might have spoiled their game by giving a hint to the GIs. Also, the girls had enjoyed having me think they were naive and could only mangle the English language.

I told Anna about how shocked I had been over the way that fourteen-year-old girl was treated at Solingen-Wald. She giggled and said that it could have been true but was probably the innocent-little-girl game. Because of the no-fraternization rule in effect at that time, the girls were far from helpless; if they yelled "rape," MPs would come. Even our Sneaky Jesus boys would not have tolerated rape, and Captain Warren would have hung offenders out on the line. Anna also pointed out that the girl was not being tempted with food: only with candy and cigarettes. Germans had been heavily rationed at the time, but they certainly were not near starvation.

I had the feeling that Anna was taking some delight in introducing me to Bad Aibling reality. I had been seeing German women from a GI point of view and was upset about the way the poor girls were being abused. Anna showed me that it was a game in which everybody cheated and everybody won.

She told me about another version of the innocent-little-girl game. As with Mike and Stud, I knew the boys who were being manipulated. The two girls were roommates, not related, and didn't look much alike. The game had been developed while they were dating Luftwaffe cadets. The taller, twenty-something-year-old girl became a thirty-five-year-old mother living with her young daughter; the husband/father had been killed in Russia. The young cadets saw a touch of evil in dating both mother and daughter; the girls loved improvising and polishing their act. When one group of cadets graduated, the "daughter" would become a virgin again and the "mother" would be prim and proper. They made a few modifications when the GIs came. The Americans seemed to enjoy melodrama more than the Luftwaffe had, so the "mother" occasionally staged a fine performance in which she was "forced" to watch her "daughter" being "deflowered."

The little show had run for so long that it was a staple of the gossip among the women of Bad Aibling. Counting all of her acts for the Luftwaffe and U.S. Army, the daughter had become a virgin six times. The big puzzle for the gossips was why the boys always rewarded the shocked mother with more cigarettes, candy, blankets, and food than they did the poor daughter.

It was a wonderful tale, but I wasn't comfortable and didn't quite know why. There was something sad about the whole thing. Maybe it was because the mother/daughter or sister/sister had no real protection. There was no husband or father or brother to burst in and straighten things out. What was funny about women being forced to fend for themselves?

Anna was disgusted with me: "Oh, come off that holy attitude, Leon. They are enjoying life. They like getting food and cigarettes, but the real pleasure comes from independence, being able to control their lives. Under National Socialism, women were only supposed to raise children and keep the house clean. It was a dull life. When the men went off to war, we enjoyed doing what had always been men's work. Besides, this won't last. When the men get back, we will have to become Bavarian wives again."

I wasn't really sure what Bavarian wives were supposed to be like but agreed that Inge and Hilda were having a ball and were in complete control.

Anna said, "Well, they will return to Stuttgart soon. Why should they care what people here say or think?"

What *did* people here say and think?

Anna hedged a bit but said that the women in Bad Aibling had never been afraid of GIs. There had been a little apprehension about the possibility of looting and rape, but it soon vanished. Even on the first day, the GIs were friendly and considerate: firm in their demands but not unreasonable. Yes, there had been some looting, but nothing terrible; there had been one rape that they knew of—the man was immediately arrested and sent off for trial.

"I grew up hearing what the French occupation was like after the other war," Anna said. "And we all know what happened in the places the Russians captured." The Russians, she said, knew only two German words: "Fräu komm." You came and did, or you died. The people of Bad

Aibling felt fortunate that their town had been captured by the Americans.

According to Anna, nearly all of the Aibling women between fifteen and forty-five felt at least some attraction to the Americans. Even the older GIs acted like kids; they were always joking and laughing, but with an underlying respect for all women. The Americans also smelled good; they had plenty of soap and used it, and they all drenched themselves with "Old Spice" after-shave lotion. And after several years of seeing only German soldiers who were recovering from wounds, the German women were impressed that none of the Americans was crippled.

The downside of this was that we were still the enemy—and would continue to be as long as German soldiers were being held prisoner. And, of course, even now, every woman wanted to believe that her man would return from Russia and they could begin a normal life. Even that was changing, though, and most of the women were ready to date GIs—after the prisoners were released. Until then, it was one thing for refugees like Hilda and Inge to go with Americans, but permanent residents feared for their reputations.

I wondered where that left someone like Anna's boss. Mrs. Bachmann, the bakery owner, was dating Pete Riley, a captain in quartermaster. Anna was always telling the customers how awful it was that Mrs. Bachmann had to go out with the American captain so the shop could have bread for them. They pretended to believe her despite knowing that he was with the Bad Aibling base and the grain came through Military Government at Rosenheim. Captain Riley was handsome, spoke excellent German, and drove a jeep (the regulation required that he use a driver, but he ignored that). Colonel Bachmann had been gone for three years. Mrs. Bachmann was having a wonderful time with the captain. She was a little worried about his friendly attitude toward her seventeen-year-old daughter, who was enjoying the attention. Mrs. Bachmann would soon have to lay down strict rules for both the daughter and Captain Riley.

Anna didn't really have an answer to my question, even though it applied to her as well as to Mrs. Bachmann: she had told me that Bad Aibling was a nice little town and that she was thinking about staying there permanently, as a partner in the bakery. "Hilda and Inge say I'm crazy.

They think that as soon as there's enough flour for other bakeries to make more bread, everyone will stop buying from Mrs. Bachmann—and me. But maybe they are wrong. As I said, things are changing. It's not just the question of the prisoners, you know. Most of the women here speak very little English. When you can't understand three words a man says, it's hard to pretend you like him for his personality."

I couldn't see what that last remark had to do with Pete Riley and his fluent German, and I was pretty sure that I didn't want to be included in it either. "Anna, I speak German with your neighbors every time I see them."

She laughed. "Leon, your German is atrocious, and you insist on using that Austrian mountain slang. You were only making things worse. Now the women like you. They still look on you as a kid, but I tell them how much I'm learning. My English is improving. I can translate and interpret American poetry. I'm an authority on Bryant. You've got to teach me another poem soon because I've almost worn out 'Jedem, der aus Liebe zur Natur. . . .'"

By now I recognized this as part of the game. Listening to Anna's stories, I had long since realized that I hadn't chosen her as a girlfriend; she had selected me and controlled our relationship as strongly as Inge and Hilda manipulated their GIs. Why had she chosen a shy kid like me? She had different answers at different times: "Maybe it's because you don't remind me of Hans. The war's over, Hans is dead, and it's time to start living again." Or: "Maybe it's because I don't want to go back to the old system where a woman must obey her husband, absolutely. You Americans treat a woman more as a partner. Maybe Germany will change." Or: "That's what all the gossips wanted to know, what I saw in such a kid. But you were the only one I met who could joke with me and who didn't seem to be obsessed with sex. They said, 'Don't be a fool, Anna. All men are obsessed with sex; he's just more subtle.'" (I wasn't sure I liked that last one.)

I knew that Anna's story had some holes in it, but I didn't want to see them. Anna admired handsome officers. She couldn't get one, so she selected a skinny, philosophical young rifleman. Anna was stretching the truth, but so was I. She probably knew that I had colored my combat record and literary knowledge. We had chosen each other for our own reasons and were both lucky.

"Ship me somewheres east of Suez, where the best is like the worst,/ Where there aren't no Ten Commandments, an' a man can raise a thirst." Kipling was a good man. I appreciate Anna. We weren't in love, but "I learned about women from 'er." I learned a lot more than that. She was leading me gently into an adult reality where I would have to decide what was right or wrong. This was my first adventure outside of a strongly structured system. The Ten Commandments did exist east of Suez, but I would have to interpret them. Who else was there? Surely not Major Muller, or even our chaplain, who was shocked at everything the Germans did.

Anna wasn't trying to make rules for me, but she was a big help in explaining how this new game was played. In her adult world, beer-drinking, sex, gossip, and plotting were healthy components of life. Enjoy them all in moderation, but make the rules for yourself. I remembered the theme of a long-ago sermon. The preacher had said: "You will meet temptations in which it seems that you can cheat just a little and no one will know. That is a mistake; one person will know: you." He was right, but the rules had been much clearer back then. I was a long way from Sunday night BYPU in Clinton.

7

FOR THUS SHALL THE LORD DO

On my next visit Anna said, "Wait here, Leon, the girls have a surprise for you." Inge came out wearing a man's hat and carrying a stick that she used as a cane.

> With my high starched collar, and my high-topped shoes,
> and my hair piled high on my head,
> I went to spend a jolly hour on the trolley. . . .
> With his light blue braid and his combat jacket,
> He was quite the handsomest of men.

The "light blue braid" referred to me, with infantry braid on my garrison cap. Stud wore the beige braid of quartermaster on his cap. Inge was singing with a British imitation of an American accent, and doing very well. Then Hilda joined her in "Drinkin' Beer," both of them using a terrible imitation of my Mis'Sippi accent.

I enjoyed it all, glad they could now be honest with me and impressed at how well they spoke English. They rolled into a good rendition of "The Yellow Rose of Texas," which went well until they reached the phrase about "the sweetest rose of color." They stopped and asked what it meant.

I thought for a minute and said, "Well, the German translation of that song would probably be 'The Half-Jew of Bavaria.'"

They were surprised that the song was about a *Neger*. I pointed out that they should avoid that word, which wasn't derogatory in German but sounded too much like "nigger." Then I had to explain why it was acceptable for black soldiers to call each other "nigger," that I thought "colored" was a politer term, but that the official description was "Negro." Inge argued that the German word for "colored" was *farbig,* which could mean black, red, green, or purple. It turned out that she knew quite a lot about American race relations. I suppose she just wanted to see me squirm.

One thing Inge mentioned was that during the last months of the war, newspapers had carried horror stories about the Americans using black soldiers as assault troops—cruel savages climbing into windows with knives in their mouths. I had to laugh as I tried to picture combat troops running into a town with sharp knives in their mouths. Inge was a little peeved: "I didn't say we believed it, but that is what we were being told."

She said that everyone in Bad Aibling had been terrified when American tanks rolled into town—and black soldiers climbed out. But within an hour children were scrambling over the tanks, eating chocolate candy, chewing gum, and sucking on sugar cubes. The children learned very quickly that the Americans didn't mind being called *Schwarz*—in fact, they seemed to like it. After that there were no problems. The tank company stayed for about two days and completely won the hearts of the town. Most of the black troops who had come to Bad Aibling since then were well-behaved, competent, and very friendly. This was the point Inge had been working toward: the American Military Government was promoting democracy in Germany and condemning National Socialism for racial hatred, but it segregated black Americans and, except for a few combat units, gave them the most menial jobs.

I tried to think of an argument, but there was none. These people knew black troops as very nice and caring people who were not being treated fairly: and they were absolutely right. "Inge, I don't have a reasonable answer; maybe things will change."

She just smiled. "I know, but try to remember that when you talk about the Germans and the Nazis."

I was ready to change the subject. "Bad Aibling likes the black troops, but will they ever treat white GIs with some decency?"

Hilda laughed at me, "Only sluts date GIs! That includes me, Inge, and sweet, proper Anna."

The three women switched into German, arguing, yelling, and laughing. When they returned to English, Hilda said that nearly everyone in town admired and appreciated the American soldier, partly because of the alternatives: the Russians, French, or British. They were amazed that such a group of sloppy, friendly, and freewheeling kids could have won a war. No one doubted that it was the powerful American army that had defeated Germany; the surprise was our less-than-military bearing. The cadets at the Luftwaffe base had been much more disciplined and impressive. They never played with the children, gave away candy, or joked with anyone. (I should add that all of the cadets training there were Prussians and apparently had very little respect for anybody but other Prussians.) The American army had made some awful blunders while it was learning to run the town, but that had nothing to do with people's attitude toward the GI.

One mistake that particularly incensed Inge was the Military Government's policy on denazifying the movies. The censors didn't know their ass from first base (a phrase she'd picked up from Mike and Stud). Only a few of the German wartime movies were Nazi propaganda. Before the war there had been some strange productions about the glorious service of the Hitler Youth and a few about how horrible the Jews were, but that sort of thing had gotten old. During wartime the Germans went to movies to forget about the hard realities of life. They enjoyed stories of beautiful women dancing and going to wonderful banquets. There were fantasy adventures of living in a tropical paradise, eating pineapples and watermelons. Inge couldn't see how that sort of thing could be considered Nazi-related. I couldn't either, but I hadn't seen any of those movies.

I have recently read a report that suggests Inge's account was a fairly accurate description of Goebbels' attitude about wartime entertainment. He used crude propaganda in speeches and news stories, but movies were directed at escapism. (Also, Goebbels liked beautiful actresses and had affairs with several of them; he was short and crippled, but women liked his quick wit and, I imagine, his power.) Toward the end, Hitler had him make some heroic "hang-in-there-until-we-win" movies, but Goebbels didn't think it was a good approach.

Much of what Inge and Hilda had to say about local women and the GIs mirrored what Anna had told me: Refugees could get away with dating us, but native Aiblingers, even though many of them might be ready to, simply couldn't afford it—certainly not while we were still holding German prisoners. It was a quiet, conservative, patriotic town. They had sent sons, husbands, and boyfriends off to fight in a war for the survival of their country. Thousands of badly wounded soldiers had been treated in the bath hotels. Most of the cadets who trained at the air base had been killed, either while defending German cities against Allied bombers or trying to stop the Russian hordes. Even people who were disgusted with the Nazi Party were deeply loyal to Germany and to the men who had died in defense of their homeland.

Inge added some advice about the local men. "Leon, maybe your work crew likes you and doesn't oppose the idea of your dating a German woman—if she isn't their sister or wife. Aibling men who have been discharged, who are crippled, discouraged, and can't find a job, don't look at you in quite the same way."

I knew that this feeling existed and had read some of the small posters that mysteriously appeared overnight and were quickly removed in the morning. They varied from sad poems to bitter protests to abusive threats, but the theme didn't vary: For many years the German soldier had fought bravely against invaders of the homeland. They had suffered in the snow and mud, they were wounded, they retreated slowly, but they never surrendered. The brave German women were beginning to surrender for a few cigarettes, some coffee, and chewing gum. This outrage would never be forgotten.

Anna apparently thought that Inge's advice didn't go far enough. She warned me very seriously not to assume that all Germans, women or men, were friendly. She strongly suggested that I avoid dark streets.

"You're saying there are people here who would kill me if they could?"

"Probably not in Aibling. In Munich, sure." Munich had been the center of the Nazi movement and, according to Anna, now harbored a lot of very bitter people.

Anna had grown up hearing about the French occupation; I remembered tales of the Yankee invasion and Reconstruction. Mother's Grandpa Mills had been a prisoner on Ship Island, one of the barrier islands off the Mississippi coast. The prisoners had been worked to absolute exhaustion and nearly starved, but one damnyankee guard had been especially mean.

When the war ended, the discharged prisoners learned that the guard was planning to settle in New Orleans. Three of them drew straws to see who would kill him. The winner told the others to read the obituaries in the New Orleans paper. They did, and a couple of weeks later there it was: the former guard had been found dead on a dark street in the French Quarter.

I knew that my work crew liked me. I had trouble believing that any German, even in Munich, would really want to kill me. But after the discussion finally wore down that night, I had plenty to think about on the two-mile walk back to the barracks.

The topic of attitudes toward Americans came up on another long night from another angle. Hilda and Inge began telling about the air raids on Stuttgart. Anna hadn't talked much about the raids, partly because her son and parents had been killed in one of the early ones, but maybe also because she had left the city before the bombing became really awful. There had been early raids on the Daimler-Benz plant on the edge of Stuttgart, but the heavy raids didn't begin until the summer of 1944. By then everyone realized that the Nazi Party had sucked Germany into a catastrophe. The Americans were roaring through France, and the Russians not only had not been defeated but were destroying whole German armies. Hilda's brother returned from the eastern front paralyzed from the waist down. One arm was nearly useless, and he was blind. He wouldn't talk about the war except to say that Germany could not win; at night he would groan and cry in his sleep.

When the citywide air raids began, British bombers flew at night and the Americans came during the day. The very name "Flying Fortresses" was terrifying. The planes bombed from such altitudes that you could hardly see them. Occasionally antiaircraft fire would hit one, but that was rare. The planes did seem to be fortresses.

Everyone had an air-raid bag with their personal papers, a change of clothes, a little food, and a book to read; you never knew how long an attack, or a series of attacks, would last. Another precaution was to leave a few clothes at a friend's house, in case yours was destroyed. In the shelters people would joke and sing, trying to ignore the noise and shaking of the ground. If a bomb landed very close, there would be a sudden swish of air into the bunker. That was followed by a swish outward, the suction so strong that your hair would stand up. The man in charge of the shelter had telephone communication with a central command; unless the wire was broken, he could keep them informed about the progress of the attack. During severe raids he would risk an occasional glance outside to see what was happening nearby.

The girls said that the greatest shock was to climb out after a raid and see familiar buildings in ruins, while hoping that their own homes were still standing. This was the time when they (everyone, including Inge and Hilda) had felt deep hatred for the "air gangsters" who were destroying homes and cities for no good military purpose other than to punish the German people. The Americans dropped leaflets saying that the bombing would continue until Germany surrendered. How could anyone believe that terrified women and children might persuade Nazi officials to surrender? Inge remembered hearing of an American flier who had been shot down in her neighborhood; he had surrendered to the civilians, who beat him to death with clubs. Inge hadn't wanted to go look at the body, but she had felt no sympathy for him. Air gangsters deserved death.

My mind drifted again to tales of the damnyankee occupation soldiers, who set fire to almost every house in Jackson—after the town had surrendered. My POW group maintained that if not for the massive American aid to Russia, they could have won the war in the East. These girls probably felt the same way, and they had spent a horrible year under massive terror bombardments by American planes or British planes using American bombs; the only purpose had been to break their spirit. My grandmother hated the Yankee occupation troops until the last day of her life. I knew that this was different, that the Nazi rule had been brutal, that we had liberated Europe, including Germany. But I still wondered how people like Anna, Hilda, and Inge could ignore the bitterness that must be stored inside them.

I began to realize that, although there were emotional scars, most of my own bitterness from the war was gone. Maybe a better way of putting it is that I was running out of people to blame. Those SS kids weren't very bright and had been taught some strange racial ideas, but they were ordinary boys. I was finding that I liked the German people more than I had the French or English. But I didn't know the English well, and the French hardly at all. I could still blame the French for being so harsh on Germany after World War I, and the British, and us: for doing nothing to protect Germany. I blamed Hitler and the Nazi Party for massive atrocities, but they were dead or in prison.

I had seen war as a combat soldier. Now I was learning that war hurts everyone. It is a terrible way to settle anything. The war had caused extreme suffering for people of both sides. It had forced us all to commit inhuman acts. But the time for war was over and the time for peace was at hand: the voice of the turtle is heard throughout the land.

The next morning I encountered reality again. It was time for our weekly "occupation indoctrination."

When Patton was relieved of his command for being too easy on Nazis, he was replaced by General Truscott. Eisenhower told Truscott that the denazification orders were to be carried out both in spirit and to the letter. He also said that occupation troops were to be reminded that all Germans were responsible for the barbaric conduct of the war. For us, these reminders came through Major Muller.

Muller had begun with a campaign aimed primarily at the new troops who had seen no combat; he assumed that anyone who had actually fought against Germans would hate them already. (I will concede that Muller's ridiculous lectures were based on Truscott's orders, but it doesn't necessarily follow that he wasn't a jackass.) Muller had a two-part program: everyone must (1) attend the weekly orientation programs and (2) take the tour of Dachau. I went to the programs because there was no way out, but I kept postponing my Dachau visit and never did go.

A training film, which Muller enjoyed and showed us repeatedly, explained the attitude we should hold toward the Germans. All Germans were Nazis in the sense that they had supported the actions of the Party and believed the racist dogma of Aryan superiority. We were to show that the Americans (the American race?) were above such attitudes. We were to be fair but hard, respect the local laws, but never let the Germans forget what awful things they had done. After World War I, the German people believed that their political leaders had betrayed the army by surrendering. Many German soldiers said that they could have won in a few more months. This time we were to be sure that everyone knew Germany had been utterly defeated.

When the film was over, an officer would lead a discussion to see that we had understood the message properly. I kept out of trouble by remaining quiet during the lecture and venting my disgust later to Mike and Stud. I came close to getting them mad after a different movie and lecture, on the Malmédy massacre. During the Battle of the Bulge a German armored patrol had captured about a hundred Americans near the northern Belgian village of Malmédy, taken them into an open field, and opened fire with machine guns; some seventy of the prisoners were killed, and the rest escaped.

"All right, Stan, you surely can't defend the Nazis on that atrocity."

I assumed my old combat tone and prepared to lie. Actually, I agreed that Malmédy had been a horrible, inexcusable crime, but I enjoyed shocking Mike and Stud: "The Infantry School used to have a stock answer: 'It depends on the situation and the terrain.' As I understand it, that SS unit was operating in a confused area where there was no front line. They surprised a group of Americans who should have fought but surrendered instead. They had no place to send prisoners and couldn't afford to leave any guards. Their stupid act was to use machine guns at a place where there might be witnesses. They were so poorly organized that they let a third of the men escape to tell what had happened. In the same situation, American troops would have taken the prisoners along until they came to a deserted house, crowded them into a few rooms, and used some hand grenades. If there had been only a few prisoners, they might have taken them to an isolated place and reported them shot while escaping."

I had never, even in hospital yarns, heard of more than three or four German prisoners being shot. In King Company, Captain Warren would have court-martialed anyone who shot a prisoner. The Malmédy incident was an inexcusable lapse of discipline. The Americans had arrived in vehicles with plenty of fuel, both of which the German army needed badly; the obvious solution was to load prisoners on their vehicles and move them to the rear. I was bluffing. Mike and Stud were still in awe of anyone as tough and battle-hardened as me.

One morning the officer in charge of guard details told me to take my

group by truck to the Bad Aibling railroad station, where we would receive a shipment of prisoners. That was strange because prisoners usually
arrived on a rail line that ran directly into the base. I also wondered why
we needed a prisoner detail to help receive other prisoners; it seemed to
me that a few guards could simply direct the new arrivals onto our trucks.

I soon learned why: this was a shipment of prisoners from the Russian
camps. The poor, starving men had been packed into the boxcars so tightly
that they could only stand. When the doors were opened, the prisoners
looked out with blank stares. One of our orientation sessions had included
a film strip of SS guards receiving starving Jews at an extermination camp.
What I was seeing now seemed like a reenactment. The stench of human
filth was awful; thin, pale, expressionless men crawled out of the boxcars
and stood in lines. Slowly, some of them developed smiles as they realized
that we were Americans. After the group trudged to the waiting trucks,
my prison detail climbed into the boxcars to remove the weak, wounded,
sick, and dead.

I stood there ashamed and nauseated. We, the Arsenal of Democracy,
had supported and supplied the Russian army so that they would be able
to do this. I had seen training films on how terribly the Russians had suffered during the war, but there was no justification for anyone treating
humans with such brutality as those prisoners had endured. Vaguely, in the
back of my memory, I could hear the old revival preachers telling of the
punishment the Lord God dealt to enemies of the Jewish people. I remembered how we joked about the Old Testament war stories. After some
battles all of the men, women, and children had been killed. Sometimes
the women were kept unhurt but the men were blinded or had their tes-
ticles crushed, or perhaps both. We joked because we thought those were
just tales. No one could actually be that cruel.

"For thus shall the Lord do to His enemies." But what I was seeing
was pure, vicious brutality. Surely God does not mean for us to take
vengeance in this way.

8

SHOWTIME!

When I arrived, the Bad Aibling base was part of a good vaudeville circuit. A young woman named Maria had contracted with Special Services to give weekly shows along a string of four or five American bases that included ours. We were used to the dull USO shows with their old, stale jokes. Big-time entertainers such as Bob Hope played in Munich to audiences of thousands. We got the over-the-hill groups who were willing to play to audiences of fifty or seventy-five. Maria was not USO. She and her entire team were German.

Maria had been a cabaret entertainer in Munich, but because there was no civilian market for her profession at the moment, she had put together a troupe and developed the little circuit it traveled. The performers probably received a little pay plus room, board, and transportation. It wasn't a way to get rich, but they could survive until times got better. Why Major Muller allowed them to include our base in the circuit, I don't know; who can understand the mind of such a man? Initially, the girls were eating in the officer's mess but that was canceled because someone pointed out that allowing Germans to eat officer-quality food might be considered coddling them. After that they ate with the enlisted men—not exactly with us, but at a table in our mess hall. We were not allowed to talk with them. Even "Hi, I enjoyed the show" was prohibited.

The program always drew a pretty good crowd—not a packed house, but the material was varied enough to offer a little something for every GI taste. Well, almost every taste: Maria was working under a few restrictions. Some of the program was standard entertainment, but she included efforts at introducing us to Bavarian culture; we thought the yodeling songs and folk dances in traditional costumes were pretty silly. Maria opened every performance with the same phrase: "Hi, gang, I am Maria, and it's showtime!" She would introduce the performers and, usually, begin with a torch song. Maria seemed to model herself after Marlene Dietrich and sang a very soupy "Lili Marlene." The song is a German soldier's lament about missing his girl back home, dreaming of when he and his Lili Marlene will be together again. During the war the German propaganda radio had included it in music beamed at American troops; we loved it and adopted Lili Marlene as our own. Because most of us knew at least some of the words, Maria encouraged us to sing along with her.

One night she translated the song, not literally but for the full meaning. I remember the feeling she put in "Wenn sich die späten Nebel drehn": "When the fog of this horrible war finally drifts away." Then she sang the entire song, not in her usual cabaret fashion but as a slow dirge, an evocation of the horror and loneliness of war. The misery of war is something that all soldiers share regardless of their uniform. Tears came into my eyes; I looked around and almost everyone was crying. Maria was reminding us that we all suffer when countries try to settle their differences through combat.

Maria also loved to sing the Marlene Dietrich song from *Destry Rides Again:* "See what the boys in the back room will have,/and tell them I died of the same." She had a torch song called "Soldier, Soldier, Come with Me," which we didn't know but which was very sexy. I have heard that the original song was Hungarian and entitled "Sailor, Sailor." It had been translated into German during the war and was now being modified for the victors.

Maria's only instrumental accompaniment was a little concertina, but that was enough. She would squeeze on the thing, yell a little, and start us all laughing. One of her favorites was the Spike Jones version of "Der Führer's Face." During the war, the BBC had used it to introduce propaganda broadcasts aimed at the German people. Now that the war was over, Germans seemed to enjoy singing it. Maybe it offered a way to laugh at their problems and blame them on Hitler. Maria would have her girls goose-stepping around the stage while she played. She spoke excellent English, but for this song she used a heavy accent: "'Is dis Nazi land so good? / Vould ve leave it if ve could? / Ja, dis Nazi land is good, / Ve vould leave it if ve could!' Boy, would we! Do any of you New York boys want to take a nice German girl home with you? See me after the show. No, I won't go to Texas. I've seen too many Bavarian cowboys. Come on you guys, I can't hear you singing. Do you want people to think you're Nazis? Let's sound off for Goebbels and Goering and Streicher: 'Not to love der Führer is a great disgrace, / So ve heil, heil, right in der Führer's face!'"

Some of the performances were very much vaudeville: a mix of magicians, dancers, and comedians. "I was dating this GI back during the no-fraternization period. Not exactly dating: I was trying to get some cigarettes from him and he was trying to get something I had. He saw a MP coming and shoved me into a doorway. I said, 'Warum? Warum?' [Why? Why?]. 'Any old room, baby, any old room.'"

One night her leading dancer was doing a slinky torch-style number that the audience loved. As we clapped, she got sexier and the dance became an artistic striptease. It wasn't a vulgar bump-and-grind, but a striptease by any definition. When it was over Maria came out with her usual jokes, but she was a bit sober: "That wasn't in the script, I promised the Major to keep it clean. Please don't let word of this get out." But we did, and the next week GIs were lined up to get in. We had a movie instead of Maria.

We were furious and tried to find who had canceled our show. The clerks at battalion headquarters didn't know. Miracle Muller would have been the best bet except that he always took copious credit for everything he did. The self-righteous chaplain was a possibility, but he didn't have much clout with Muller. Later I got a much better picture of the situation from a contact in Munich; Maria had gotten into trouble over something only vaguely related to the performance.

Because Munich was only about thirty miles away, it became almost a second home base. The army ran buses on a regular schedule. If I had an overnight pass, I could eat at the transient mess and sleep at the Hotel America. It wasn't exactly plush—several large rooms with rows of double bunks—and the food at the transient mess was awful, but the alternative was a late-night ride to Bad Aibling.

Instead of taking the bus to Munich, I preferred hitching rides on GI trucks. These were usually quartermaster-company trucks with black drivers. The truckers liked having someone to talk with, and I enjoyed swapping stories with them. Talking with the drivers from the South was like a visit home. On one of these rides I met a man who became a friend and introduced me to an exciting army subculture.

As I climbed into the truck, he stuck out his hand and said: "Emory, Sam'Le'."

I said: "Standifer, Leon."

I knew he was pure southern. His name was Samuel Lee but Sam'Le' is the proper way to pronounce it in Mississippi.

Sam'Le' was a staff sergeant, tall, loose-boned, but obviously tough. His face was one big smile: "Man, you sound like Mis'Sippi. Where you from?"

"Clinton, a little town out from Jackson."

"I'm from Purvis. You know where that is?"

"My Granpa Moore started the Baptist church there."

"Did? I don't know any Moores there."

"That was a long time ago. He left in about 1905 or '06. As soon as he got one church started, he would start looking for another town that needed one."

Sam'Le' thought for a minute and started grinning. "He the one broke the clock?"

"Nah. God did that. He was the one told God to do it."

We both laughed. The courthouse clock in Purvis was a piece of local legend. The story goes that in 1904, a revival preacher passed through and set about lambasting the town for its sins. He called Purvis the Gomorrah of Mississippi and warned that God would visit his wrath on the place. The next day a tornado destroyed several houses and stopped the clock. Supposedly, the town fathers decided to let the clock remain stopped as a warning to sinners. Whether all of this is fact or not I don't know, but a tornado did stop the clock in 1904, and as of about ten years ago it hadn't been repaired. Granpa Moore didn't go to Purvis until several years after the tornado, so my guess of 1905 or 1906 was wrong, and he probably didn't start the Purvis Baptist Church. But "Granpa started the church there" was a gambit I often used to establish south Mississippi connections.

Purvis is about fifteen miles from Hattiesburg, where I had lived for three years during my early teens. Sam'Le' and I talked a bit about people we both knew and about the Hattiesburg High football team. Colored schools couldn't afford football teams, but the Hattiesburg High Tigers had a strong teenage black following. Sam'Le' asked if I had known the football stars who were my age. I had moved to Clinton after the ninth grade but knew most of the boys he mentioned. I told some stories about them and ignored the fact that they had been mean, tough bullies.

We hit a pause in the conversation. If the subject of race was going to be mentioned, it was up to me to do it. If I didn't, Sam'Le' would assume that I thought the same as a lot of other white Mississippians, and our talk wouldn't go much farther. I said something about Bilbo—I can't remember what, but it wasn't complimentary—and we took it from there. It was a friendly discussion; we both looked at segregation as a fact of life and knew that blacks weren't getting a fair shake. The county was supposed to fund black and white schools equally, but abuse was blatant. Sam'Le' was a very sharp man, but it would have been absolutely impossible for him to get an education equal to mine. He didn't blame me for his problems. They were part of a system that we couldn't change.

Then he said, "See you're wearing a Combat Badge. Where'd you fight?"

"In Brittany first. Then they moved us to Germany after the Bulge."

"Man, that was one cold place in January, wasn't it?"

"Where were you?"

"I hauled ammo up to the divisions for Third Army. Had a Yankee lieutenant hated our guts. We called him Lieutenant Whitey. He never found us a decent place to sleep. Kept saying, 'Men on the front are sleeping in the snow!' Hell, we knew they were in the snow, but that was no reason to have us freeze. Man, I didn't join the army to drive a truck. When I went to Shelby, I told the man I wanted to go to the Buffalo Division. He said they were full up. Army don't have many places where a colored can fight."

He lit a cigarette, then: "Last August I was hauling jerry cans of gas on the Red Ball line. Man, that was some kind of rough! One day my buddy and me were driving in Normandy and a German plane came in to strafe. We didn't even have time to jump out. He hit the truck but not the gas."

I remembered our "Blue-Star Commando" song in England: "Take down that gold star, mother, / Your son's not going to die. / He's a blue-star commando in the service of supply."

" 'Course, it wasn't just the Germans," Sam'Le' went on. "The French would set up a barricade, stop you, and steal your whole truck. Some men in my outfit went out and just disappeared. I don't know whether they were killed or sold the truckload and became Frenchmen. I never tried to find out. You know the French are a whole lot nicer with colored than some Americans are."

"Yeah." There wasn't much else to say.

"Well, it's rough, but I didn't ever think about quitting. My mama has a flag in her window, say 'Serving Proudly.' I don't wanna be a French-man. I'm not saying I never did sell anything. I figure the army owed me a little something. I sold a few cans of gas here and there. Blankets'd bring a good price. I got me some of those warm shoes: shoepacs. They sold good. Kept one pair myself for driving that cold truck. We had to hide them when the lieutenant was around. He kept giving us that crap about the boys at the front needing 'em."

The lieutenant had been right. The boys at the front had needed them; our feet froze in the old combat boots. I decided not to argue with Sam'Le' because he was right also. The Red Ball Express had accomplished miracles in hauling supplies and ammunition. Two-man teams drove con-tinuously for days. They ate and slept in the cab, stopping only to refuel and swap positions. The army really did owe him something.

As we got into Munich, I asked Sam'Le' where he stayed and if I could stop to visit sometime. He smiled: "Yeah, come by this evenin' for supper. We got a cook will make you think you died and gone to heaven."

I had to beg off because I had a date in Bad Aibling that night, but about a week later I was back in Munich and decided to take Sam'Le' up on his offer. The "company street" of his outfit was exactly that: one block of a street in an undamaged middle-class neighborhood on the outskirts of Munich. The "barracks" consisted of about twelve houses. One had been converted into a mess hall, and another seemed to be roughly (very roughly) a "company day room," something of a recreation house. One end of the street was barricaded, the other blocked by a guard shack. "Yeah, what you want?" The black guard's New York accent told me that no matter what I wanted, he wasn't going to help me. I was scared enough to turn around and leave but couldn't; I had to answer his question.

"I'm looking for Sergeant Emory. Sam'Le'."

He looked me straight in the eye, no expression at all: "He ain't here. Why you want to see him?"

"He's a friend. Said that if he wasn't here, I should ask for Big Willie Martin."

He didn't like it but led me over to the company headquarters. "Sergeant Martin, Charlie here wants to see you."

First Sergeant Martin was the black equivalent of a good, tough southern sheriff, medium height and heavy-set, not fat, about 250 pounds of muscle. He sat at his desk, looked me over, and said nothing.

"I'm Leon Standifer. Sam'Le' Emory invited me over and said that I should look you up if he was gone."

That was good enough. He stood up, shook hands, and said: "Yeah, Sam'Le' told me about you. Think he said you were from Hattiesburg. Call me Willie."

Willie was from Meridian, about eighty miles northeast of Hattiesburg, and it took me maybe two minutes to learn that he loved to talk football. I didn't care very much for the game but could hold up my end of a discussion, and luckily one of Willie's football heroes was "Goat" Hale, who had played for Mississippi College in Clinton. Willie's stories must have come from his father because Goat's college football career began in 1915. He was on a baseball scholarship but was allowed to play football because he enjoyed it.

Back then, Ole Miss was scheduling M.C. as a breather, an opportunity to test new players and plays before the "real" games began. Goat Hale beat Ole Miss 74 to 6. Tulane, a football power in those days, fell by 20 to 8. When World War I began, Goat volunteered. He came back from France with shrapnel wounds in his left knee and both feet. For two years he just bummed around. LSU, Ole Miss, and Mississippi A & M offered him scholarships, but he didn't want to play as an invalid. In 1921 Coach Robby persuaded him to return to Mississippi College and give football another shot. In the first game he played, or tried to play, for two minutes. After that he lasted a bit longer in each game, slowly rebuilding his strength and confidence. In his senior year, 1922, Goat scored twenty-four touchdowns and rushed for 2,160 yards, more than 350 of them in the game against Ole Miss.

I enjoyed sharing these bits of yore that I had heard from my own father, who graduated from M.C. in 1911. But at one point Willie was quiet for a moment before saying: "Damn, I wish I could have played."

I just shook my head: "Yeah, I wonder if it will ever happen." Both of us knew that we were talking about more than football.

Willie glanced at his watch. "Man! Time to eat."

At the mess hall First Sergeant Martin and PFC Standifer walked to the head of the line. Willie spoke to the mess sergeant: "This is Charlie Standifer. He's a friend of Sam'Le's." Calling me Charlie was a sincere, if backhanded, compliment. To most blacks of that time, "Mista Charlie" was a generic term for the cruel white boss. When the guard had called me Charlie, he intended it as an insult and I took it as such. Willie, using the same term, was introducing me as okay—white, but acceptable.

The food was great: big thick pork chops, creamy mashed potatoes (there was an art to cooking dehydrated potatoes properly), and greasy slabs of cornbread. A rich peach cobbler for dessert. The cook was excellent, but he also had good kitchen equipment (Willie said that it was taken from a bombed-out hotel, but he smiled just a little) and top-quality ingredients. Willie's company drove the trucks that carried rations and PX supplies in the Munich area. The more important officers liked good food and had the clout to get it, but that required cooperation from the quartermaster clerks and drivers, which in turn required that they be allowed to share in the better things of life.

Sam'Le' came in just after we got started, and I met the other men at the table. Fats McLean was from Georgia. He was nearly as large as Big Willie but almost solid fat. Fats was a master at telling jokes. He knew that the beauty of a story lay not in its final point, but in the art of spinning the yarn. Sometimes it was obvious from the beginning where the story was going and what the punch line would be, but he would drag it out in shaggy-dog fashion, piling on extraneous details and building suspense until—zap!—he hit the punch line. He also used the old trick of stopping in the middle to laugh about the joke: "Oh, God, I'm sorry, I got to start over." He would start again and get a little farther before cracking up; his timing was beautiful.

Fats said that his mother had named him John Henry McLean but had changed the name in 1933, "when Mr. Roosevelt freed the slaves." His new name was Franklin D. Roosevelt McLean. He liked playing the dumb country boy, which he wasn't. He had grown up in a city or fair-sized town and had a good education. He read voraciously and could recite poetry for hours, but his forte was "pore folks" tales. He and I hit it off immediately, and before I knew it we were swapping memories of southern summer childhood games. On hot dry afternoons the neighborhood kids would play "stickerweed." Stickerweeds grow in yards that are never fertilized or watered, and not mowed very often. The challenge was to see how far we could run, barefoot, through a patch of stickerweeds; it wasn't actually a contest because once you started into the patch, you had to keep running until you got out. The real competition game was "sidewalk": how long you could stand still on the hot sidewalk while someone counted, very slowly.

Fats started giggling and said: "I s'pose you white folks had lots of fine swings and slide boards for recess at school?" It was a test, a batting-practice pitch just to see what I would do with it.

"Fats, you're talking about those high-tone rich folks' schools. We had a nice shady spot where we could pitch washers."

He smiled. "What kind of holes you use for washers?"

"Well, you dig one just a little bigger than a Vie'enny sausage can, slip that can in, and pack dirt around it."

"I swear fo' God, Charlie, you sho' do know how to country. A Vie'enny sausage can is the best kind for a washers hole!" I knew he was ham-boning; so was I. But the next pitch had some curve on it: "Say, Charlie, how good are you with a nigger-shooter?"

I took a long drink of coffee, studied his grin, and decided to keep playing: "Well, Mista Fats, I'll tell you the truth." The table was absolutely quiet. "My mama never 'lowed me to use that word—actual, she did 'low it but only when I felt like having my mouth washed out with soap. I tell you what, next week I'm going to whittle me out a slingshot, and you and me will have a contest."

Fats giggled and shook. I had knocked the ball over the fence, just as he had 'spected. Then Sergeant Cornel Young spoke up: "Say, Charlie." That name again, but this time full of venom. Cornel was a sharp-looking dude, another of the company's New Yorkers. I had been watching him fume as Fats and I joked. He resented a white devil being allowed to eat with them, and he particularly resented my being able to make fun of the teasing lines Fats fed me. Most of all, I think, he resented having to be a truck driver with this bunch of what he considered to be corn-fed, big-foot niggers. "Say, Charlie, when was the last time you saw a lynching?"

I sipped my coffee and started planning what I would say. The possibility of telling the truth got no consideration. Long ago, in Hattiesburg when I was about six years old, I had been walking along Mobile Street—the black business section—beside my father when a car drove by with the horn blowing continuously. Four white men were yelling obscenities from the windows. A rope tied to the back bumper was dragging the flaming body of what had once been a man. Daddy took me into a drugstore and held me in his arms until I stopped crying. The scars of that incident were still a part of me, but I blamed the system and would not accept the bigotry of blaming all people with white skin. No, Cornel would not hear that story from Ole Charlie. I was going to use a joke.

But Fats popped in first: "Cornel, you welcome to play in this game, but what you need to know is that you are way outta yo' league. Charlie here is like Br'er Rabbit. He was born and bred in that briar patch." Everyone relaxed. Fats had covered for me so well that anything I said would be safe. I didn't say anything, though, because I looked over at Big Willie. His face had absolutely no expression, but it spoke loud and clear: Keep your goddamn mouth shut. He turned the same stare on Cornel, who looked down at his plate and started eating. I was disappointed and wanted to appeal the ruling but knew that The Man had spoken.

After that, Fats and I carried on in a quieter, more serious vein. The first thing he told me was obvious: Big Willie ran the company with an iron hand and could beat the hell out of anyone who doubted it. The only officer in the company, Lieutenant Whitey—I never heard him called anything else and don't know if he was the same man Sam'Le' had complained about—came by every Friday to sign papers and pass on any orders that had come down to him. In an emergency, such as a surprise visit from some brass, Willie could have someone locate Whitey at the Officers Club. The company stood reveille and roll call every morning. Willie had his own method of punishment for anyone missing roll call. I asked Fats what it was. "Lord, I don't know and ain't goin' to find out." Every Saturday afternoon the company spent two hours at close order drill. I don't know of any other outfit in the Munich area that drilled on a regular basis. Apparently they were very good and had been featured in some Munich parades.

The company ran a little club that Fats called the "Naughty Nigger" (I called it the "Naughty Who'd-a-thought-it"). The actual name was the Schwarze Kater, the Black Tomcat. After supper we went there for a beer. When we sat down, the waitress-bartender came up to Willie. He turned to me: "This is Lili Marlene. Lili, this is Charlie."

I deadpanned: "I've heard your song."

She laughed. "I've heard a lot about Charlie—nothin' you want to hear, though." Lili, blonde and slender, spoke with the soft accent of a central Mississippi black woman. Her whole attitude was one of friendly confidence; she was Big Willie's woman and nobody was going to mess with her. Over the course of a few visits, we became fairly good friends, but she never let me see any aspect of her personal life. I don't know her real name. She was a Munich native and apparently had worked in supper clubs as a singer, general hostess, and possibly booking agent. "Supper clubs" is not quite accurate. Lili would probably have said cafés or cabarets. I am referring to a club where the upper middle class would go for light snacks, drinks, and diverse but talented entertainment. I am using "supper club" to distinguish such a place as something more sophisticated than the "Kit Kat Club" in the musical *Cabaret,* but the distinction may not be valid. It is only my impression of Lili's background.

Lili ran the Black Tomcat for Willie, using his strict discipline. Anyone who began to get drunk or argumentative was sent home. No threat was needed: when Lili said it was time to go, they left. About half of the men brought German girlfriends with them. Some of the girls were polite, and some were pretty raunchy. (To be honest, a lot of the men in the company were pretty raunchy too.) Once in a while a girlfriend would decide that she could tell the arrogant hostess to shut up. Any girl who tried to sass Lili got a slap in the face, after which the frightened boyfriend apologized to Lili and made a quick exit. I have a strong suspicion that Lili made a bundle of money while running the club, but she did an excellent job. There was never any violence at the Schwarze Kater.

Lili brought me a full liter stein of beer. I decided to nurse it very slowly. This was not the place for me to get drunk. Sam'Le' said: "Say, Charlie, how's the crop of women in Bad Aibling?" I blushed a bit and wondered if he was baiting me by trying to bring up the topic of interracial dating. I decided to hedge.

"We got a bumper crop, but the quality's not all that good. The young ones ain't got any sense, and the older ones got too much. I found me one that's pretty good, but she's a little old and a little heavy on the Nazi side."

Fats smiled. "Yeah, the pickings are pretty slim here, too. There's a few that look good and are ready to play mama and papa—a little too ready— but they still got a lot of Hitler showing."

We were waltzing around the real subject. I was ashamed of not being able to say that the rules back home didn't count, that Fats and Sam'Le' were good enough for any girl they wanted to date. I couldn't say that because I wasn't sure how I felt. Fats had covered for me by hinting that he wasn't dating because the girls he might want were still racists. The truth was probably more complicated. I think most of the Germans were re-thinking their ideas on race, but not to the point of dating black soldiers— although some had certainly reached that point: there were six or eight girls in the room while we were talking.

After Fats had some beer in him, he stood up and started us in singing "Vive l'Amour": "Let every good fella come fill up his glass / And drink to our rotten and miserable past." I wasn't surprised that Fats knew a

college drinking song; he obviously had a college education. Almost everyone joined in. I couldn't carry a tune in a bucket but had a great time pretending that I could.

Then Fats said, "Lili, get your squeeze box, me and Charlie and Sam'Le'
want to sing a song." He hustled us all into the back room "to practice,"
closed the door, and said, "Cornel and them Yankee dudes are getting their
ass outta joint about Charlie being here." He hummed a bit of "The Old
Gray Mare" so Lili could get the tune right. Fats wanted us to do a little
song and dance act; he showed what he wanted, but I couldn't get my feet
to work that fast. We practiced some, not nearly enough, and went into
the front room. The three of us lined up and sang: "Now, Old Jim Crow,
he ain't what he used to be. . . ." Fats stepped out front, wiggled a bit and
did a few quick steps: "Old Jim Crow was sitting in a ca'box, acting like a
crazy fox, looking for a place to go." Sam'Le' took over, did some dance
steps, and sang another senseless verse. Fats said, "Mista Charlie!" I stepped
out, raised my hands, tried a jitterbug step, made a mess of it, and sang:
"Old Jim Crow went floating down the Delaware, pulling off his underwear to see what was under there." It didn't fit the theme but was the only
parody I could remember.

We were a smash hit. It was a perfect joke; Fats and Sam'Le' were fantastic dancers, and Ole Charlie was an excellent counterpoint: a clumsy,
clodhopping peckerwood. Jim Crow was alive and well, both back home
and in Germany, but not in the Schwarze Kater.

Pretty soon I realized that Ole Charlie was getting tipsy and had to
catch the bus—I had guard duty the next day. Big Willie invited me back
for the next Saturday, when I could spend the night with the company:
"We got a little party planned for the back-room bunch." He had a big
smile on his face, which may have meant that I would enjoy the party or
may have meant something else.

I wasn't exactly afraid of spending the weekend with the company; I
guess you could say I was apprehensive. Willie, Fats, and Sam'Le' were
friends. Some of the other southerners were pretty crude, but they were
home folks and I could get along with them. Men like Cornel hated my
guts. If I made a fool of myself—well, I didn't know what would happen,
but I was determined to be very careful.

I got off duty Saturday at noon and caught the bus to Munich. Willie requisitioned a rifle, belt, and helmet liner for me: I had to drill with the company. I wasn't all thumbs in the standard commands that took up the first hour, but the second hour was fancy drill; they let me sit that one out. I had seen squads of black troops drill back in England, so I expected Willie's men to be good—but they were fantastic. They created a whole new meaning for close order drill. They swung rifles like batons, they half-stepped, they side-stepped, they put their rifles on the ground and jitter-bugged, and they sang—boy did they sing! I loved it. If they had marched in Prague, the Russians would have been humiliated.

I was thoroughly impressed. Big Willie's company was the sharpest, most tightly disciplined, and loosest outfit I had ever seen. Captain Sim-mers' King Company back in training wasn't even close to them in pre-cision or unit pride. Willie knew how to get the very best out of his men.

At supper we ate, laughed, and teased; all of the jokes were directed at me. "Hey, Charlie, you should have stayed with us. Maybe you could have taught us a few high-class white-folks steps!"

" 'Course, that was just practice. We do a good job when we have a band!"

"We goin' to have a real party tonight. Sam'Le' and old Fats here are going to show you some toe-tappin' fun."

I hoped that was all they were planning, but something in the tone of their jokes said . . . I didn't know what it said. I wanted to back out and go home but knew it was too late for that. We went over to the Black Tomcat at about seven and had a couple of beers in the main room. They put some Phil Harris records on the "GI jukebox," and we sang along: "Oh Lord, if you can't help me, please don't help that bear!" Phil Harris was the only white man loose enough to put real fun in black songs. I think he may have been one of the first rap artists. He followed the writ-ten lyrics, roughly, but improvised with words much as Louis Armstrong did with music. (Okay, it wasn't rap, but it had a little of that kind of sound.)

After a while twelve sergeants and one PFC adjourned to the back room, where the real party would begin. The club had once been a neigh-borhood beer hall, and the "back room" was simply a storage area. It had been converted into what was very roughly an NCO club; lesser breeds, without the stripes, were sometimes admitted, space permitting. There was a small stage and four tables; the total seating capacity was sixteen, leaving room for a small dancing area. About every two weeks, Lili would bring in a few performers, somewhat like Maria had done—they both drew from the Munich supper-club talent pool. Lili's presentations differed from Maria's in that Lili had absolute freedom with respect to censorship. Maybe I should say that she seemed to have freedom. The only racial jokes were about Lieutenant Whitey and the company's reputation for precision drill. There were no Nazi jokes and no MP jokes; black soldiers had grown up under unreasonable discrimination and saw nothing funny about it.

Big Willie didn't come, but Sam'Le', Fats, and I took a table together. Lili bounced up onstage, told a few jokes, sang a song, and called three girls out for introductions. "Girls, this is the gang, the famous Black Tomcats. Put on a good show or you'll answer to Big Willie. We have one visitor Willie swears is a mean black tomcat, but his mother used to wash him in bleach. Let's have a big hand for Tomcat PFC Charlie. Stand up, Charlie!" This was entirely for show—everybody in the room already knew me—but I stood, held my hands over my head like a boxer, and got a mixed reception: some clapped, a few smiled, and some showed no expression at all.

The program was about what I thought a freewheeling Munich supper club would have done. The girls seemed to be more relaxed and were better performers than those Maria had used. They told a few risqué jokes of about the level we had sniggered over in high school, like one about two elephants watching a man bathe: "One elephant turned to the other and said, 'How do you suppose he eats with that thing?'" There was a rinky-dink piano that one of the girls played while all three of them sang various American songs. They did a good rendition of "As Time Goes By," from the movie *Casablanca*. It was one of the American movies being shown for GI audiences but not to Germans because the story was based on Gestapo operations; anything related to the war was usually banned.

I was beginning to relax and enjoy the program, fairly sure now that Lili wasn't planning to embarrass me. I was wrong. One of the girls went over to the little record player and started Glenn Miller's "In the Mood." Lili said, "Okay, girls, showtime!" When Maria had said "showtime," it was simply an introduction. Lili meant it in a more literal sense. I had thought striptease music was supposed to be slow and sensuous, or brassy and raunchy; surely they couldn't use "In the Mood." But they could— and did.

The first girl to dance was tall and slender. She kept up with the fast rhythm and began removing bits of clothing; when the song ended she was down to panties that were not much more than a G-string. She smiled and bowed as everyone clapped. Lili motioned toward our table and said, "Sam'Le', the dancin' man!" "In the Mood" started again. Sam'Le' grinned, went up on the stage, and started jitterbugging with the girl. He was an excellent dancer, and she followed him beautifully, bouncing, whirling, laughing. I was amazed that a German girl could jitterbug and shocked at seeing a naked girl act like that. I blushed for a while but then realized how funny it was, and that the whole room was cheering them on.

The music stopped, the girl went out to dress, and Sam'Le' came back to the table exhausted and laughing: "Hey, Charlie, they don't do that sort of thing back in Purvis."

No, they didn't.

Lili was back onstage: "Showtime!" The next girl was stocky, very buxom, and all smiles. The music was "String of Pearls." Lili called out, "Charlie, this dance is for you!" I grinned mindlessly until it hit me what she might mean. I blushed, turned pale, and began to get nauseated. I remember thinking that if I were to throw up, everyone would laugh but maybe Lili would take pity on me. I couldn't dance very well, couldn't jitterbug at all, couldn't possibly dance with a naked girl, and couldn't possibly back out. The audience was cheering and laughing. I stared down at the table, wondering how many of them were watching Ole Goodtime Charlie. The music stopped. My heart stopped.

Lili walked over to our table: "Now, Mr. Five by Five—Fats McLean. Showtime!" Fats waddled up onto the stage and started a hilarious dance, so funny that the girl simply stopped and watched. His big belly rolled, he shook, laughed, and squealed. I was amazed at how agile such a fat man could be. Once the girl joined in, she made a good partner for him: hefty and full of jiggles but fast with her feet, laughing and squealing with Fats. I especially enjoyed the dance because Lili hadn't made me go up there; she had only been teasing me. Then I realized that there was still one more girl, the one at the record player.

As Fats stepped down amid shouts and applause, Lili motioned to the music girl: "Ilsa, get your little ass over here!"

She scurried up to the stage and said, "Ohh, I can't do that sort of thing."

"It's showtime. What are you going to show?"

"You told me to get my little ass over here. They don't want to see it— do they? It's awfully little."

Lili looked her over. You're right, it's little and it's awful." A vaudeville routine ensued, with Ilsa saying she didn't know how and was shy and Lili trying to comfort her by saying it was easy. Then Lili showed her how to start. Gradually, Ilsa worked the Tom Sawyer gimmick: Lili was down to her bra and underpants, and Ilsa hadn't taken off anything. "Miss Lili, I don't think I can do that." Everyone laughed, and the girls came out to sing a song while Lili dressed. Showtime was over, praise the Lord!

Lili came to our table: "Well, Charlie?"

"Miss Lili, I don't think I could do that. And that's the gospel truth."

The three performers had gone to the front bar and brought back steins of beer for everyone. Now they were circulating among the four tables in the little room, talking and joking. Lili sat with us for a while, keeping an eye on things. Some of the boys were demonstrating new dance steps. There was a little horseplay, but the girls could handle it. One boy went a bit too far. Lili just shook her head and he stopped.

I was curious about Lili's troupe and about the act I had just seen, but Lili didn't really say much, just suggested that I come back sometime when it wasn't so crowded (which I interpreted to mean when we could be alone). It was Fats who filled me in on most of the details. The girls were friends of Lili's from the supper-club days and had asked her for help in learning to jitterbug (the German term was "swing dance"). She recruited Sam'Le' and Fats to develop some sort of demonstration. Although swing music had been pretty much forbidden during the past several years, it had been very popular in the early Hitler times and would come back strong when the economy improved. The girls were good professional dancers and knew that when German supper clubs revived, there would be a demand for performers and instructors. While watching GI dancers, they noticed two things: first, the German girlfriends couldn't quite catch the loose spirit of the steps, and second, the very best GI dancers were black. "Lili tol' 'em that me and Sam'Le' were the best dancin' cats in the whole army," said Fats. "And, you know, she was right!"

They practiced with the girls twice a week and had a lot of fun. The only problem for Lili's friends was that although jitterbugging had some fundamentals and a distinct rhythm, most of the steps were improvised to fit the moods of the dancers. As supper-club entertainers, they understood the art of improvisation in comedy acts but had no experience with unstructured dance routines. They were pros, though, and caught on fairly quickly, enjoying themselves in the process—they loved the dancing. Before long, Lili could tell Willie that she was ready to stage a Saturday-night program. Originally, it was going to be a few songs, some jokes, and a jitterbug session featuring Sam'Le' and Fats and the two girls, who were still learning. Afterward, the girls could dance with the audience and pick up some more steps. (Lili was also very much in favor of her GIs getting to know some decent German girls.)

Lili's plan changed after my visit to the club. The next day Willie told her that he wanted the show to have some spice—enough to embarrass me a little. Lili met with Fats, Sam'Le', and the girls to discuss what might work. Fats thought it would be funny to have me teach the girls some "white folks" steps, but Sam'Le' pointed out that, as a dancer, I wasn't even good enough to warrant teasing. It was the girls who suggested a strip show. They had never done one but knew that GIs liked it and thought it might be fun to try. Lili opposed the idea; she didn't want the program turning into a stag show.

Even outnumbered four to one, Lili was the boss, and she said no. Then Sam'Le' suggested that they ask Big Willie. The mere suggestion was enough to change Lili's outlook: Willie had said he wanted spice. Her only restrictions were that the strip show be a surprise and a one-time event; she didn't want any gossip. The rest of the boys had known only that a jitterbug session was planned.

I asked Lili about the routine with the third girl. She brushed it off as an afterthought, something to end on a comic note. The girl was a singer, piano player, and comedienne but not a dancer. Lili didn't want to have three strip acts—she hadn't even wanted two. The program would have been stronger if both girls had stripped together and danced with the boys at the same time. She had used the two-part idea purely to frighten me. But what about her own little striptease? Had Big Willie known about that?

"Charlie, nothing happens around here without Willie's approval."

That night was the only real excitement I saw at the Black Tomcat. I went back three or four times, was always welcome and always teased about something. Big Willie kept wanting me to invite them to eat at Bad Aibling. "Willie, we're starving to death over there. You see how skinny I am? I used to weigh two hundred pounds!" It made a good joke, but we both knew the truth: First Sergeant Martin wouldn't be allowed to eat in our mess hall. Willie, Sam'Le', and Fats didn't hold that against me, but they were probably the only real friends I had in the company. I think the others resented my stopping by; I had nothing but a few stale jokes to offer in exchange for the friendship.

Maybe I should change that a bit. Fats and I had a lot to talk about together—for example, church back home. I was a Southern Baptist, and Fats belonged to the segregated version (some of the black Baptist churches were independent, others were with the American Baptist Church). Theologically, and socially, the two versions were almost identical. The black ministers were trained at summer courses taught by white ministers, and even the sermons were very similar, except that black preachers tended to deliver them with a bit more flair. Socially, middle-class communities, whether black or white, were dominated by the church and its attitudes.

Fats said: "Charlie, when you get back to Mis'Sippi, what you going to tell folks about the way you lived over here?"

I thought it over. "Well, I'm going to do what any good Christian would: lie!"

He said: "Man, when I get back, I'm going to wait until the first big revival meeting. When the preacher calls folks down to rededicate their lives to Jesus, I'm going right down, step up on the podium, and confess that I have sinned and fallen short of the glory of God. I'm going to tell, in lurid detail, the terrible sins that I committed while serving my country in Germany. I'm going to fall down on my knees and beg the church family for forgiveness!" Fats sat there, smiling. "And you know what, Charlie? Every woman from sixteen to thirty-six is going to try to get dates with me, just to see if I really have repented."

Fats was a good friend who understood me well. He knew that my grandfather had been an old-time Baptist preacher. He didn't know that one of my great-grandfathers had been a slave dealer: the kind that bought slaves right off the boat from Africa, taught them about the ways of their new life, and sold them to planters. Fats's ancestors might have been trained at my great-grandfather's new-slave bargain center. I think, hope, that Fats would have looked on the possibility as funny, but he never found out because I wasn't willing to put our friendship to such a test. I was scared.

I thought of Lili as a friend, too, and maybe she considered me one, but she was cautious about serious discussions. I took her up on the suggestion of coming back when the club wasn't so busy, and we had some interesting talks about the operations of the entertainment circuit, but even then she said very little about herself. (I did notice that, when it was just the two of us, Lili dropped the black dialect and spoke the standard American that was used on Armed Forces radio. Or maybe the reverse is more accurate: she dropped her standard black dialect and used the radio dialect.)

It was Lili who gave me the real story on the Maria mess. In contrast to what I had thought, Maria had despised working for Special Services. The job didn't pay well and allowed her very little freedom for innovation. She had to prepare a complete script for each performance and couldn't deviate from it. Maria argued that she didn't know what GIs liked and would need to improvise; the Special Services man said he knew what they liked, but they were going to get what the army wanted them to like.

Officers had been a nuisance at every base. Some propositioned the girls, others tried to work up black-market contacts. Maria began losing control over her troupe. Performances were getting sloppy. Finally she just gave up. She decided that if the Americans wanted her to supervise a black market, that's what she would do. Then she learned that the CID (the army's Criminal Investigation Division) was collecting evidence on her. The officers who had pressured her into the black market would be safe, but she could go to jail. Maria quit and dropped out of sight. The strip act may have been an outburst of defiance, but the real problem was disgust with Special Services.

According to Lili, professional entertainers hated working for the army. But they also liked to eat, and there was no civilian entertainment market. That was why the little semiunderground theater circuit had developed. Each performer was paid a standard fee, plus cigarettes, coffee, meat, sugar, or flour as a bonus. Initially, the only clubs were those supported by officers who could siphon off extra rations. But such transactions could not be hidden from the men who filed the forms and delivered the cartons, and soon there were a few enlisted men's clubs, such as the Black Tomcat.

That brought up a subject I had wondered about ever since my first ride with Sam'Le', when he mentioned the truckers' extracurricular commerce in gasoline and blankets. I'm not sure how I brought it up to Lili; maybe I commented that the men in the outfit always seemed to have a little spending money on hand. She had probably already decided that even the CID wouldn't recruit someone as naive as me, but she gave me a long, hard look before conceding (very vaguely) that she occasionally "brokered" some cigarettes and a bit of coffee and sugar for the boys—"nothing big, no one's getting rich, Charlie." A Jewish businessman came by regularly to pick up the supplies and pay a good wholesale price. Former concentration-camp inmates were the backbone of the black market— not because they were Jews but because, politically, the Military Government found it hard to prosecute men who had survived such horrors.

There was one other facet of company life that I wanted to learn more about. "Lili, what's the deal with the day room?" I was talking about the last house on the block. I had already heard plenty of rumors, but I wanted Lili's version.

She gave me another long look, and then a roundabout story. "You're in the army, Charlie, you know how it is. Half the men in any outfit, German or American, like to get drunk, fight a little, and finish up with some

'tang. Some don't, but Willie has to deal with those who do. He wants
them to stay near the company area as much as possible because the Munich MPs are brutal with colored soldiers who get drunk, especially when
one is with a white woman, even a prostitute. It's a goddamn shame."

So Willie had come up with, or gone along with, the idea of the "day
room"? Lili explained that it was "the other company club." It even had
a name: Das Katzen Haus. It was basically Lili's operation, just as the Black
Tomcat was. "We have a bartender, who is also the bouncer. He stops
fights but serves drinks to anyone who is able to stand, or at least crawl to
the table. The house has six bedrooms and a few maids who try to keep
them reasonably clean. Do you understand?"

I did.

"Charlie, I don't and won't run a whorehouse!" Lili said. But the truth
was a little more complicated. As with the black market, Lili had a contact: a woman who brought in girls, usually from small nearby towns. Lili
hired them for a few weeks, sent them home with a nice nest egg, and
hired some more. She ran a whorehouse but wouldn't admit it.

Although she was defensive about her "brokering" business and Das
Katzen Haus, Lili was proud of the Black Tomcat. It belonged to her and
she ran it exactly as she pleased. True, Big Willie was the boss, and she always cleared her ideas with him—but he almost always agreed. His only
stipulations were that she run a tight club and provide top-rate entertainment. "Top-rate" is a subjective term, and Lili had to experiment in
balancing the talent she could get with what her boys would like. But the
club was earning a good reputation on the circuit because the audience
was small, lively, and well-behaved. It was also very close-mouthed. Willie
didn't want publicity because that could start investigations. It wasn't that
he was afraid of army officials—he had some very good files on where
certain PX supplies, rations, and choice steaks had gone. But his philosophy was that clout is much more effective if you never have to use it.

I was impressed, to the point of awe, at what Lili was doing. I am pretty
sure that she was making a pile of money, but her club was orderly and
never very crowded. I am also fairly sure that she controlled Big Willie
much more than he or she wanted me to realize. And although there was
certainly sex involved, to a very large extent Willie had selected Lili be-

cause she could show his boys a better aspect of Munich life than they would ordinarily get. He trusted her judgment, and she protected his image of being strong and tough.

I don't know if Lili actually had such good contacts with the Munich supper-club circuit as she claimed, but she had me convinced. Her performers seemed to be good, and they were well paid (on the night that I went, each one got a thick package of steaks and some coffee besides the standard salary in marks). I believe the entertainers enjoyed working that club and that they were fairly tolerant about race. Obviously, this is what Lili wanted me to believe. In my mind it is the truth.

Certainly it was true of the girls who did the strip/jitterbug act with Sam'Le' and Fats. At first I hadn't known quite how to categorize them. Fats had said that the strip show was their idea. But Lili made it clear that they were legitimate entertainers. They had made good money in the supper clubs and hoped to do so again. They didn't do stag shows—that would have gotten them banned from the legitimate side of the business. But at the Black Tomcat, they had felt free to push the boundaries a little; no outsider was likely to hear about it. And like most performers, they lived for the attention and applause of an audience. The strip act had been a fun and slightly naughty adventure that guaranteed audience enthusiasm.

But that wasn't the whole story. The two young women were like many others I was hearing about in postwar Germany. Neither had been able to date a man she liked for more than a year. One had been engaged to a young man who disappeared at Stalingrad. The other had a boyfriend at Bad Aibling, but he was a Waffen SS officer and wouldn't be released for a long time. Sam'Le' and Fats were fun, but neither girl wanted to be thought of as dating the enemy. Then one of them had an idea: they couldn't date Americans in Munich, but what if the "date" took them to some other town? They could dress like tramps, act like tramps, and have a good time. They told Lili their idea and asked her to mention it to Fats and Sam'Le.

"I didn't want to encourage that sort of thing," Lili said to me. "Still, I can't be responsible for actions I don't know about." She smiled because she did know, and now I knew. Last week Fats and Sam'Le' had gone on a three-day pass to . . . somewhere. They said they had rented a cabin in the mountains near a little town and just rested.

Lili said one more thing about the strip act. Fats had claimed that she was the main opposition. That wasn't quite the truth. She wasn't enthusiastic about the idea, but the real worrier had been Fats himself. He had been very concerned that the show would come as a double whammy to a white boy from the Mississippi sticks. He didn't want to strain our friendship over what amounted to a joke.

I appreciated her telling me. Since that night I had run through a jumble of ideas on what I thought of the whole thing. I had seen plenty of German whores with black soldiers in Munich, and it hadn't bothered me at all. The thought of dancing with a naked girl in front of an audience had terrified me, but that had nothing to do with race. Seeing my friends dancing with naked girls had bothered me a little, but I couldn't decide whether it mattered that they were black. Back home I would have been shaken, maybe because of the violent reactions it would have caused, maybe because I was still more of a bigot than I wanted to be.

After talking with Lili, I simply put the question out of my mind. She had left me with a more comforting memory: Sam'Le' and Fats had shared food, friends, and entertainment with me although I could offer nothing in return. In their final decision about the program they were most concerned over whether I might be insulted or hurt. We remained friends during my stay in Germany, but I didn't try to contact them after I got home. I suppose I could offer reasons why not: I knew that Big Willie had decided to be regular army and stay in Germany, and probably stay with Lili. I knew Sam'Le' was planning to move "up north" and get an education on the GI Bill. I never did know where Fats lived in Georgia.

But those are just excuses. As Lili said, "It's a goddamn shame."

9

NEVER SHEATHE IT WITHOUT HONOR

The last chapter may sound as if my Munich activities centered around visits with Sam'Le' and Fats at the quartermaster company. They didn't. My primary Munich enterprise had an entirely different focus. I visited the quartermaster boys when I was in Munich on other business. Because I was stationed at the POW Discharge Center for only four months, most of my accounts of Munich and Bad Aibling represent experiences that were parallel and overlapping. I began exploring Munich within a few days after I was assigned to Bad Aibling.

As a small-town boy, I was usually intimidated by cities, but Munich was so bomb-devastated that it was hard to think of it as a city. It was . . . the adjective *peaceful* comes to mind, but *quietly interesting* may be more accurate. I had gone through heavily bombed cities on trucks and seen a lot of the destruction on the train trip down to Czechoslovakia, but in Munich I had a man-on-the-street perspective; I could walk through the rubble and poke through the remains of shops. There had been a cabaret, or possibly one of the supper clubs that Lili had worked, built beside the old city wall at the Isartor (the gate leading to the River Isar). The building was a pile of bricks, but the fortresslike city wall had withstood the bombing. There was something incongruous about seeing a medieval wall painted with the marine-life decor of a cabaret.

We had bombed Munich ninety-two times, using a total of more than 9,000 planes and 25,000 tons of bombs. More than 6,000 Germans died in the raids. So did a lot of Allied airmen. I remember the emotional conflict: fascination with the dead city, horror at imagining what the massive bombing raids must have been like. During the war there had been a popular song, "Coming In on a Wing and a Prayer." It told of a bomber that had blasted its target—"What a show, what a fight"—but had been badly shot up in the process. Now the crew, with "our trust in the Lord," was struggling to return to their airfield, "coming in on a wing and a prayer."

The images of simple Christian faith, a glorious show, and an honorable fight had inspired me, back then. Now I was walking the streets from which helpless civilians had watched the glorious show. They had prayed to the same Lord while their children and city died. The cost to Munich was more than death and flattened buildings. It included shattered lives and broken spirits. I grieved at the costs and was fascinated by the devastation.

Although large sections of the city were simply rubble and burned-out hulks, areas here and there showed only a little damage. People were busy cleaning up, repairing buildings, reopening the stores. The electric trolleys ran from dawn to dark, very slowly and with no fare charged. I enjoyed touring by trolley, getting off when I saw shops that looked interesting. Only a few had things that I could buy. One place sold old, valuable stamps and series of Hitler-time stamps; I bought an entire set of stamps with pictures of Hitler and another that commemorated the various combat arms of the Wehrmacht. I paid regular visits to a secondhand store that dealt in all manner of jewelry, paintings, bronze sculptures, watches, and the beautiful long-stemmed pipes that the Bavarians loved. The shopkeepers were amused at a young American who wanted some *lange Tabackpfeifen*. Those were old men's pipes, the kind for sitting and meditating. Back in the barracks I loved to lounge in an overstuffed lobby chair, fill the large bowl, and smoke for a half hour—just sitting and day-dreaming. I especially liked the briar bowls with hunting scenes carved on them, but the porcelain bowls were also nice.

I wandered around large, impressive buildings that looked like museums, and I went frequently to see the noontime glockenspiel on the big Rathaus clock. It was a marvelous show, and the building was in good condition, with only a few shrapnel scars on it.

Munich after dark was one big flesh market. The streets teemed with prostitutes, who plied their trade with opening lines that ranged from the blunt "You want it? I got it" to "Hi, Joe, you new to Munich? Let me show you the town, won't cost you a thing, I just want to practice my English." I was told that none of these girls was operating on her own. The entire business was overseen by a group of mean and efficient former DPs. They housed and fed the women, paying them on a commission basis. The pimps were real pros and ran a tight ship. Word among the GIs was that if you argued with the girls or tried to cheat, there was a very good chance someone would follow you to a dark street.

Thinking back, I wonder just who these prostitutes were and what their lives were like; at the time, I saw them as only dangerous trash: a chance for catching VD or, worse, fathering a child who would grow up under those conditions. I suppose many were small-town girls who had been recruited for money, food, or from fear of threats (I have read that some of the men would discover or fabricate evidence of former Nazi activities and use it for blackmail). Regardless of how the girls got there, their lives must have been a nightmare. Besides being fundamentally brutal (most of the good DPs had gone home by then), the pimps probably hated all Germans and enjoyed humiliating young girls.

The other sleazy attraction was sex shows. A civilian man would sidle up to a GI and suggest that he knew of a show with some real action. I don't know just what "real action" meant.

None of this was illegal, in a military sense. The army wasn't strongly opposed to the prostitution or sex shows, although it was very concerned about the high rates of VD. With cooperation from the prostitutes, the military carried out a strong campaign to promote the use of condoms. The German slang for these items was "close combat gloves," which the girls shortened to: "Joe, you got to wear your gloves." The busy streets were patrolled by MPs, who were pretty good at keeping order. In general Munich after dark was very, very foul but not really dangerous, except for those GIs dumb enough to go into dark, deserted sidestreets, against which we had all been warned. The Bürgerbräukeller, where Hitler had started the failed 1923 putsch, was now a Red Cross Club. The front room, where they served coffee and doughnuts, had a large fireplace, and the walls were being redecorated with murals of Bavarian scenes. Another large room behind that one had a bandstand where a small orchestra played every night. The club sponsored local tours and offered some mimeographed sheets on the history of Munich. They weren't allowed to serve beer and couldn't afford to pay for local talent shows, but the Red Cross girls were very innovative. They had some sort of special event every week. Their GI Dog Show was a great success. During the war, soldiers had taken in hungry dogs out of pity, but with peace they had become more sophisticated in the selection of pets. Wartime Munich must have been a mecca for dog fanciers, and the hobby was being taken over by GIs. The dogs were acquired in all of the ways one can imagine: "liberated," purchased, or temporarily adopted; I know of one instance where a GI simply rented a dog from a breeder in exchange for mess-hall scraps for the man's other dogs.

I knew almost nothing about purebred dogs but went to the show out of curiosity. I remember that there were dachshunds in all sizes, colors, and hairstyles, some beautifully groomed, others ratty looking. There were some magnificent Doberman pinschers, a breed that I associated with concentration camps. They, too, came in a variety of sizes and colors but were much more orderly and well-behaved than the dachshunds. Dobermans dominated the obedience trials and the jumping of hurdles. I was impressed by their intelligence and training. But I learned the downside: they were well trained because an undisciplined Doberman is very dangerous. I don't know what became of the GI dogs after everyone settled down to occupation duty; I assume they were returned to Germans. Shipping space was too scarce for anyone, even officers, to justify bringing a dog home. (Even so, a few dogs were flown back to the States: Air Corps crews could smuggle almost anything.)

Occasionally, maybe twice a month, the Red Cross Club sponsored a small afternoon dance where we could meet girls who had been students at the university and would return to it when it reopened. They all spoke a little English. It was becoming socially acceptable for such girls to dance with (white) American enlisted men, although dating was still a "maybe" question. The girls wanted to dance and to learn the swing steps that had been forbidden during the war. Most of them really wanted to begin dating again, but Mama and the returning German soldiers strongly opposed the idea—which didn't necessarily mean that the girls weren't dating, only that Mama didn't allow it.

I went to one of the dances. My chances of finding a date there were pretty slim, but I knew what kind of luck I would have on the streets. I didn't want a whore or even a girl to party with. I was hoping to find an ordinary girl who would wander around Munich with me, explaining what it was like before the air raids, listening to my yarns, and maybe doing a little loving. Or maybe no loving would do. Anna was beginning to pressure me for a bit more than I cared for. We didn't really argue about it, but her expectations were more than I was ready to accommodate.

At the dance I looked over the possibilities and quickly eliminated the pretty girls who were flirting and practicing their English. A homely, awkward, twenty-year-old PFC who couldn't dance well stood no chance at all. My only real hope was to try the bargain basement, a corner of the room where quiet, shy, plain-looking girls were sitting and hoping. Focusing on skinny, tall glasses-wearers, I picked out a likely prospect.

I was still trying to adjust my Sudeten German into Bavarian. "Grüss Gott, mein Name ist Leon."

She smiled and replied in English. "Hello, I am Bridget." (She was probably saying Brigitte, but I understood her name to be Bridget.) Because I couldn't dance, we sat, drank coffee, and ate doughnuts. I found that she spoke awful English, mainly stock phrases—"In America, where are you from?" My Mississippi drawl was so foreign that she couldn't understand a thing I said. We switched to German and did a little better. I had developed a pretty good vocabulary, but still knew very little grammar and couldn't handle the Munich pronunciations.

After a while she asked, "Do you have ze cigarette?"

"No, I don't smoke."

"I no like ze smoke also, but zey are needed to trade for things."

Bridget had switched back to English. I didn't know why, but she obviously wanted to buy or trade for cigarettes. I didn't care much for black-market deals but had nothing against selling, trading, or even giving her a few packs. I usually had two packs with me and tried to keep at least a carton available for barter purposes. Bridget's approach seemed to indicate that she wasn't looking for a few cigarettes or just one pack.

I went over and got more coffee because I needed time to think. I had come there looking for a female companion who would talk with me. Bridget seemed to be a good prospect for that. She was interested in developing a friendship with me, but I was beginning to realize that we had different goals, and wondered whether they were compatible. I couldn't understand why she was being so cautious. What was she trying to do? This quiet little girl with a twinkle in her eyes was making me curious. Did she have something valuable to trade? Probably not; big-time trading deals were made with officers who had access to large stores of supplies. If she only wanted a few cartons of cigarettes, I wasn't quite sure what she planned to trade for them. I wasn't in the market for sex and already had more money than I was allowed to send home. Bridget was witty and smart. She was planning some sort of deal. I decided to play along, at least until I found what she had in mind.

"I could bring some cigarettes next week. Should I meet you here or somewhere else?" I had switched back to German because her English was so poor. Bridget wanted to meet me at her place. I should go to the first block beyond the Feldherrenhalle and turn left. She had a room at a building in the second block. That was on the edge of Odeonsplatz, the center of the theater and opera district. It had once been a fine residential area, but I knew it as mostly walls with no roofs. "Isn't that bombed out?"

"Yes, but this building wasn't hit very badly."

I hesitated, wondering if I should back out. Those bombed-out areas were dangerous. There were no lights, and rumor said ex-SS lived back in there. They called themselves *Werwölfe*—werewolves—and used women to lure GIs into dark places. I remembered what Anna had said about Munich being dangerous. I remembered Fats's warning: "Charlie, they's some bad cats in those bombed sections." Because I had already decided to learn what Bridget was planning, I rationalized a little: it wasn't very far from the lighted areas, and I wasn't going to stay very late. The SS would use whores as bait, not shy little girls like Bridget.

The next week I went to Munich with a whole carton of cigarettes. Following Bridget's instructions I walked passed the Feldherrenhalle, the Rathaus, the wrecks of theaters and opera houses. I had been back here once before, and since then I had read the Red Cross leaflet on the early history of the Nazi Party. Now the story was coming to life; the ghost of Hitler seemed to be here. The morning after the putsch at the Bürgerbräukeller, the future Führer had walked onto the Odeonsplatz with Göring, Ludendorff, Rosenberg, Streicher, and the Storm Troopers to face the army and take control of Bavaria.

Hitler thought everything had been arranged, but the front ranks of the army didn't move. The army and the Nazis stood face to face. Streicher grabbed at a soldier's rifle, someone yelled, and someone fired. Thirteen people were killed, Göring was wounded, and the party was defeated.

The Feldherrenhalle was a memorial to German heroes of the past. Anna had stood somewhere along here, under the smoky glare of huge torches at midnight, and watched Hans receive his SS commission. They had presented him a sword with Meine Ehre Heisst Treue on the blade and a certificate that said, "Never draw it without cause or sheathe it without honor." To the left at the far end of the Odeonsplatz ran Brienner Strasse. About a block down it were the ruins of the Brown House, which had been the Nazi Party headquarters. Hitler had lived over on Prinzregenten Strasse. I walked down through Odeonsplatz and turned left. There were no houses on the first block, only shells and rubble.

A house in the second block still had a roof. I went up the stairs and knocked on the door. "Come in quickly." Bridget closed the door and said in clear American English, "Okay, Leon, what have you got?"

This was not the mousy little college student I had met at the Red Cross Club. Here, Bridget was a grown woman, well-groomed and a little sexy (not very sexy, though; she was still skinny, with no figure). Looking back, I realize that she was a consummate actress, huckster, yarn-spinner: liar. I don't mean a compulsive liar: Bridget lied for pure artistic pleasure. After I came to understand her, it was interesting to watch her pause in the middle of a story, considering the various possibilities for improvement. She told excellent lies; I never quite knew where truth ended and fantasy began. But it didn't matter to me. I think, maybe, her stories were factual in the overall atmosphere of the time, but the beauty of a Bridget yarn lay in the glorious details she adorned it with. She was probably in her late twenties and had grown up around the university community. I don't know if she had actually been a student, but her stories of university life, both in the early days of the Nazi Party and during the war, were reasonably close to historical accounts.

She explained her use of poor English at the dance. "I took English in school for four years, but it was with a British accent. When the Americans came, I studied your speech and changed. That was easy because I also studied drama at the university. Then I found that GIs were suspicious of girls who understood everything they said. That made it hard for me to do my cigarette deals."

She did know English grammar rather well, and she had developed a bit of American accent, but her overall command of the language was only slightly better than mine of German; she certainly hadn't taken four years of it. And there was no reason why being able to speak English should be a hindrance in buying cigarettes. I have no idea why she liked pretending that she couldn't speak English.

After some small talk, she asked what I wanted for the cigarettes.

I said, "What about fifty marks?"

"For only one carton? I would go broke dealing with you. Thirty-five is my top price."

I knew that fifty marks (about five dollars) was the absolute minimum street price for cigarettes, but they had only cost me ten marks and I was selling them out of curiosity about Bridget. I agreed to thirty-five marks with no argument. That surprised her. Now she was curious about me. She asked if I thought she would include a little sex with the price. No, I had enjoyed talking with her at the Red Cross and wanted to visit again; she wanted cigarettes, so I brought some.

When she realized that she could have gotten the carton at an even lower price, she asked about buying some coffee and sugar. I could easily get coffee through Sam'Le' or Fats, but I didn't want to play the black-market game. That didn't make sense to her. If I sold cigarettes, why not coffee? In my mind it made sense. The cigarettes were my ration; the coffee belonged to the army. I wasn't going to do it. We argued awhile and reached a compromise: I would bring coffee and sugar on my next visit but wouldn't sell it. She would keep some coffee on hand for us to drink while we talked. She could sell or use the rest but would always keep enough for my visits.

That was our arrangement: she traded dramatic tales for coffee, sugar, and cigarettes. I can't say that there was no aspect of sex between us. She enjoyed tempting me, and I was not above yielding to temptation, just a bit. We sparred and joked; she called me a prude and I called her a slut, but nothing, much, happened. Bridget thought I was being faithful to my Bad Aibling woman, which wasn't true but was close enough. I was comfortable and satisfied with the personality of my quiet, relaxed Anna. Bridget was interesting but too much of a challenge for me. She was continually scheming and lying.

Bridget's stories of the Nazi era in Munich were full of fantasies about famous people she had met at parties and seminars. Ignoring questions of accuracy, she told wonderful anecdotes and provided plausible information on university life under the Nazis. Her attitudes about the Nazi era varied to fit the story she was telling. On some nights she was an intelligent, sensitive anti-Nazi. She could also be a firebreathing racist/nationalist Aryan. Above all, she was a good actress.

Bridget pointed out that Bavaria was the birthplace of the Nazi Party and Munich was always its home. Berlin had been the seat of government, but here was where the party lived, the *Hauptstadt der Bewegung:* Capital City of the Movement. She had heard professors at the university say how foolish Hitler had sounded in the early twenties. He had always been an excellent speaker, but he spewed wild hatred of Jewish-Bolshevism, capitalism, Catholicism, and urban life. In those early years Hitler was a local character. People invited him to parties for entertainment. His slogans became the current campus jokes. The jokes stopped when he took over the government in 1933.

During the early 1930s, the university became a stronghold of Nazi support. Most of the faculty saw behind the Hitler facade because they had watched him develop from a common rabble-rouser, but many of the students loved his idealistic concepts and agreed that the old democratic government wasn't suitable for Germany. They were greatly concerned about the depression; people needed jobs and food; people needed hope. They needed an authoritarian government that could take money away from the rich war profiteers and build a beautiful new Germany. Some students objected to Hitler's virulent racism, but most of them agreed that the Jewish Bolsheviks were a threat to Germany; everyone knew that Jews had been the force behind the party that took over the Bavarian government and tried to make it Communist. Even after the war started, there was strong student support for Hitler, but it began to fade as stories filtered back from the Russian front.

There had been the rough equivalent of an ASTP unit at the university. Oriented toward medical training, it was called simply the "Student Company." The boys studied medicine in the winter and served in Russia as combat medics during the summer offensives. They brought back a different picture of "National Socialism in the New Territories." At first, the Ukrainians had welcomed the invasion as a way to get out from under Stalin, but that changed when the SS "action squads" began slaughtering entire villages. The SS plan was to make room for new German communities by removing the current inhabitants. A group of university students began printing antiwar leaflets and posting them around Munich. At night they painted freedom slogans on the walls along Ludwigstrasse. This group, called the "White Rose," lasted for only a few weeks. The landlady of the house where they were printing their leaflets reported them to the Gestapo.

A few days later, morning classes were dismissed for a meeting of the entire student body. The announcement was very brief: some students had been distributing defeatist leaflets; they had been apprehended and executed. The entire student body began pounding on their desks—the equivalent to American clapping and cheering. But it wasn't long before the significance of students being executed for simple protest sank in, and the attitude on campus changed. In fact the incident was the turning point for sentiment toward the Nazi Party. Although there was no more open defiance, the student body became increasingly anti-Nazi. The dream of National Socialism was dead, and they began looking forward to liberation at Allied hands, hoping the Russians wouldn't get to Munich first.

I told Bridget about Maud's praise of Hitler's slogan "Common good goes before personal advancement." She said the fallacy lay in the definition of common good. If you were a true German (Bavarian, anti-Communist, family-oriented, heterosexual), the common good suited you perfectly. The problem was with people who didn't quite fit the mold.

People who were more Jewish than German had problems, as did Russians and Poles. The university community of Munich had been shocked when the so-called pornography and degenerate art were burned. The Storm Troops had also transformed the lifestyles of virtually all of Munich's homosexuals in one day by arresting a group and shipping them to the concentration camp at Dachau. Heterosexual arrangements were made immediately, and there was no cheating because no one knew who was a spy.

"Going to Dachau" had an ironic meaning. Before the war, Dachau had been an art colony. Students weary of discipline and stress would drop out for a while and go to Dachau. Food and lodging in the quiet, picturesque town were reasonably priced; the coffee shops made interesting places to discuss life's problems. Then the SS took over an old munitions plant and converted it into a training center. A little later they began expanding to include a camp where political prisoners were to be re-educated. SS guards started using the coffee shops, trying to pick up female students, and arguing with almost everyone. The Dachau atmosphere had changed.

Did the people of Dachau know what was happening at the camp? Bridget said that it would have been impossible not to know. Thin, weak, ragged workers were marched through the streets on their way to work assignments. Guards and other staff members talked about outbreaks of disease that sometimes killed nearly everyone in a barracks or group of barracks. The crematorium would belch black smoke for days. The residents of Dachau tried to ignore everything. With the students gone, the town's economy depended heavily on the camp. Besides, everyone knew what was happening to people who criticized the government.

Listening to all of this, I realized how completely the Germans had been tricked and dominated by the Nazi Party. I told Bridget that someone had described the American Civil War as a few politicians leading the South up Fool's Hill. She said it hadn't been that simple in Germany: in many ways Hitler had been a good leader. Again I got to hear about *Volksgemeinschaft*. Even people who opposed Hitler's racial ideas believed in the importance of the "national community." Bridget remembered how proud she had been of the autobahns and other construction projects that provided jobs for everyone, of the welfare program, of the system to care for unwed mothers. She had watched Germany grow strong enough to demand the return of its land. She had cheered when the new army crushed France and England so quickly. She hadn't wondered about the large supplies of French wines and cheeses that showed up in the stores. All of this was despite her distaste for the harsh "military necessity" measures that were being installed.

Then Bridget said a strange thing. "Dachau. Yes, I think that most of us in Munich knew what was happening there. But it doesn't really matter whether we knew or not. You must understand, Leon. It wasn't possible to be a part of the Germany that did those good things, but not the one that did the rest."

I could not understand how building good roads and caring for unwed mothers meant that you had to invade your neighbors and set up concentration camps, but maybe Bridget was trying to say that if the basis of a "national community" was collective pride, that also implied collective guilt. Or maybe she and I were involved in a different version of an exchange that I had heard often, and disliked, between GIs and German prisoners. When a German said he was "nicht Nazi," the GI would laugh: "'Nicht Nazi.' You say that now because Hitler is kaput. Last year you weren't 'nicht Nazi.'"

Or maybe Bridget was simply right. Maybe all Germans had actually been like those stupid SS boys we knew in Czechoslovakia.

As Bridget and I got to know each other, she began inviting friends over to drink my coffee and talk. By then she had persuaded me to bring flour, canned milk, and butter so that she could make cookies for us. I remember two of the girls were former students who were going to be students again when the university opened but had spent the summer as "rubble women" helping to clear the streets of debris from the bombing. Usable bricks and stones were put into one pile, and the rest was hauled off to the dump. The work was not exactly a civic volunteer effort: the Military Government issued extra food-ration tickets to people engaged in heavy labor. On the other hand, it was not drudgery. The rubble women took frequent breaks, sang parodies of the old Hitler-times songs, told jokes, and gossiped.

Now that the streets were nearly clear and cold weather had stopped most of the rubble work that remained, the girls were acting as what they called "marketing assistants." The truth was that they were helping in an art scam being run by an antique dealer. The dealer would give them a cheap painting, which they would offer to some American officer. Their tale was that a once-rich friend was now on the verge of starvation and desperately wanted to sell the painting. How much was it worth? They didn't know. It was probably valuable, but they weren't art experts. Oh, but wait—they knew an antique dealer who would appraise it in exchange for a few packs of cigarettes. The officer would then have a basis on which to decide whether it was worth buying and what to offer for it.

The antique dealer, of course, would recognize the painting as an extremely rare piece of art and suggest a price that the officer should pay if he were to be fair with the owner. But the officer didn't want to be fair; he would get it at a much lower price and gloat over the deal he had made—at least until he tried to sell the painting back in the States. I knew the antique shop and had bought some pipes there. The man had beautiful items, and they were all very expensive. I had the impression that he didn't really want to sell the fine material but was buying or trading for investments that would be valuable long after cigarettes and occupation marks had lost their importance.

I asked the girls how they managed to persuade officers to fall for a scam that seemed so obvious. "Leon, men will believe anything after they have fed the *behaarte Venusmuschel.*" We were speaking the usual polyglot GI/German language: mostly German with the GI term for any word that I wouldn't understand in German. There was a pause and all three girls watched while I half smiled, trying to understand the joke. I hated to admit defeat but didn't get it at all: "The hairy what"? They laughed. "Hairy Venus mussel. You would call it a clam". I kept the half smile; they had given me a clue but I still didn't see anything. Venus was the goddess of love; in English the term could mean—then I understood, then I blushed. It was a funny description, a good joke, but I was blushing because women shouldn't talk about things like that.

The girls had other stories that weren't funny at all. Some friends of theirs had been sent to Dachau for various offenses. None had died, but they worked long hours on starvation rations. Under those conditions disease would sometimes kill off an entire barracks (I later learned that in 1944 and 1945, typhus alone killed 15,000 prisoners at the camp). The girls discounted GI stories of "death ovens" at Dachau. Those were crematoria where bodies were burned to reduce the spread of disease. The ovens were conventional, one-corpse-at-a-time affairs. Dachau could rightly be called a death camp but mainly because exhausted, emaciated human beings were easy victims for disease. Toward the end of the war, substantial numbers of the inmates were killed outright and cremated, probably thousands, but not tens or hundreds of thousands: one-at-a-time cremation ovens aren't very efficient.

I didn't know how much of that was true. I also didn't know whether to believe the girls when they said there was no real animosity toward Americans because we had gotten rid of the Nazis and allowed a freer style of life. Gradually, though, I realized what they meant by "style of life" and why their friends had been put in Dachau. They had been hinting at it all along, but it took me awhile to catch on. They laughed at my embarrassment when I finally realized that they were the Sodom and Gomorrah type of girls!

Looking back, I see that the girls were probably surprised at my reaction, although they were absolutely delighted to see me blushing. They must have wondered how anybody could be so naive. All I can do is repeat that I came from a very sheltered background. During my army career, I had known several homosexual boys. Stevie, back in basic training, had been completely open with his close friends: he was homosexual, had a boyfriend in the navy, and wouldn't risk our friendship by making advances. To me, it seemed perfectly normal; Stevie was queer but not strange. Somehow, this attitude did not extend to homosexual girls. Logically, I must have known that some girls were that way, and of course there were plenty of barracks-room jokes on the subject. But that such women really existed—much less that I might know them—was a possibility I had never even considered.

Bridget and her friends had unusual slants on a lot of things, including the war. Hitler's invasion of Russia, for example, was a case of bad timing but had been absolutely the right thing to do. Someone had to stop Stalin, who had been converting a primitive society into a powerful, menacing nation. He had taken over the Baltic countries and was trying to grab the Rumanian oilfields. The Finns were fighting against brutal Russian attacks aimed at the nickel mines. Churchill was the stubborn bastard who prevented Germany from defeating Russia. If he had surrendered, Britain, and maybe the U.S., would have joined Hitler in stopping Stalin's invasion of Europe.

I just sat and listened. I knew absolutely nothing about those manipulations. I suspected they were pulling my leg but wasn't sure. I heard the same ideas in 1957 from a graduate student who had been in the Hitler Youth, but by then I knew a little more about the history. Germany and Russia had made their pact because they were mutually dependent. Germany needed grain, meat, petroleum, and other raw materials. Russia needed manufactured goods, including military supplies. The Skoda Company in Czechoslovakia had been under contract to Russia to produce weapons, and the contract continued after Germany took over the country. Apparently Hitler, against the advice of economists and military advisers, decided that he could capture Russia in a short assault much like the one against France. Diplomats throughout Europe repeatedly warned Stalin about the planned invasion. The British, having broken the German diplomatic code, even gave him the exact date. Stalin had no plans for invading Europe—in the near future, at least—and refused to believe Hitler was planning to fight him; it simply made no sense.

The girls were disgusted that we were still ignoring the Soviet threat. "Now Europe is so weak that you are the only country strong enough to oppose Russia. You're treating them like allies and giving them all of eastern Europe. If you don't wake up soon, you'll still be fighting them twenty years from now." I argued for a while, but without much enthusiasm; I didn't think they had a very good understanding of world politics.

On one of my visits with Bridget, I stayed so late that I was afraid of missing the midnight bus, which left from the Bahnhof. I decided to take a shortcut through the bombed-out area; it wasn't a very dark night, and I knew the general direction. Pretty soon I saw two men standing on the sidewalk. I was already walking in the middle of the street but worked myself over toward the far side. Then a man stepped out of the shadows and said, "Eh, Ami."

I thought, "Now I've done it. These men are the *Werwölfe*. This is what everybody tried to warn me about."

I tried not to panic. Two men were on one side of me and one on the other. My only weapon was a pocketknife. Running was hopeless. As a last resort I could yell, "GI in trouble!" You never knew where a GI might be sitting with a girl.

I couldn't just stand there, so I said, "Grüss Gott."

The man laughed and said, "Haben Sie Zigaretten?"

"Nein, tut mir leid. Ich rauche nicht."

That was all. Nothing happened. So I walked on, boldly and aggressively. But I no longer felt like a brave Combat Infantryman.

10

AND THE LIVES YOU LIVED WERE MINE

I suppose Bridget wondered why I suddenly stopped coming by. The "Eh, Ami" experience had absolutely terrified me. On my next visit to the Black Tomcat, I impressed the boys with my stupidity. Fats said, "Charlie, I told you to stay away from those wild women." Lili took on a very serious tone in telling me to stay away from that area. She said that the ex-SS Werewolf tale was just GI rumor, but there were a lot of black-marketeers in there who had no qualms about killing anyone who happened to get in their way. Most of those men were Polish and Russian DPs who had escaped from the DP camps to avoid being sent home. They were well armed and robbed German homes, stupid GIs, and (occasionally) ration depots. Big Willie had absolutely forbidden his men to wander around as I had; I don't know why he hadn't sat me down and talked sense into me.

I had another reason for breaking up with Bridget: Anna knew what was happening and didn't like it at all. I had no trouble convincing her that I was sleeping at the quartermaster company rather than with Bridget; Anna knew me pretty well. The real problem was that she had was tired of hearing Inge and Hilda tease her about my "other woman." I promised that all future trips to Munich would be for shopping and visiting with the boys.

I was still enjoying my work with Arbeits-Kommando V. As I was bringing them in one afternoon, a GI said, "Hey, Standifer, one of the PWs that we got from the Russians is asking for you."

For me? I didn't know anyone who was a prisoner of the Russians.

The POW, named Kurt, had said that his sister lived in Bad Aibling and he wanted to contact her. The prison grapevine had told him that a guard named Standifer was dating her.

It had to be Anna's brother, who had been engaged to Inge. I was glad to know he was alive but wondered what he would think of the new arrangements Inge had made.

As I walked over to his compound, I tried to remember what I knew about Kurt. He and I were the same age; Anna had shown me a photograph taken two years ago, when he was eighteen and had just gone into the service. He had been an excellent student; he spoke English as well as Inge did and was fairly fluent in Russian. He had been reported missing over a year ago, but some friends wrote that they thought he had been wounded and captured. That was slightly encouraging. The Russians often tortured and killed German prisoners, but they were said to be more tolerant of men who spoke Russian. Even so, Kurt wouldn't be in good condition. Prisoners got no medical care except for what their friends could give. I thought of Hilda's brother, who had returned from the Eastern front blind, with a useless arm, and paralyzed from the waist down.

Although I had been a guard for about six weeks, this was my first time in the cage compounds. I had to leave my rifle with the gate guard and sign an entry permit telling my purpose and estimated length of stay. As I walked by the barracks of my work group, they razzed me about being a new prisoner. We had a running joke that my German had become so good the guards would mistake me for a Bavarian; it was entirely a joke.

Kurt was in the "Russian" compound, a sort of isolation unit for men who had come in from Russian camps. Medical technicians checked their health and kept them on reduced rations until their stomachs could adjust to regular meals. I hesitated at the barracks doorway, worried about what I might find. Would Kurt be a dirty half-human like the Russian-camp returnees I had seen earlier? Would he be bitter that his married, proper, twenty-nine-year-old sister was dating a young enemy soldier? Or would he ever again be capable of shock? I took a deep breath and opened the door. An emaciated but clean and neat man came up. "My name is Kurt. I assume you are Standifer."

I had expected him to be badly underweight, but I honestly could not recognize this skeleton as the proud young soldier in Anna's photograph. His left leg had been amputated at the knee; he had a hand-carved wooden peg leg with blanket padding on top. His face bore a bad scar, but his eyes were bright. I forced a smile and said, "It's good to see you alive, Kurt. Anna and Inge told me a lot about you, but we were afraid you were dead."

Sitting on a bench outside the barracks, Kurt explained that the compound grapevine had told him all about me, including what I could probably do to help. He had a note for me to give Anna but hadn't known that Inge was in town—the grapevine didn't realize that the teenaged girl was his fiancée. I decided to let her tell him about Stud. Kurt wanted me to let them know he was in pretty good condition. He said he had been in a well-run prison for the last few months, but life had been rough before that. His leg had been amputated by a German doctor working without anesthesia and with no medicine. He decided that I should also tell Anna and Inge that he had lost weight.

I said that I could probably get permission to take him to see them tomorrow, but he wanted to wait. I then learned how well the grapevine understood procedures and where red tape could be cut: Kurt wanted me to get him permanently freed as soon as possible. He gave me the name of a GI who was a clerk in the discharge office. I knew the boy and was sure he would help.

Anna and Inge were ecstatic to hear that Kurt was alive. They wanted to see him that night or certainly the next day. They knew that it took around a month to process a discharge and didn't believe I could do better than cut that in half. I didn't think so either, but the next morning I went over to see the clerk. He and I had occasionally done business in "war trophy" medals. My POW crew sometimes traded their medals to me for cigarettes or extra food. I had also accumulated a collection of Gott Mit Uns belt buckles. (The slogan was traditional in the German army. It came from a speech by Bismarck in which he warned other countries that Prussians are a peaceful people, but if they are attacked, "God will be with us.") Newly arrived GIs eagerly bought authentic souvenirs from combat veterans but were less enthusiastic about medals POWs had sold to a clerk.

The clerk could sell the medals if I would vouch for a good combat story to go with each one. It was a fun game in which everybody won.

The clerk outlined how I could walk the paper work through and went ahead of me to smooth the operation with promises of combat souvenirs. First, I needed a stack of forms, plus Kurt's available military record. That night, Anna and I went to Mrs. Bachmann, who signed a paper saying Kurt would work for her as a baker. Pete Riley was there, and he and I signed an affidavit stating that Kurt had never been associated with the Nazi Party or the SS. Then Anna filled out a lodging form saying that Kurt would live with her. At eight the next morning I was in the discharge office with everything Kurt needed except his food-ration card. I walked the papers through the various offices, and by midafternoon, he was ready for discharge. In twenty-four hours we had accomplished what usually took a month. Even so, Kurt couldn't be discharged until the next day because he was being cleaned up. His uniform was washed and dried while he was given a hot shower and dusted liberally with DDT. It was his third treatment with the magic insecticide that immediately killed all fleas and lice, carriers of typhus.

After Kurt received his discharge and ration card, we walked over to Anna's little two-bedroom house. I watched them hug, laugh, and cry, and then I left. Kurt still didn't know about Stud. Until now, Inge's affair with a GI had been just a game because both she and Anna thought Kurt was dead or would die in a Russian prison. But it was a game that couldn't be ended abruptly; besides furnishing entertainment, Mike and Stud had been keeping the household generously supplied with staple rations. Stud still believed that Inge was fifteen, had never dated a boy before him, and understood only the crude, vulgar English he had taught her. He was also the kind who would raise hell over the idea of his girl dating a Kraut soldier.

I don't know how Kurt took the news initially, but afterward he handled himself beautifully. When the boys were around, he spoke no English and generally ignored the two girls, who had supposedly been thirteen when he joined the army. He treated me as the man of the house because, functionally, Anna was the girls' aunt, so logically, I was their uncle, only five years older than them but much more mature. I'm not sure what Kurt's actual attitude was toward me. He seemed to accept me as a friend who was going with his older sister; it didn't seem to matter that I was a GI and much younger than Anna.

Kurt was the only German ex-soldier I knew who refused to discuss the war. His attitude was that it was over and everyone should look toward the future. Because I had seen his service record, I knew more about his trauma than did Anna. He had been in some harsh battles and had been wounded twice before being captured with a bad leg wound in Poland. During about six months in the first prison camp, almost half of his unit had died because of brutal treatment: beatings, starvation, and no medical care. He survived because he spoke Russian and was able to get a little sympathy from the guards.

At night, after Mike and Stud left, Kurt, Inge, and Hilda would visit with Anna and me. We spoke English because I would have limited them too badly in German and because Kurt wanted to learn American idioms. I was continually amused at Inge's speaking absolutely correct British English, whereas when Stud was around, she mutilated vulgar GI phrases. I had been embarrassed over what they had taught her to say but now realized that Inge was fascinated with the strange language. She was curious as to the significance of one popular phrase: "Fuckin' A!" What did the *A* stand for? I didn't know. "Fuckin' A" meant "You are absolutely right"—maybe the *A* was for "absolutely." In GI language, *fuckin'* was an essential and meaningless adjective. We also said things like, "Kilroy was here," "Oh, my achin' back!" and "Big-assed bird." The GI vocabulary was vulgar and unique, but the terms had no deeper meanings. They were just things we all said.

I don't remember any especially significant discussions from our "family" gatherings at Anna's. We talked about the common topics of the day: how long the occupation would last, when the civilian government would phase in, whether the French would try to annex Stuttgart. Did Kurt still want to study engineering, and if so, what would it cost?

Anna and Kurt were the only surviving members of their family. Their parents had died in the raids that had killed her son. Their brother had died in Russia during the first year. Of course, there was still the question of Anna's husband, Hans, and it led to a difficult moment for all of us. Anna had decided to accept the probability that Hans was dead. Now, even though Kurt had survived Russian captivity, Anna did not want to return to the pain of wondering if Hans might come home, and in what condition. One night Kurt pressed her on the subject. He argued that Hans was very sharp and had good survival instincts, that the Russians were beginning to send more prisoners home, and that Hans might return soon. I expected Anna to start crying. Instead she lashed out at Kurt about the problems of never knowing whether she was married or not. She said that Hans was SS, rather than regular army; the Russians would never release him alive. Kurt got mad, switched to German, and said, "Hans is alive. He will come back and find that you are an Ami whore!"

I was shocked and ashamed. Kurt was surprised at having said it in front of me. He apologized: "I didn't mean that the way it sounded. It just came out." I knew that he was sincerely sorry, but I also knew that he was right. Neither Anna nor I could justify what we were doing. I remembered a song from back at Fort Benning:

> In hurried words, her name I blessed,
> And breathed the vows that bind me.
> And in anguish pressed against my breast,
> The girl I left behind me.

Hans and Anna had breathed vows, and I had helped her to break them. Conversation stopped for the night, and I went back to the barracks more than a little ashamed of myself.

In February the army started sending 50-point men home. I would be leaving almost any day. I was more than ready—homesick and sick of the army. Besides, things were changing at Anna's house. Hilda and Inge had gone back to Stuttgart. Before leaving, they sold Mike and Stud to some local girls. They asked for bids on the two GIs with good food connections, introduced the boys—who knew nothing about what was going on—to the highest bidders, added some compliments, and left. Kurt and Anna were preparing to return to Stuttgart as well. Kurt had decided that he liked baking as a profession and had persuaded Anna that she would never be fully accepted in conservative Bad Aibling. They planned to apply for a loan to rebuild her bakery. He would marry Inge. Anna had agreed to wait for two more years before deciding that Hans was dead.

I was marking time waiting for orders home when, instead, an assignment came down that filled me with dread and reminded me that, for some men, the war wasn't over. The Bad Aibling camp had about two hundred Slavic soldiers—Rumanians, Ukrainians, and a few Russian nationals—who had joined the German army. The summer before, the United States had returned a number of such men to the Russians, who promptly shot them. Since then, officials had been negotiating to assure that any further returnees would at least receive trials. The prisoner grapevine had concluded that because these men were German soldiers, they would be discharged as such in the American zone. But now, suddenly, the bulletin board listed fifteen men who would serve as guards on a train taking the Slavic prisoners, plus some DPs, to Poland, where they would be turned over to the Soviets.

My name was on the list. We were to meet that afternoon for instructions and leave early the next morning. At the meeting we were told that a small cage had been built at the doorway of each boxcar, just big enough for a cot and one chair. Two guards were to stay in each cage, watching to see that the prisoners did not try to escape or commit suicide. We would have a telephone with which to report every half hour. One of us was to be awake and alert at all times; the trip should last about two days. The officer also said that the prisoners thought they were simply being transferred to another prison. I wondered if he really believed that; the grapevine knew the entire story.

I was terrified; we were going to be guarding men who knew they would be shot, or possibly tortured and then shot. The cage wasn't very strong, and the mesh was wide enough for a man to stick his arm through. What would happen if the prisoners caught us dozing and grabbed the rifle? What would happen if they all rushed the cage at one time? A telephone, connected by wires that could break, was not much protection. Would the prisoners kill me in order to escape? Sure they would. (In writing this, I went back to my letter home to see why they were putting us in the cars instead of simply locking the doors, with guards stationed in separate cars. The letter gives no explanation.)

I chose a reliable man as my partner, and we stayed up late that night making plans. There really wasn't much we could do. We packed books to read (for the person who wasn't guarding) and plenty of food, so that we could share some with the prisoners. We decided that if they tried to break into the cage, we would jump off the train and run.

We were lined up to get our car assignments when an officer came up with four new guards. "The following men will come with me for transfer to a new unit. Standifer . . ." I was going home! My instructions were to pack up and be ready to leave the next morning. I never knew how my buddy made out with his trip to Poland.

That night I took my extra food, a carton of fruit juice, and some cigarettes over to Anna's house.

There wasn't much to say. "Should we write?" I asked.

Anna shook her head. "No. We needed each other here, but the time is over. You helped me through the worst parts."

Yes, but she had helped me too. The idea of being an occupation soldier like the Reconstruction Yankees had been hard for me to accept. Anna had given me new insights on adult relationships; being grown up involved much more than sex and being able to do grown-up things. I gave her my home address in case I could ever help, and told her that I appreciated what she had done for me.

At eight the next morning I slung my duffel bag into the back of a truck, climbed up, and sat down. It felt strange because all I had was the duffel bag. For the first time in two years I was relocating without a rifle, cartridge belt, and helmet liner. The war was over and I was going home. Actually, I was only traveling about seventy-five miles to join the 71st Infantry Division, which would take me home. I had hoped to be put back in a rifle company, but we went to an artillery outfit: Battery C, 608th Field Artillery. Battery C was stationed at Lauingen, a small town northwest of Augsburg. It was about the same size as Bad Aibling, clean and neat, but without the beautiful mountains. We were quartered in the school because every home was packed with refugees from the cities. To me, it seemed even more crowded than Bad Aibling. The place teemed with women and young girls. They had been around GIs for a long time, spoke vulgar GI English, and were far too wild for me.

Early one morning two weeks later, we loaded onto 40-and-8 box-cars, eighteen men to a car, carrying only our fart sacks and some K rations. Our duffel bags went on a separate car. This trip was even better than the one from Düsseldorf. We had a small Coleman stove on which we heated water for coffee, we lounged on the straw, we dozed. At every station we piled off and visited with anyone who would talk to us. We traded cigarettes for anything of value. Cigarettes were becoming useless to us because we were headed home!

I spent a lot of time sitting in the door of the boxcar, just dreaming. I was looking forward to home, but I had come to love Germany:

> Now the cathedral is standing, standing squarely in the light.
> The suffering is gone, that tore our people apart.
> Our song makes us strong and sure.

That song was of the Hitler Youth, it was for the Hitler times, but now it had taken on a deeper meaning.

The shattered towns no longer had any effect on me, they were simply part of Germany. I was part of Germany, or perhaps Germany had become part of me. The war seemed far back in my past. I had fought tooth and nail, just as the Germans had. I had watched them fight and die, courageously. I had swapped yarns, lies, and jokes with the POWs and with the kids, girls, and women. They had taught me about true courage: the ability to face hardships, shock, and humiliation with hard work and jokes. I had come to love the crazy Bavarians, who loved the crazy GIs. The Bavarian hillbillies, Texas cowboys, Mississippi rednecks, Nebraska cornhuskers: we made quite a team. I was glad to be headed home, but part of me would always be Bavarian.

Kipling had a short poem in *Barrack-Room Ballads* that was meant for India, but I changed the words to fit my Germany:

> I have eaten your bread and sausage,
> I have drunk your beer and wine,
> The deaths you died I have watched beside.
> And the lives you lived were mine.

AFTERWORD AND THANKS

I wrote this "with a little help from my friends." To be honest, it was more than a little help—so much that I don't know where to start.

Günter Bischof, associate director of the Eisenhower Center at the University of New Orleans, continuously helped and encouraged me with the manuscript—to the point of taking an early draft with him when he was on assignment as a visiting professor at the University of Munich. Faculty and students in the Amerika-Institut read the material, offered constructive criticism, chuckled at my spelling of German words, and urged me to submit it for publication; they felt that it offered an interesting view of that first occupation year, a view that German women had been reluctant to acknowledge. Günter also provided me with some excellent German-point-of-view material that helped me achieve a more balanced understanding of the things I had witnessed or been told. That a professional historian kindly lent me a hand should not be taken to imply that the book is a sound, scholarly historical account of those times. I have tried hard to maintain the viewpoint of a twenty-year-old boy who was still trying to figure out what was happening.

Members of the 94th Division Association helped me tremendously. I should especially thank Bob Cassel, editor of the *Hoodlum News,* the newsletter of the 301st Infantry Regiment. Bob inserted many notes informing his readers that "Leon is trying to get more information on the DP camps we ran"—or on the Prague parade, or the men who were with me at the POW discharge center, or whatever. I received many interesting letters and phone calls because of these notices.

Our annual division reunions include a Friday night "Rally" at which tables are set aside for the various rifle companies, plus artillery, medics, and various other units. Large, refillable pitchers of beer are provided, plus a few snacks. I usually sit at the King Company table, ask questions, and listen. By pooling our poor memories, we have figured out the real names of Milky and Kevin, and what became of them. Milky (his actual nickname) was the true hustler of the pair, the instigator of several profitable scams; he later joined the paratroops and (we think) was killed in Korea. Kevin was the one who just went along; Bill Henry thinks he became a banker after the war and died a few years ago. (Bill also thinks Kevin was an ASTP boy who went overseas with the company; I still think he was a replacement.)

Everybody remembers the debacle of me and the tank, but Jim Carey thinks I got it stuck between two buildings—damaging both of them. I asked Carl Nance about the incident in which a replacement tried to refuse to act as scout on a patrol, and Carl threatened to shoot him. That is exactly what happened. Carl is a little embarrassed over it, but at the time it seemed to be the best answer. The boy followed orders, did a good job, and became a good soldier. We have had long talks about the SS kids we slaughtered, and have discovered that one German division we wiped out was composed entirely of Danish troops, who might have been forced to serve under the threat of imprisonment of their families (or they might have believed Hitler's dream of a pure Germanic race).

One night someone reminded me of our King Company Sportsmen and Weapon Collectors Club. I had forgotten about it, and we had a lot of fun trying to remember the details. We also enjoyed remembering the "secret document" that we composed for the benefit of the Rosenthal girls. In actuality, Bill Warren had been replaced as company commander by the time we pulled that stunt, but I kept his name in the account for simplicity.

I haven't found anyone else who remembers the ASTP reunion at L Company. This fact may mean that it wasn't nearly the big event that I remember, that it happened somewhere else, or that it happened fifty years ago. I took a poll of what we felt, after fifty years, was the greatest individual price of having been riflemen. Consensus generally favored loss of our youth—that we had left as adolescents and returned as old men. On the positive side, almost everyone agreed that we came home with a sense of pride at having been able to serve our country as combat troops. There was no consensus about attitudes toward the Germans: as combat troops or as a nation. A few of the group are still bitter toward Germany, and specifically toward the 11th Panzer Division.

I am grateful to the Hitler-time Germans I met in Bad Aibling on my visit there in 1992. Hilde Hofer, now deceased, owned the Café Arnold in 1992 and had been working there in 1945—her father was the original owner. She didn't remember me or anything about Anna, but she agreed that this was probably the place where Anna and I went: it was in the right location, an area called "between the bridges," and had been the only beer hall around there at the time. Hilde showed me where Mrs. Bachmann's bakery had been and recalled for me what the woman's real name was; the building is now a television store. We decided that Anna had probably lived in the houses built for NCOs from the Luftwaffe base. It was Hilde who explained to me about the street signs being removed and told me that one street had been named after the Red Baron; I don't know whether Anna actually lived on that street.

Gerda Kopliks, who served as our interpreter (she had worked for the U.S. Army immediately after the war), had grown up in Bad Aibling and was able to explain the early attitudes of Aiblingers toward American soldiers. Although she did not date Americans during that first year, she was criticized for accepting a job with the enemy. Gerda was also my source of information about the BDM knitting socks for soldiers on the Russian front. She told us where the Hitler Youth Home had been. It was built on the banks of a pretty stream and probably had a large play yard, which is now shaded with trees.

Most of the material on combat in Russia is from a friend who was in the Waffen SS but doesn't want his name used. He had just finished writing a manuscript, parts of which he shared with me, about his experiences on the Russian front and as an inmate at the Bad Aibling Discharge Center. He was one of the SS men who worked for the signal company and wore American uniforms into town. We had our picture taken with me holding an old photo of him as a young SS officer. I asked when he had realized that the war was lost: "When we got orders to surrender." He had been totally imprinted with the idea that they would win if they kept fighting. He felt very strongly that they could have beaten the Russians except for American intervention. I can't vouch for the validity of that idea but have included it as an example of what some German soldiers believed. When I asked what he thought would have happened if Germany had won and Hitler had continued in power, he just laughed: "God help us if that man had won!" He asked that I not include his name as one of my sources. Even in Bad Aibling there is still a lot of animosity toward men who fought as SS; he hopes that after another generation his manuscript can be published.

Hermann Böhme, eighty years old in 1992 and now deceased, had been an officer in the Luftwaffe. He was not a prisoner at the Discharge Center but told me about the German pilots' practice of landing at the Bad Aibling base with the wheels retracted in order to destroy the planes. He said there had been no particular hatred of the Americans; the men simply didn't want good planes to be used by the enemy. Böhme had been stationed at Berlin until just before the war ended, but he didn't want to remember those days.

My accounts of Inga and Hilda are fairly accurate, although the names are fictitious because I remember only their personalities. "Mike" and "Stud" are also fictitious; I remember their real names (almost, maybe) but see no reason to take a chance on embarrassing them. I borrowed the nickname "Stud" from a GI I knew in Aibling. He was one of the boys who were being conned in the "mother/daughter" scam. I remember enjoying his tales of the escapades, knowing that he was being fooled.

My description of wartime student attitudes toward Nazism came largely from a medical doctor in Bad Aibling, 1992. She had been a student at the University of Munich at the time of the "White Rose" incident. The story is exactly as she told it to me. She and her friends had supported Hitler and applauded the announcement that the White Rose students had been executed, but the incident eventually made them rethink their attitudes and gradually turn against Hitler. I gave the story to Bridget because it seems to fit my memory of her.

I should add that Bad Aibling was, and still is, a very conservative town. I suppose the only people who wanted to tell about the Hitler Youth were those who had fond memories of the experience. My "primary sources" in Bad Aibling may thus have been a biased sample, but I feel confident that they were being honest with me. I know of at least two Aiblingers who had information I wanted but were still so bitter about the early American occupation policies that they wouldn't talk with me. On the other hand, Bad Aibling women who remembered good times from the occupation enjoyed telling me about them. They particularly wanted me to know how nice the black soldiers had been to them. I have been unable to identify this unit. My initial impression was that the men were with the 761st Tank Battalion, an all-black unit that fought as part of the 71st Infantry Division, but the president of the 761st's reunion organization told me that the battalion was never in that area. He suggested that the unit might have been from a tank destroyer battalion that was attached to the 3d Infantry Division; however, I discovered that neither of the TD units with that division was composed of black troops. Louise Arnold-Friend, reference historian with the Army Military History Institute at Fort Carlisle, took up my search and found that the first American troops in Bad Aibling were from the 101st Cavalry Recon Battalion, but photographs showed that this was not a black unit. I sent this information to Gerda Kopliks, asking if the men could have been dark-skinned "white" troops. Gerda was unequivocal: they were black African Americans (although she did see some white soldiers in the afternoon of that first day).

In 1992 the old Luftwaffe base was still under control of the U.S. Army. The security officer, Will Daisy, took me on a tour of the base and helped me to locate the buildings that I remembered. The barracks where I stayed has been converted to a hospital. The beautiful lobby with the big fireplace is gone, replaced by a series of offices. From looking at old photographs I realized that the fireplace had been only a facade; there was no chimney on the roof. The old mess hall is now the base club and is still impressive. The only substantial change that I noticed was on the terrazzo floor in the entrance lobby: a circle with a blue star in it has replaced the large swastika. The theater where Maria had performed is a bowling alley. The aircraft hangers are storage facilities, and the airfield where the cages were located is a pasture. The bricked areas where planes were serviced is now a children's play yard, with several picnic shelters.

Marie (his wife) and I went to Munich for a day of touristing. The Feldherrenhalle still overlooks the large Odeonsplatz, with no evidence of it having been a Nazi shrine. The structure is only the facade of a building. Steps flanked by two stone lions lead to a columned entrance about thirty feet deep by fifty feet wide. There is a statue of someone— I failed to note who it was—and plaques commemorating the dead of the Franco-Prussian War and "The World War"; there is nothing about World War II. When we were there, people were sitting on the steps eating lunch. A warning sign is posted on this shrine where SS officers took their oaths of loyalty: No Skateboarding.

Following my fifty-year-old memories, I tried to locate the area where Bridget had lived, but with no success. I think it was on the left, about halfway down the Odeonsplatz. That section is now one of expensive apartment houses, although most of them seem old enough to have been repaired after the war. In any case, I couldn't match them up with the bombed-out ruins that I remembered.

Marie and I watched the Glockenspiel on the Rathaus clock and were told that the parade of knights now includes the figure of an American GI in combat uniform, in appreciation of an American soldier who organized a project to repair the clock immediately after the war ended. We did not try to find the Bürgerbräukeller because it is across the Isar River, a long way from the city center. Some people have tried to convince me that the Hofbräuhaus was "Hitler's beer hall." It is true that he held rallies at this much larger hall, but that was after he came to power.

I didn't even know where to begin looking for the company area of the black quartermaster outfit: my letter home said only that it was on the edge of Munich. In reading that and other letters, I was a bit surprised that my friendship with the black soldiers didn't seem important enough to write about. I mentioned eating with them several times, and that I spent a weekend there and tried to do close-order drill with them, but there was almost nothing about individuals. I'm not sure why—possibly because my family wouldn't have seen having black friends as a big deal.

They were loyal to the segregation rules, but within those restrictions we always had close ties with middle-class black families.

The names I use for the black GIs are fictitious because I am not quite sure of the real names (and perhaps I don't want to embarrass anyone). I have tried to describe the personalities and the incidents accurately, but undoubtedly there is some embellishment because I am working from impressions rather than recorded facts. I wanted to create the atmosphere as I remember it. I have shown this account to several black friends. Their opinion is that my description of the situation is plausible. Most southern middle-class blacks would have looked on me as "home folks"; they were certainly not trying to con me—I had nothing to offer them. Southern poverty-level blacks would not have resented me but might have been a little intimidated.

I hope my account does not imply that "Ole Charlie" was popular with everyone in the company. Sam'Le' and Big Willie accepted me as a friend, but we didn't have much in common beyond football stories. Fats and I were close because we came from the same culture: a Protestant, church-oriented community. Fats was better educated than me, and we both enjoyed spinning "country boy" yarns, but our strongest tie was old-time revival songs. My most vivid memories of him are in singing those songs. Fats had a good voice, and mine was scriptural—I made a "joyful noise."

Oliver Patton, a West Point graduate who served in Germany during the early occupation, made many helpful comments on the manuscript. Concerning my account of driving a tank, he pointed out that a German tank that had been idle for several weeks was extremely difficult to start; it would not have been a simple matter of a mechanic cranking it up for me. I suppose the motor pool had already checked out the vehicles and managed to start the tank before they sent us out. I don't remember the mechanic having any great problems with starting it. Patton also provided me with better information on the Malmédy massacre, including the fact that there were several American trucks at the scene that could have been used to transport prisoners.

In 1994 I went to Templin, a small town about forty miles north of Berlin, in hope of finding some basis for comparing the Russian occupation soldier with the GI. No comparison is possible. In that rural farming and resort area, the standard policy was to allow Russian soldiers a few weeks to obtain vengeance: loot, pillage, rape, and murder. This happened even in villages where there had been absolutely no resistance. After that, the troops were quartered in a large camp surrounded by a barbed-wire fence and were allowed out only for guard duty. The German civilians did not get to know any ordinary Russian occupation soldier: they all remembered too clearly what he was like during those first awful weeks.

Russian cultural affairs officers, who spoke German and knew the cultural traditions of the area, designed occupation policy. They assigned German civilians to municipal and educational duties, telling them exactly what to do, teach, and think. Because the alternative was to have the Russian soldiers released again, everyone tried to conform. Fifty years later I found a generation of young people who believe there was no Russian "occupation," that the German people were liberated from Nazism and were justly punished for their sins: "Vengeance is mine, saith the Red Army." The Germans I met in and around Templin seemed to have no quarrel with how they had been treated; in fact, some criticized the "soft Americans" for not punishing the Nazis severely enough. I suppose I should have anticipated such an attitude.

Finally, I must add the Louisiana State University community to my list of helpful sources. This community has been my home for thirty-five years, and I have no hesitation about asking friends to criticize my ideas and provide leads for other concepts. I have depended heavily on Karl Roider for historical guidance. Quentin Jenkins and George Ohlendorf were my primary sociologists. I received solicited and unsolicited opinions from the Horticulture Department's Unit for Abstract Research (the coffee-table group) regarding flaws in my thinking. The staff of LSU Press has helped me in so many ways that I cannot list all of the names. I am especially grateful to Gerry Anders, who has wasted a lot of his time listening to my ideas. To the rest of the Press staff: many, many thanks.

SELECTED BIBLIOGRAPHY

The following is not intended as an exhaustive and scholarly bibliography. It is simply a list of some books that I found to be interesting and would recommend for others' reading.

NAZI PERIOD

Baird, Jay W. *To Die for Germany: Heroes in the Nazi Pantheon.* Bloomington, Ind., 1990. Two chapters give excellent descriptions of the Hitler Youth. (This is the source in which I found the words to Hitler Youth songs. I hope the reader didn't think I actually remembered them from fifty years ago.)

Beck, Earl R. *Under the Bombs: The German Home Front, 1942–1945.* Lexington, Ky., 1986. My stories of life in Stuttgart during the bombing raids are based on accounts of the two girls I call Inge and Hilda. Beck gives a fascinating documentation of similar experiences, with German women remembering life in the ruins as a fight for *Überleben*—simple survival. From Hilda and Inge's stories, I had assumed that Stuttgart was severely bombed, but Beck lists it as one of the places only moderately damaged.

Breitman, Richard. *Architect of Genocide: Himmler and the Final Solution.* New York, 1991. An excellent biography. Breitman argues that Himmler was the driving force behind much of the Nazi racism and was probably directly responsible for developing the extermination camps. The author leaves little doubt that Hitler knew and approved, although at that stage of the war he was more concerned with military matters.

Fest, Joachim C. *Hitler.* New York, 1974. A superb, detailed account of the man as he was understood by an excellent writer who lived through that era.

Grunberger, Richard. *The Twelve-Year Reich: A Social History of Nazi Germany, 1933–1945.* New York, 1971.

Kershaw, Ian. *The "Hitler Myth": Image and Reality in the Third Reich.* New York, 1987.

Koch, H.W. *The Hitler Youth: Origins and Development, 1922–1945.* New York, 1976. A good factual account of the origins and development of the organization. Koch describes it as being much more fragmented and less focused than I had assumed.

Koonz, Claudia. *Mothers in the Fatherland: Women, Family Life, and Nazi Ideology, 1919–1945.* New York, 1987.

Santoro, Cesare. *Hitler Germany as Seen by a Foreigner.* Berlin, 1938. A heavily biased, idealistic account of Nazi Germany in 1937. Santoro describes only the good aspects of Nazism and often implies that nothing brutal was going on. The book's main value for my purposes is that it presents Germany as it would have been presented to the Hitler Youth.

Sereny, Gitta. *Into That Darkness.* New York, 1983. Postwar interviews with Franz Stangl, commandant of Treblinka, and with his family, friends, former SS men, and several survivors of the camp, combined with extensive research on Treblinka and other camps. A fascinating, horrifying, sickening account.

Seydewitz, Max. *Civil Life in Wartime Germany.* New York, 1945.

OCCUPATION PERIOD

Bischof, Günter, and Stephen E. Ambrose, eds. *Eisenhower and the German POWs: Facts Against Falsehood.* Baton Rouge, 1992. The basis for my understanding of why the American troops and the German POWs were on such limited rations. I remembered that we were always hungry, but I had not realized what a difficult problem Eisenhower faced. Collectively, these essays destroy sensationalistic claims that we engaged in mass starvation of German prisoners.

Blumenson, Martin. *Patton: The Man Behind the Legend, 1885–1945.* New York, 1987. The source of most of my information on Patton.

Botting, Douglas. *From the Ruins of the Reich: Germany, 1945–1949.* New York, 1985. A useful and detailed account of the American and British occupation policies that is, unfortunately, sensationalized with stories of corruption, sexual license, and stupid mistakes. The stories are probably true, but I feel that history should be more evenhanded.

Ziemke, Earl F. *The U.S. Army in the Occupation of Germany, 1944–1946.* Washington, D.C., 1975. A well-written official account of the problems, successes, and failures of the army during that trying period. The chapter "The Army in Disarray" is a frightening description of our difficulties during the winter of 1945–1946. Ziemke's reading of German civilians' opinion of American GIs is very different from my impression.

THE WAFFEN SS

Browning, Christopher R. *Ordinary Men: Reserve Police Battalion 101 and the Final Solution in Poland.* New York, 1993. A chilling account of how ordinary men became an SS death squad.

Höhne, Heinz. *The Order of the Death's Head.* New York, 1971. A good overall view of the SS as it was developed by Himmler. Höhne gives a vivid picture of the brutal, amoral SS command structure. He devotes a long chapter to the Waffen SS, laying the blame for the escalation of war atrocities in the Ukraine squarely on the shoulders of that organization.

Organization of Former Waffen SS. *When All Our Brothers Are Silent.* Munich, 1975. This collection of wartime photographs with German and English captions has a detailed foreword by Colonel-General Paul Hausser, the senior general *(Generaloberst)* of the Waffen SS. His account is clearly biased but gives an excellent defense of service in the Waffen SS. The title is from an SS marching song.

Sydnor, Charles W., Jr. *Soldiers of Destruction: The SS Death's Head Division.* Princeton, N.J., 1977. Whereas most popular histories on this subject are, in my opinion, badly stereotyped and sensationalized, this scholarly work is well documented, well written, and well balanced.

Walther, Herbert. *Die Waffen-SS.* Bisses, Ger., n.d. Primarily photographs (with captions in German and English), but an introduction includes some excellent evaluations of the SS, its officers, and its enlisted men.

Weingartner, James J. *Hitler's Guard: The Story of the Leibstandarte SS Adolf Hitler, 1933–1945.* Carbondale, Ill., 1974. A full, scholarly, and balanced portrayal of the Adolf Hitler Division.